More Critical acclaim for *The New Rules of Marketing:*

"In order to thrive in today's competitive retail market, it is essential to know who your customers are and retain them by offering the merchandise they want coupled with exceptional service. Fred Newell does an excellent job of demonstrating why customer knowledge is inherent to successful marketing and why capitalizing on repeat-customer visits is key to survival."

> *Marvin Girouard*
> *President and Chief Operating Officer*
> *Pier I Imports*

"*The New Rules of Marketing* is a classic in the understanding and importance of building customer relationships. Fred Newell gives us the reasons, the know-how, and the direction for successfully implementing relationship marketing. His soft-spoken counsel has been an important element in the success of those with whom his paths have crossed."

> *Joseph Dugan*
> *Chief Executive Officer*
> *Colony Shop*

"Fred Newell has taken a complex subject and communicated it in a vernacular all can relate to. An understanding of database and/or relationship marketing is crucial to all marketers as we enter the 21st century. This book makes that a much easier task."

> *Sandy Josephson*
> *Executive Director*
> *New York Market Radio Broadcasters Association*

"It's about time Fred Newell put his thoughts on paper. *The New Rules of Marketing* is a no nonsense . . . common sense . . . read on how to stay focused on the future ... by understanding the customer! Newell's 'blue print' is a must read for marketers who look to 'thrive' vs. 'survive' in the 21st century."

> *Thomas A. Conway*
> *Senior Vice President, Marketing*
> *Television Bureau of Advertising*

"When you think about who could possibly author a book on 'the new rules of marketing,' Fred Newell's name tops the list. Fred, who has seen it all, and most importantly knows what does and does not work, is uniquely qualified to chronicle this new wave of 'one-to-one' relationship marketing. Fred's unique perspective and engaging presentation manner, makes this must reading for any marketer who wants to be around for the next millennium."

> *Ernest V. Speranza*
> *Senior Vice President Advertising and Marketing*
> *Toys "R" Us*

"Few retail marketers understand the language of 'consumerspeak.' This book is written in it!"

Neil Kennedy
Chairman
European Advertising Agency Association

"*The New Rules of Marketing* is a very loud and very important wake-up call for every marketer in any business. It is essential reading. Those who are willing to set aside the tired old paradigms, and follow new rules, will be the ones to prosper in this ever-changing marketplace."

Douglas E. Raymond
President and Chief Executive Officer
Retail Advertising and Marketing Association
International

"Few marketers understand the difference between information and knowledge. Fred does. This book is about the knowledge era, how to make a customer, how to keep a customer, how to earn a profit. Good stuff!"

Ray Jutkins
Chief Executive Officer
Rockingham • Jutkins • Marketing

"Fred provides an entertaining perspective on the importance of understanding and building successful relationships with today's customer. *The New Rules of Marketing* is a creative blend of the principles, practices and lessons behind the process of database marketing and relationship building. Everyone can learn from this book."

John Goodman
Vice President
Helzberg Diamonds

"A realistic approach transitioning from traditional mass marketing to a twenty-first century, customer-centric, database-driven approach. Bravo, Fred Newell."

Don E. Schultz
Professor, Northwestern University

THE NEW RULES
OF MARKETING

THE NEW RULES OF MARKETING

How to Use One-to-One Relationship Marketing to Be the Leader in Your Industry

FREDERICK NEWELL

McGraw-Hill
New York • San Francisco • Washington, D.C. • Auckland
Bogotá • Caracas • Lisbon • London • Madrid • Mexico City
Milan • Montreal • New Delhi • San Juan • Singapore
Sydney • Tokyo • Toronto

Library of Congress Cataloging-in-Publication Data

Author:	Newell, Frederick, date.
Title:	The new rules of marketing : how to use one-to-one relationship marketing to be the leader in your industry / Frederick Newell.
Published:	New York : McGraw-Hill, 1997.
Description:	p. cm.
LC Call No.:	HF5415.55 .N49 1997
Dewey No.:	658.8 21
ISBN:	0786312289
Subjects:	Relationship marketing.
	Database marketing.
Control No.:	97009622

McGraw-Hill

*A Division of The **McGraw·Hill** Companies*

2 3 4 5 6 7 8 9 0 DOC/DOC 9 0 2 1 0 9 8 7

ISBN 0-7863-1228-9

The sponsoring editor for this book was Jeffrey Krames, the editing supervisor was Donna Namorato, and the production supervisor was Suzanne W. B. Rapcavage. It was set in Times Roman by Carol Woolverton Studio in cooperation with Spring Point Publishing Services.

Printed and bound by R. R. Donnelley & Sons Company.

This publication is designed to provide accurate and authoritative information in regard to the subject matter covered. It is sold with the understanding that neither the author or the publisher is engaged in rendering legal, accounting, or other professional service. If legal advice or other expert assistance is required, the services of a competent professional person should be sought.

> *—From a Declaration of Principles jointly adopted by a Committee of the American Bar Association and a Committee of Publishers.*

McGraw-Hill books are available at special quantity discounts to use as premiums and sales promotions, or for use in corporate training programs. For more information, please write to the Director of Special Sales, McGraw-Hill, 11 West 19th Street, New York, N.Y. 10011. Or contact your local bookstore.

This book is printed on recycled, acid-free paper containing a minimum of 50 percent recycled de-inked fiber.

For my wonderful friends and clients from whom I have learned so much, and for the young, next generation of marketing executives who will be leading us through the new century.

CONTENTS

FOREWORD

If your business deals with consumers, this book is must reading. For those of you who are already marketing with a database, this book will open up new uses to keep you in a leadership position.

If you don't have a database, you will not fare well in the next century. This book explains why marketing with a database is essential to success in today's highly competitive world, how to get started, and how to use it.

Fred Newell has been involved with database marketing for over 25 years. Many firms with database capability are only using a fraction of the potential that exists in their marketing database for more sales, building customer relationships, and more efficient use of their marketing dollars.

This book is written in a clear and concise manner that illuminates the power and multiplicity of uses hidden in your database. Here are just a few of the areas covered:

+ How to increase sales with fewer marketing dollars.
+ How to measure advertising results.
+ How to develop customer relationships.
+ How to increase share of wallet.
+ How to gain market share.
+ How to search out new customers.
+ How to get a database started.
+ How economic and social trends are driving database usage.

Newell's book covers all this and more, plus four great case histories and many examples that show the varied uses of a database and how the database tool can impact virtually all areas of your business.

Having been involved with marketing databases since 1961, I know their importance and power. I strongly endorse this book's clarion call, which sounds the importance of a database to marketing success, today, as well as in the next century.

PAUL LEBLANG, Ph. D.

PREFACE

A confession is in order. I grew up in the retail business. Following the real-life experience of working "in retail," I have spent the past 20 years sharing the marketing challenges of a great many wonderful folks: department stores, men's and women's specialty stores, jewelry stores, children's stores, gift stores, shoe stores, appliance stores, furniture stores, electronic specialty stores, sporting goods stores, national and regional chains, auto supply stores, farm and home stores, home handyman stores, off-price stores, discount chains, ten dollar stores, shopping centers, restaurants, catalogers, cruise ships, banks, newspapers, advertising agencies, computer companies, software companies, chemical companies, manufacturers, and The Metropolitan Opera Guild.

When I first got involved in catalog marketing and learned how much the catalogers knew about their individual customers, I decided there was an enormous opportunity for *every* kind of marketer to know more about his or her customers. We didn't even know the phrase "database marketing" then.

It took a while to get anyone to listen. Finally, I persuaded STS Systems in Montreal to build the first desktop customer profile system for department stores and specialty stores, and then for other marketers. I couldn't write a software program even if I went to school for the next 10 years, but I could, and did, tell them what customer data the marketer needed to capture, and how we would need to access the data for customer marketing. I became known as the "father" of the first desktop database marketing system that is now in place in hundreds of companies in North America.

Since that start, I have been criss-crossing the continent as a missionary for this new, customer-driven marketing. It was a tough sell. I was telling folks to change the rules. Converts came slowly.

Now, database marketing, relationship marketing, and customer management represent the fastest-growing marketing investment in North America, in every field. It is changing everything marketers ever thought about marketing.

It will no longer work to market to the *averages*. We must learn to market to the *differences*.

The mass communications, so well developed in this century, will no longer serve to communicate to the new customer. Marketers must change the rules and find new paradigms of marketing communications and new models of understanding customers. This calls for an understanding of the new rules of marketing.

To understand these new rules requires an understanding of the evolution of the tools and strategies that now give the marketer the ability to gather enormous amounts of information about the customer and to turn that information into knowledge.

This book develops a complete understanding of the basic concepts of relationship and database marketing, bringing the exciting principles of the new rules of marketing into fresh focus, and offers a view of how marketing leaders are putting these tools and strategies into action to increase sales and profits in every industry.

The purpose of this book is to simplify an otherwise complex subject—to show by lesson and example how the best and the brightest are learning to market from the customer database. By presenting a definitive overview of the marketing trends impacting the new century, I hope to help marketers learn how to make these trends friendly and helpful for growing their businesses. Beyond that, the reader will learn the analysis tools and measurement techniques so vital to the customer management process.

Unlike many database marketing studies already in print, *The New Rules of Marketing* is not for a limited audience of techies or database managers. Though it is filled with hands-on explanations of sophisticated customer analysis techniques, it is written for the thousands of business people who are looking for effective, efficient, customer management tools, and an understanding of the state of the art of database marketing, today. It is important reading for CEOs, sole proprietors, middle management, and those just starting marketing careers.

While many of the examples that follow are taken from the experience of our consulting clients, this is not a book just for retailers. The principles involved in the examples for all of the different industries cited hold true for every kind of business. These exciting principles of new-century marketing are critical for every business whose success depends on selling to customers: consumers, business-to-business, any and every kind of customer.

The new century has dawned. Answer the wake-up call!

FRED NEWELL

ACKNOWLEDGMENTS

My sincere thanks to the companies that cared enough to share stories, numbers, and insights. They are the ones who are operating, today, with the new rules of marketing. They are helping us find the way. They care enough to "give back" to help our marketing industry grow. I salute them.

This book could not have been written without all of the help I received from friends and business associates. First among these is Paul Leblang, President of the marketing consulting firm IBJ Associates, former Senior Vice President of Marketing for Saks Fifth Avenue, and honoree of the DMA's Edward N. Mayer, Jr. Award in recognition of his many contributions to direct marketing education. Paul spent hours and days reading early drafts, always providing exactly the right incisive comments and suggestions.

Equal thanks to "Pete" Hoke, Chairman, Hoke Communications and *Direct Marketing,* who helped me to find my way through the history and development of the direct marketing concept.

Most of all my thanks go to the many Seklemian/Newell clients who, over the years, have taught me more than I have been able to teach them, and my late partner, Sek Seklemian, who was telling us to love and understand the customer—and surely understood relationship marketing long before it became cool.

Thanks to Doug Raymond for his constant help and support, Stanley Marcus for his great thoughts on leadership that fit the challenge of the new rules of marketing, Jennifer Barrett for her knowledgeable help on the privacy issue, and my Argentine associate, Mario Ascher.

Special thanks to the database marketing pros, Spencer Joyner, Ray Jutkins, Emily Kelso, Leo Rabinovitch, Francey Smith, and Brian Woolf, for all they have taught me; my associate, copy editor, coach, and severest critic, Helen Dunham; and my research assistant Nita Krygier for tireless hours spent to save me from errors.

My agent, Ed Knappman, for finding the good folks at McGraw-Hill and, of course, my editor, Kevin Thornton, for forcing me to sharpen my thoughts and for helping me through the roughest spots. I learned quickly why God gave us editors.

And, finally, my wife Harriette for her patient sustenance, constant smile—and for dragging me away from the computer by three or four each afternoon to *make* me eat some lunch . . . and our three great children and their wonderful children for enthusiastic support throughout the effort.

F.N.

CHAPTER 1

Frogs, Toads, and Lizards

Marketers, since the 80s, have worshipped at the shrine of service, then price, then frequent buyer points—and customers are fed up.

Once upon a time there was a young boy named Tim. In his third-grade classroom, Tim was sitting four rows back from the teacher's desk by the window. He spent a lot of time gazing out of the window. This bothered the teacher, who thought Tim was daydreaming about all the fun things he could be doing out in the sun and fresh air. But Tim wasn't thinking about the sun and fresh air. His thoughts were all about the fresh, pretty, freckle-faced, red-headed classmate who sat in the same row, a little farther from the window.

He wanted to be her friend. He looked out the window only because he was too shy to look at her. He wasn't thinking about the sun and fresh air. He was thinking about how he could impress this delightful creature whose name was Jenny. He knew he needed something better than walking on fences.

He decided he needed to find a special gift that would impress Jenny.

That very afternoon Tim went down to the pond and spent hours trying until he finally caught a frog. With great care he put the frog in a jar with grass and food, and air holes in the lid. Timidly, the next day, he gave

1

the frog to Jenny. She was less than thrilled. "Well," he said, "She doesn't like frogs. What else can I catch?"

That very afternoon, he went into the meadow and spent hours trying until he finally caught a toad. With great care, he put the toad in a jar with grass and food, and air holes in the lid. The next day, he gave the toad to Jenny, only to be rebuffed once more.

"Well," he thought, "She doesn't like frogs and she doesn't like toads. There must be something she likes. I'll try one more time."

That very afternoon, he went into the marshes and spent hours trying until he finally caught a lizard. Lizards are longer than frogs and toads, so with great care he put the lizard in a shoe box with grass and food, and air holes in the lid. The next day, he gave the lizard to Jenny. She said, "Ugh."

Tim didn't know the new rules of marketing.

———

In the 1980s a quiet, family-owned specialty department store, born of a Seattle shoe chain, began expanding successfully, majestically, and profitably across the United States. Sellers of goods of every kind watched in wonder and decided they had found Nirvana. The Nordstrom level of customer service would make every kind of business successful. It was that simple. CEOs across North America memorized the now famous Nordstrom "Sales Associates Policy Manual," printed on a single card (Figure 1-1).

At every marketing conference, attendees heard the story of Nordstrom senior management telling sales associates, "If a customer comes in to return a defective automobile tire, smile, say thank you, and cheerfully refund her money. Then roll the tire out the back door and throw it away." (Powerful testimony, of course, because Nordstrom sells only apparel.)

Business leaders made speeches about their new plans for superior customer service. Human Resource teams rewrote policy manuals, but, as one might suspect, it was not that simple. Few businesses have ever achieved the Nordstrom mystique. One reason, of course, is that the Nordstrom mystique involves much more than good customer service. It is also selection and presentation, fair pricing, a very special understanding of the customer, and caring, quality people.

At a Nordstrom stockholder meeting in the late 80s, a stockholder asked the late Jim Nordstrom, "The Nordstrom sales team is so outstanding, can you tell us who trains them?" Mr. Nordstrom replied, "Their parents."

Then somewhere in the early 90s, as a difficult business economy

FIGURE 1-1

Nordstrom Employee Handbook

NORDSTROM
EMPLOYEE HANDBOOK

WELCOME TO NORDSTROM

We're glad to have you with our company.
Our #1 goal is to provide
outstanding customer service.
Set both your personal and
professional goals high.
We have great confidence in your
ability to achieve them.

Nordstrom Rules:

Rule #1: **Use your good judgment in all
situations.**

There will be no additional rules.

Nordstrom

Reprinted from Robert Spector & Patrick McCarthy, *The Nordstrom Way* (John Wiley & Sons, 1995), p.15.

slowed the selling pace, the warm whisper of "Service" gave way to the shrill scream of "Price." Auto makers shouted rebates. Long distance phone carriers competed with the lowest cost per minute, even bribing customers as much as $50 to switch to their service. Airlines started disastrous fare wars, and retailers brought out their biggest, blackest newspaper type to proclaim discounts and mark-downs. They might as well have spent their time down by the pond chasing frogs.

Packaged goods marketers kept pace with discount coupons. They would have been just as well off spending hours in the meadows, looking for toads.

Businesses that weren't trying to give away their products with discounts began to eye the airlines. If customer service wasn't the trick, surely the Frequent Flyer points and rewards programs would make every kind of business successful. It was that simple. Unfortunately no one seemed to understand—the free ticket the airlines were offering cost them $30–$40 in extra meals and paperwork, but was perceived as a $400–$600 value by the consumer.

No one stopped to realize that this consumer purchase choice represented the spending of other people's (employer's) money—it didn't come out of the consumer's pocket; two ingredients hard to match in any other industry. And no one seemed to notice the millions of dollars the airlines were losing. So, like the children following the Pied Piper, businesses lined up to develop Frequent Shopper Programs.

S & H Green Stamps would have been proud of the vindication. The marshes were crowded with folks looking for lizards.

One company I interviewed told me that when they decided to create a loyalty program to increase their retention of best customers, they started the process by talking to customers and asking questions. One of the key questions was, "How much would you value a frequent buyer reward program?" Customers told them, "Please don't clutter up our lives. We just want someone to care about us and know what we want."

As Tim learned, spending hours at the pond looking for frogs, or hours in the meadow hunting toads, or hours in the marshes capturing a lizard didn't mean much if Jenny didn't want his thoughtful gift.

The new rules of marketing will be that simple and that complex.

They are what this book is all about.

PART ONE

An intense focus on price by marketers has been prevalent, yet with a few exceptions this approach has not built exceptional profit growth. Too many companies that have made it this far into the 90s have done so by cost cutting and downsizing—not the road to long-term success. A recent study of the 1,000 largest U.S. companies, comparing the stock market performance of successful cost-cutters with that of successful growth companies, found that investors will pay considerably more for a dollar of profit generated through revenue growth than for that same dollar generated through cost reduction.*

This is not a book about price discounting, and it's not a book about downsizing. Rather, its purpose is to help companies find a better way to take advantage of the new rules of marketing to become successful growth companies by increasing not just sales but *profitable* sales.

The first new rule is the importance of understanding the buyer—the customer—and that customer is changing. He or she is not the same customer as in the 70s, 80s, and early 90s.

Part I will build the foundation for understanding the new customer, explain the process of turning customer information into knowledge and knowledge into marketing strength, and examine the tools marketers are using to harness this new marketing power.

Part II will get into the fun of what some real-life

---

*Mercer Management Consulting, *Strategic Direction,* November/December 1996, p. 4.

marketers are doing with sophisticated customer files. Finally, Part III will look into the near future.

To build the foundation, we'll start with some very important trends that will help to explain the changed customer.

We're not in Kansas Anymore

Why marketers can't find the Yellow Brick Road.

Not so long ago, American marketers started a courtship with American consumers that hasn't ended yet. We hope it never will.

It was a time of simple needs, simply met, a time of face-to-face relationships. There was an innocence to life, not so long ago. And while much has changed, much has remained the same. It's more comfortable that way.

Then, something happened. The old, warm relationships didn't seem to apply. Once well-known faces were lost in a shifting, faceless crowd. Even Toto could have told us we weren't in Kansas anymore!

Americans swarmed off the farms, and they deserted the inner cities. They created a brand new country, transported by station wagon, framed by the picture window, and equipped with wall-to-wall kids.

These were good days for American marketers, who were still refilling the pipelines from all the pent-up needs from war shortages. We could sell all we could make or get. There were still perceived differences between brands and between stores. We believed we had "loyal" customers. It was easy to convince ourselves we were great marketers.

The 70s made us a bit less sure. Discount retailers escalated their offerings. Private brands began to make a dent in brand manufacturers' longtime customer franchises. But, for the most part, brands and stores still owned "loyal" customers. Marketers got a bit more promotional, but there was still profitable business between the manufacturers' coupons and the retailers' sales.

Then, in the 80s, department stores became the discounters.

I remember when L. S. Ayers, the Indianapolis department store chain, held its first, shocking one-day November event. They "gave away the store" for one day just prior to Thanksgiving and had a $5 million dollar day; something unheard of. I was working with them at the time. We thought we were heroes. We produced the biggest day in the history of the store.

The truth was we created a monster. The retail industry went from there to the 14-Hour Sale, the Night & Day Sale, the point of sale (POS) percent off mark-downs sale. Doing this every week, they trained the consumer to shop on sale.

Automakers were no better. They escalated the sale ethic with rebates. Brand manufacturers accomplished the same customer seduction with coupons.

We think of coupons as being a modern concept, but the truth is they are a hundred-year-old habit. In 1884 Coca Cola gave out coupons for a free glass of Coke at local general stores, and a year later C.W. Post offered penny certificates to get customers to buy its new Grape Nuts cereal.[1]

In 1984 there were 83 million US households, and the packaged goods industry gave each one $485 in coupons. That was just a start. In 1990 there were 92 million households, and the industry gave each one $1,400 in coupons. That's 279 billion coupons with a total face value of $125 billion. In 1992, that jumped to $336 billion. In 1994 there were more than 310 billion coupons, saving customers a record $4 billion dollars.

Ninety-nine percent of U.S. Households surveyed say they used coupons in the past year. One-third of these consumers say they wouldn't go grocery shopping without coupons.[2]

Some signs suggest this growth in couponing has now run its course. According to NCH Promotional Services, coupon distribution and redemption fell 6 percent in 1995. Distribution declined to 291.9 billion coupons; redemption dropped to 5.8 billion coupons.[3]

Procter & Gamble Company started a three-market test at the beginning of 1996. In Buffalo, Rochester, and Syracuse, New York, P&G went cold turkey: no coupons for P&G brands. It has been reported that P&G has reduced their national coupon spending 50 percent in the last five years.[4] And remember, these were the folks who shook up the packaged-goods marketplace with experiments like this in everyday low pricing. This latest zero-coupon test could bring big changes industrywide.

One might suspect that the smart folks at P&G are assessing the marketing fact of the 90s—that price has become the consumer's point of difference, and that marketers have been killing brand equity by overdiscounting. As one smart marketer told me, price is the only guaranteed unsustainable competitive advantage in the world.

Now many marketers are as confused as Dorothy in Oz. Everything has changed. Few have been able to find the Yellow Brick Road.

To go forward we must do more than overcome our bad discounting habits. The facts are that we are facing a new consumer and that pre-2000s consumer trends are changing everything we ever thought we knew about consumer marketing. These trends involve virtually every link in the marketing chain, from the manufacturer, through the retailer, to the customer. They are tearing apart the efficient, delicate marketing process that has worked for the past 60 years. It calls for new rules of marketing.

We must have the ability to accept change.

Marketing leaders must find ways to change the rules. Listen to Brett Shevack, President and CEO, Partners & Shevack: "Even when there is great risk inherent in change, it is the responsibility of leaders to shake things up. To be truly successful we have to learn how to deal, react, adjust, survive, and be comfortable with change. Change before you have to."[5]

The new rules of marketing we will be studying will require us to change many old habits in order to understand and serve the new century customer. Before we begin to look at the new marketing tools and strategies it is necessary to take the time to put this new customer in focus.

Five important consumer trends will impact the marketing scene as we approach the year 2000: limits of growth, changing channels of distribution, the changing perception of value, time poverty, and the growing importance of changing generations.

These five trends are significant enough to constitute a wake-up call. It is important to understand these trends in order to grasp the real marketing challenge we face and understand the new rules of marketing.

CHAPTER **3**

Not the "Final Four"

Four consumer trends in the new century that will change marketing forever.

The NBA knows the magic of "four." Millions of fans tune in to the excitement of Michael and Shaq and Karl and Shawn. If we didn't know what was happening in Chicago, Orlando, Utah, and Seattle, we couldn't join the conversation around the coffee machine each morning.

Any marketer who doesn't know just as much about the new consumer trends as he or she does about the Bulls, the Magic, the Jazz, and the Supersonics will be even more out in the cold because these trends will change the marketing world. Already they are in sight, and as they intensify they will force us to change most of the marketing strategies that have worked in the past.

Speaking at the 1996 International Strategic Leadership Conference in Atlanta, organized by the Strategic Leadership Forum, Alvin Toffler, author of *Future Shock, The Third Wave, Power Shift,* and *Creating a New Civilization* reminded attendees what he means by the third wave: "We are living through the greatest wave of change on the planet since the enlightenment and the industrial revolution . . . and waves cause turbulence and buffeting."[1]

Although often attributed to technological change, Toffler stressed that this third wave of change is more than merely technological—it is in the process of altering cultures, social relationships, communications, and organizational structures. Economists, political thinkers, and business leaders have yet to grasp the implications of this emerging society.[2]

He talked about "particle marketing," pointing out that the profusion of information on customers means that visionary marketers are now talking about one-to-one marketing and building long-term relationships with each individual customer.[3]

This chapter looks at the waves of change that will bring the most turbulence and buffeting to marketers. There are five trends, but we'll try to borrow a bit of the NBA magic by starting with four, saving the fifth for Chapter 4.

TREND #1: LIMITS OF GROWTH

In March 1996, the U.S. Census Bureau announced the latest news of the limits of growth. The nation's population will reach 275 million by the start of the new century. That will make the next few years the slowest growth period since the 30s. Growth will remain stable until 2025, when the U.S. is expected to enter the slowest growth period in its history.

Add to that the fact that America is already overstored, overcataloged, overmalled, and overbranded. We have gone from 8 square feet of selling space per household in 1986 to 18 square feet of selling space per household in 1996, but retail sales have dropped from $190 to $160 per square foot.[4] When Wal-Mart takes $100 billion of retail sales out of the market, everyone loses some. In October 1995, Carl Steadman, Chief Economist at Management Horizons, reported that since 1990, 100,000 retailers have filed for bankruptcy.

In the U.S. a new product is developed every 40 minutes. In the last 10 years the number of stock keeping units (SKUs) in the average U.S. supermarket has doubled from 15,000 to 30,000. Procter & Gamble introduced 81 new products either into test markets or expanded areas from January through mid-August of 1996. P&G filed for 17,000 patents in 1995.[5] They have more scientists on staff than the college faculties of Harvard, Berkeley, and MIT combined.[6]

Marketers will only be able to survive and grow by gaining market share, and the only possible way to do this in a limited growth environment is by taking business away from the competition.

Operating in an environment of limited growth requires:

1. Longer range strategic planning; finding ways to change the rules. As the old Chinese proverb states, "Unless we change direction, we are likely to end up where we are headed."
2. Better understanding of individual target markets.
3. Stronger marketing philosophy of doing business; making customers instead of merely making sales.

Anyone who shops at all is well aware of the second trend.

TREND #2: CHANGING CHANNELS OF DISTRIBUTION

The time-tested, traditional distribution scheme of manufacturer-retailer-consumer has splintered. The new channels coming into play will continue to change marketing strategies to fit the new rules of marketing.

You have only to check your own mailbox to recognize the first of the burgeoning, nontraditional channels: mail order. It's big. 102 million adults (50 percent of the population) buy through the mail order channel.[7] But total sales are relatively small compared to retail. Consumer mail order sales in 1995 were $141.8 billion compared with $5.078 *trillion* in total consumer retail sales.[8] This includes $2.248 *trillion* in traditional merchandise sales and another $2.83 *trillion* in total consumer services.

About 1993, the Direct Marketing Association's Board hired a Boston research firm, WEFA, to develop numbers which would have some clout in Washington in postal and privacy lobbying. The mail order figures, though not small, didn't reflect total sales in all channels generated by all direct response advertising in all media. WEFA took a stab at trying to study and develop a sales figure generated by *direct response advertising*. They determined that figure to be $600 billion compared to total aggregate U.S. sales of $14.5 trillion in 1995. A figure still needs to be developed for the total direct marketing process, according to Pete Hoke, Chairman, *Direct Marketing*.

In 1995, in addition to the growth in consumer sales, business-to-business sales from direct order, lead generation, and traffic generation are estimated to reach nearly $500 billion.[9] This would include sales of products such as computers, office supplies, furniture, telephones, automobiles, and trucks directly to businesses, as opposed to goods sold directly to consumers.

The term "direct order" comes from a WEFA recommendation, perhaps prompted by the DMA Board. It jumps over the problem of being associated only with mail and includes other marketing channels. For example, infomercials are mainly mail order selling directly using television—although some auto manufacturers are using infomercials to drive showroom traffic. And now the Internet enters the picture to make mail order even more outdated a term. The Internet will serve all channels of distribution, including mail (direct) order, retail, and personal selling.

Compounded annual growth rates of sales over the next five years will be 7.2 percent for sales to consumers and 10.2 percent for business-to-business.[10]

One in every 13 jobs in the United States today is the result of direct marketing sales activity. One in every six jobs in the U.S. is linked to direct response advertising support services, suppliers, and interindustry.[11]

Fourteen million U.S. businesses generated $14.5 trillion in sales in 1994, and 7.6 percent of that can be credited to direct response advertising. By the year 2000, total U.S. sales will reach $20.9 trillion, with $1.65 trillion of that coming from direct marketing.[12]

In its annual Direct Response Agency Billings Survey, the Direct Marketing Association reports that 8 of the top 10 direct marketing agencies in the U. S. reported growth, with leader Rapp Collins growing domestic billings $71 million to total $461 million. In international billings, 9 of the top 10 agencies reported increases in billings between 1993 and 1994, with Ogilvy & Mather topping the list with $560 million in international billings.

In October 1996, McCann-Erickson Worldwide tapped direct marketing pioneer Stanley Rapp as Chairman-CEO of a new global direct-services unit devoted to tripling McCann's revenue in the direct marketing discipline.[13]

Annual direct mail volume in England is on course to hit three billion items for the first time, according to official figures from the Direct Mail Information Service (DMIS), London, England.[14]

All this suggests that direct marketing may well account for several trillion dollars—quite a stake. There are those who believe that one day *all* marketing will be direct marketing, as every business succumbs to the siren song of the marketing database.

Another channel within this trend is manufacturers who compete directly with their retail customers.

Manufacturers are opening their own retail stores. Why? Because they believe they can do a better job of selling their products and strengthening their brand image than the traditional retailer can. The truth is that most often they are correct. The traditional retailer's constant price-item advertising is tearing down brand equity. In contrast, the manufacturers with their own stores are using their advertising, store design, and merchandise presentation to build quality reputations to add equity to their brands.

Examples of manufacturers doing this well are Nike, Armani, Coach, Hart Shafner & Marx, Donna Karan, and Louis Vuitton. The classic example is Ralph Lauren's chain of Polo stores. In addition to developing fine individual shops across the country, Polo created a showcase store in a beautifully restored building on New York's upper Madison Avenue then added an equally impressive Polo Sport store across the street. National publicity and consumer word-of-mouth praise for these outstanding units are adding to the Polo reputation for quality and strengthening brand equity for Ralph Lauren.

The result of all these manufacturers opening their own stores is another new channel of distribution:

Manufacturer $\rightarrow$ Manufacturers' Stores $\rightarrow$ Consumer

---

Who is missing from the middle? The odd man out is the traditional retail store.

An even bigger slice of the pie is going to manufacturers' outlet stores. Factory outlet shopping centers are no longer a fad 50 miles from nowhere. Some are now the biggest tourist attractions in major cities and destination resorts. The average distance outlet shoppers drive today is 20 to 30 minutes, as opposed to two hours not so long ago.

There are many independent factory outlet center operators, but the biggest players are the real estate investment trusts. As consolidation continues, we approach the point where a handful of developers will control two-thirds of the market. The industry started with the largest centers occupying not more than 100,000 square feet; today the average is 150,000 square feet, and new centers are opening at 300,000–350,000 square feet, including food courts.

A sign of maturity in the outlet center industry is the change from mom-and-pop food retailers to the big, national food names. National food tenants are comfortable in million-square-foot malls because the thousands of employees on site and the tens of thousands of office workers and residents near the mall will assure business beyond the normal mall traffic. One outlet center expert says, "It has been very hard to convince national food tenants to go out in the middle of a cow pasture."[15] The interest of the national food names in outlet centers now is a serious indication of the important shopper traffic these centers are generating. The average sales per square foot for outlet center food court restaurants is close to $600.

Some outlet center developers are even looking to become greater destination locations by adding hotels, theaters, bookstores, and sports recreation facilities. One expert says, "We need to merchandise to families who continue to be interested in value but are really in search of something to do."[16]

Tenants of these new outlet centers include manufacturers that have as many as 75 to 150 units in operation, like Liz Claiborne, Fila, Jockey, Magnavox, and Polo. There are even outlet retailers who combine many brand manufacturers in one store. US Factory Outlet is a "big box" outlet retailer with 24 stores that are exclusive outlets or closeout distributors for 300 manufacturers, catalog operators, and mail order companies. The word is that more manufacturers are joining in every day.

Thus we have another new channel of distribution:

Manufacturer → Manufacturers' Outlet Stores → Consumer

Traditional retailers are not ignoring this. Some are opening their own outlet stores. Off Fifth (Saks Fifth Avenue), Gap, Barney's, and Nordstrom Rack exemplify this trend.

And therefore we have a third new channel of distribution:

Retailer → Retailers' Outlet Stores → Consumer

All of this reinforces the consumer's perception that the traditional retailer is overpriced. The competitive pressure of these new kinds of retailers will force the traditional retailer to adopt the new rules of marketing.

Our next channel of distribution is electronic retailing or electronic mail order. We now accept transactional TV as a way of life. Yes, home shopping today is still primitive, but there it is, a $2.5 billion business . . . and it is still one-dimensional. One insider predicts home shopping will become a $250 billion business in 10 to 12 years, probably representing half of all retail sales in 20 years or less. By the end of 1996, 40 percent of all U.S. and Canadian households will have tried home shopping. If it is not transactional TV, it will be the Internet that will serve all channels of distribution and change the locations where sales are made. While the Net will take away from in-store sales one day, retail as we know it (bricks and mortar) will continue to be a potent force in the marketplace, despite changes in size and scope.

With the meager sales results reported by most on-line marketers, the projection of a $250 billion business for the Internet may sound optimistic until we look at a business like CUC International. Founded in 1973 as Comp-U-Card, it started as a computer service then moved to the phone, and now, has added interactive offerings through most of the on-line services. In 1995, CUC sold more than 10,000 cars, booked more than $400 million worth of airline tickets, car rentals and hotel reservations. It offers its customers 429 different TV models. It has no warehouse, no stores, and no inventory, just a giant database of 250,000 products. Customers dial in to operators who search the database for model numbers, manufacturers, or features. The merchandise is shipped direct from the manufacturer. Revenues have doubled in four years to an estimated $1.3 billion, consisting almost entirely of membership fees.[17]

And, as other retailers' fixed assets—bricks, mortar, and inventory— get more expensive, CUC's assets—computers, databases, and telecommunications equipment—are getting cheaper.

Electronic shopping is getting less primitive every day. On December 18, 1995, the Supermarket Shopping Network was launched on the World Wide Web (http://www.mysupermarket.com) with major-player partners including General Mills, Land O' Lakes, ConArgra Company's Healthy Choice, Coca-Cola Foods, J. M. Smucker Company, and Tropicana Products.

The Web site offers on-line grocery shopping from supermarkets. Shoppers can make purchases with a credit card or debit card, use on-line couponing, choose pick-up or delivery, read on-line magazine NET SAUCE, find recipes in a database, and maintain customized shopping lists, which will become target marketing tools. Shoppers can buy more than just packaged goods. Offerings include 1,000 choices of fresh produce and nonpackaged items.

The Food Marketing Institute has reported that the number of supermarket chains offering some form of home shopping services jumped from 25 percent in 1994 to 40 percent in 1995. On-line shopping services can cut supermarket operating costs by 20 percent.

This suggests that food shopping on-line will be a very big business. Pea Pod is one of the most interesting on-line services, offering "Smart Shopping for Busy People." Pea Pod was founded in 1989 in Evanston, Illinois. After six years of testing, they are now serving 20,000 members in Boston, Chicago, Columbus, and San Francisco, adding new members at a rate of 2,500 a month.

Pea Pod is the ultimate high-tech, high-touch shopping service. Members can dial in from home or from work and leave an order for pick up or home delivery. They can keep past orders in memory for quick editing for re-order. The service offers 20,000 items from major supermarket chains, provides real-time price data, allows users to check nutritional facts on any item, and even ranks the brands of an item by fat or sugar content or price before selecting. At Pea Pod, the mouse has replaced the cart. Customers can shop any aisle with the click of a mouse. They can even buy stamps, bus tokens, and tabloids. They can add personal notes to the order (6 bananas—3 ripe, 3 green), and their Pea Pod shopper will respond. Beyond all that, customers can select a narrow delivery time when they know they will be home to receive the groceries.

The average Pea Pod customer shops every 10 to 12 days and spends an average of $110. Pea Pod believes they are capturing a 70 percent share of customer, and early returns show a 70 to 80 percent customer retention rate. Pea Pod's stated objective is to amaze and delight every customer. With a customer able to complete a shopping list in about 10 minutes, Pea Pod executives like to say the customer moves from "in-line" to "on-line." Pea Pod expects to be processing 12,000,000 customer orders a year by 1999.[18]

The $6.95 monthly Pea Pod membership fee includes three hours of on-line shopping and Internet e-mail access. Pea Pod charges $4.95 plus 5 percent of the grocery total to shop, pack, and deliver the groceries.[19]

In May 1996, 590 Toyota and Saab car dealers nationwide joined the World Wide Web with the on-line host firm, Dealer Net. Gulf States Toyota, Inc., a southeastern U.S. car distributor, has signed with Dealer Net to put its 140 dealers on the Internet. More than 600 dealers are listed in the Yahoo directory. One auto maker is considering making auto service records available on-line so customers can use the Internet to check whether it is time to get their oil changed or have other scheduled maintenance done.

Travelcity, a travel service on the Net, can book tickets for 95 percent of the world's airlines—including Southwest—plus car rentals and hotel accommodations. They provide travel information on 22,000 world cities, then even offer a packing checklist and travel merchandise.[20]

Amazon.com is the world's largest book store, with 1.2 million titles. They have received orders from all 50 states and 100 countries. More than a third of their customers are repeat buyers, and 80 percent use credit cards on-line. And amazon.com is interactive. After you make a selection you are taken to a page offering reviews by amazon.com and others; then, you are offered a chance to play critic and add your own reader review. The

Eyes and Editors feature offers customers the chance to receive e-mail information about new titles. Amazon's sales growth last year exceeded 2,000 percent.[21]

The number of World Wide Web pages is doubling every 53 days. Trade sources estimate short-range growth, now through 1998, for shopping on the Internet to go from $366 million to $3.7 billion, home shopping from $2.5 to $5.4 billion, and interactive TV shopping from $33.7 million to $4.2 billion.

The Web definitely fits within the new rules of marketing, with its ability to provide two-way communication. Companies like wine cataloger and distributor Geerlings & Wade are asking on-line visitors for feedback on exactly what types of information they would most like to receive on-line. Geerlings & Wade is constructing its Web site in response to an extensive on-line questionnaire that asks respondents, for example, to rate their level of interest in domestic, French, Italian, Chilean, German, and Australian wines. The survey also asks visitors if they want information on comparing and buying wines, understanding wine ratings, how to order wine in a restaurant, matching wines with food, or how to run a wine tasting. Obviously, this marketer is using the dialog to capture valuable marketing information.[22]

So we have:

Manufacturer → Computer → Consumer

Manufacturer → TV Set → Consumer

Competitor → Transactional Message → Consumer

Again, the traditional retailer with one channel of distribution—his stores—is left out of the picture. Consumers will be able to shop for almost anything and never have to set foot in a physical store.

And then there are the big-box retailers like Home Depot, Circuit City, Staples, Office Depot, Toys-R-Us, and Incredible Universe. For a few years now, these category killers have been changing the retail game in categories like toys, home building needs, office supplies, and appliances. Now some are reaching out to take the big-box concept to new arenas. Now they are about to transform the way we buy cars. Having learned how to capture a giant share of the audio-video-appliance market, Circuit

City, the $5.9 billion retailer, is taking on America's auto dealers with big-box used car "stores."

Their first four "auto stores" opened in 1995. These CarMax super-stores specialize in great service, huge selection, and no-haggle pricing. Customers can choose from 500 to 1,000 used cars at each location (compared with about 150 at most traditional dealers). Computer kiosks enable customers to check car specifications, prices, and even photos of cars, then provide easy-to-follow parking space location directions to see the chosen car. Paperwork is all completed while the customer is out on the test drive, so the entire purchase transaction take less than an hour. CarMax has earned an amazing 98 percent customer satisfaction rating. Circuit City has announced plans to enter seven more markets with CarMax in 1996.

Ellis Verdi, president of CarMax' advertising agency, said, "The core idea of CarMax we're trying to deliver is a retail idea that develops trust where there was none."[23] Analysts project CarMax will have 55 stores by the turn of the century.[24]

Circuit City believes large-volume products of almost any kind are going to sell very well in a superstore environment. They proved that in 1995 with an estimated $288 million in car sales in the four stores.[25]

AutoNation opened its first big-box car store in October 1996 in Coconut Creek, FL with plans for 80 stores within four years. These stores were conceived by Wayne Huizenga, the founder of Blockbuster Video. It was his team that built a file of 60 million customers for Blockbuster. They understand what database marketing can do.

AutoNation plans to use a customized database to track its customers and develop a one-to-one relationship with them. A spokesperson for the agency developing the database said, "The idea is to tell customers that they will not be forgotten when they drive out of the lot. We want to show the customer that there are benefits in buying a used car from AutoNation and to help them maintain their cars. Customers who buy cars get a welcoming letter, a framed picture of themselves with the car, and a membership packet explaining the benefits of being a 'citizen' of AutoNation."[26]

There is no longer just one way to buy a car. *Business Week* has reported Auto-By-Tel brokered more than 25,000 car purchases in 1995 and will generate $3 billion in car sales in 1996. What's more, Auto-By-Tel now offers auto insurance policies from AIG, an international insurer headquartered in New York. AIG's policywriting systems can deliver quotations to customers in most states within 10 to 15 minutes.[27] AutoConnect, an on-line automotive shopping network, will enable visitors to apply for and receive confirmation of financing while on-line.[28] More than a half million car buyers have used Wal-Mart Stores' Sam's Club for referrals to its dealer network. One result: the number of auto dealerships in the U.S. has dropped from 47,500 in 1951 to 22,400 in 1995.[29]

So far, the big-box car retailers have been limited to pre-owned cars, but that could be changing. In January 1995, Chrysler started a 'test' of a new car franchise for CarMax in Duluth, Georgia.[30]

All of these changing channels of distribution we have been discussing make customer retention and maximizing sales from existing customers prime marketing objectives for every kind of marketer in the new century.

TREND #3: THE CHANGING PERCEPTION OF VALUE

America's traditional values of hard work and saving for the future were eroded by the high inflation rates of the 80s and by an unbounded optimism that there was no end to prosperity. Spend now and pay later with inflated dollars or high pay raises.

The early 90s changed all that. Today, the basic American value system is re-emerging. While optimistic, it is conservative, with a strong belief in hard work, saving for the future, and that old Yankee trait of getting full value for the money.

Medical costs, college costs, auto prices, and real estate prices all escalated in the 80s, and in the 90s consumers are taking a second look and saying, "What is that product really worth?"

Slower retail sales in recent years are not just a reflection of a weak economy. We're seeing a changed consumer, reflecting declining demand. Not even a phenomenally strong upturn is likely to return consumers to the nonstop consumption of the 70s and 80s. The American Dream of the past 40 years has given way to a new reality in which consumption plays a very different role.

In 1992, Grey Advertising surveyed U.S. households and produced a revealing study they called "Downshifting in America, A Consumer Reality That's Here to Stay." The study discovered that Americans have come to terms with diminished expectations. They no longer assume that ever-rising incomes and living standards are guaranteed.

In coping with this change, people have turned away from the nonstop consumption and ego gratification of the 80s and shifted their focus to the security provided by emotional and financial stability. It is all part of a process Grey calls downshifting—a conscious, considered effort to make everyday life more manageable and secure.

The 80s—the urge to own or experience the best of everything—are over. It was fun at the time, but those high-flying years left people emotionally and financially unprepared for the problems of the 90s. Americans are not about to let themselves get caught unaware again. They are downshifting their living standards to a level they can afford and maintain for the long term. For the first time in decades, people are being realistic about how much they earn and how much they can afford to spend. They have realized that achieving financial security makes living within their means an absolute necessity. If that means less lavish life-styles, most consumers are saying, "So be it."

The critical difference between today's approach to family budgeting and what we've seen in the past is the depth of thought people are putting into their financial decisions. People are coming to grips with what is really important in their lives. In the process, they're developing what amounts to a zero-sum mentality.

For decades, shopping has been America's favorite pastime. Whole generations have grown up in malls. But there is reason to believe those days may be over, or at least altered drastically.

Retailers and manufacturers have been confusing the consumer's value system, resorting to little else than price competition to achieve sales goals. But we are now learning that consumers shop for what they need, not just because an item is on sale or discounted with a manufacturer's coupon.

The June 1995 issue of *American Demographics* reported a survey by Professor Kelly of Wayne State University. Professor Kelly asked 2,000 consumers entering stores in Cleveland, Denver, and Seattle about their shopping plans:

- 14 percent planned to buy sale items.
- 13 percent planned to buy sale and regular price.
- 13 percent were just looking.
- 60 percent planned to buy full price items.

More recently, the October 1995 issue of the *Journal of Marketing* reported a survey of shoppers in two markets. They surveyed stores on two separate weeks after the stores had inserted sale circulars in the local newspaper. Only 13.6 percent of the respondents said they had come in to buy a sale item from the circulars. They just needed things they felt these stores would have. We must learn more about these customers.

Retail stores, brand manufacturers, and the entire distribution industry is acting as though the only value system is low price, thereby creating a growing consumer skepticism concerning the true value of merchandise and the regular price claims of advertisers. Forward-looking marketers understand the new customer and, as Brett Shevack, President and CEO, Partners & Shevack said, "Learn how to deal, react, adjust, survive, and be comfortable with change. Change before you have to."

TREND #4: TIME POVERTY

The continuing rise in the numbers of women in the workforce, the increase of working mothers, and the rise of single-parent households mostly headed by women are not new trends, but *The Wall Street Journal* reported in January 1996 that women probably constitute a majority of American workers for the first time. The time now spent on the job was once spent being the family's professional shopper. Perhaps that's why 132 million people—69 percent of the population—ordered goods or services by phone or mail in a most recent 12 months, compared with just 53 percent a year ago.[31]

This important group doesn't have time for daytime soap operas. They have less time for all advertising media. They're just too busy—too busy to shop, too busy to read marketers ads. As a result, they have become more impulsive purchasers.

When they do come to buy, they are looking for suppliers who understand their special, personal needs. This is especially significant for retail marketers. The second half of Professor Kelly's survey (*American Demographics,* June 1995) reinforces this. The same 2,000 consumers were interviewed when they exited the stores. They reported buying less than 50 percent of their planned purchases due to:

- ◆ Poor selection.
- ◆ Out of stock.
- ◆ Out of my size and color.

"Service" for the new consumer is far more than the reception he or she is given in the store. It is the layout of the store, signing, repairs, return policy, complaint adjustment, depth and quality of assortments, ease of credit, quality of fitting rooms, personal shopping, alterations, check-out speed, manufacturer support after the sale, and personalized or customized products and services.

A 1994 study by Impact Resources of 2,203 Nordstrom customers in four different markets asked the question, "What is your most important reason for shopping at Nordstrom?"

Merchandise quality and assortments	60.6%
Service	21.2%
Location	12.1%
Price	6.1%

A year later, on October 5, 1995, *Women's Wear Daily* reported their survey of why department stores are losing market share. The top reason was that other stores had merchandise the consumer liked better. The next reasons were all time-related:

♦ Other stores are easier to shop due to layout.

♦ Others show combinations of merchandise better.

♦ Too many departments to have to shop.

♦ Crowded racks make items seem less valuable.

♦ Department stores are more confusing than others.

♦ Ambiance is not as good.

♦ Service levels are lower.

♦ Less convenient.

Price was never mentioned!

This message is not just for retailers. All marketers need a better understanding of time-starved customers and their special needs.

To close this chapter and look ahead, let's review the essence of the four trends we have been discussing:

The slowest population growth since the 30s.

Channels of distribution changing faster than we can keep up—new kinds of products and services providers being invented almost overnight.

Declining demand—consumers suddenly rating emotional and financial stability as being more important than possessions.

Consumers are starved for time—too busy to read ads, too busy to shop.

These four trends are just part of Alvin Toffler's "wave" that is in the process of altering cultures, social relationships, communications, and organizational structures.

As if these trends were not enough to cause turbulence and

buffeting—to force us to change the marketing strategies that have worked for us in the past—there is a fifth trend so dynamic that it requires its own chapter.

The predictable behavior of customer age groups we have come to understand and market to has vanished. Here again, the new rules of marketing require a whole new understanding of customer behavior.

We all grew up with the sound French saying, "Plus ça change, plus c'est la même chose"—the more things change, the more they stay the same. But that's no longer true as the new century nears. Hold on. It's going to be a wild ride.

CHAPTER **4**

Ce N'est Pas la Même Chose

Why a 50-year-old in 2000 won't behave like a 50-year-old in 1980.

Things will *not* stay the same. Age, income, expectations, perceptions, and peer groups all play a role in how people spend their money, yet few marketers understand how profoundly age groups and generations differ. This reality is reflected in our fifth trend.

TREND #5: THE GROWING IMPORTANCE OF CHANGING GENERATIONS

The differences among the people we sell to are important; it will no longer work to market to the *averages*. We must learn to market to the *differences*. Marketing to an "average consumer" will no longer work. We must market to the *individual,* and to accomplish that we must understand how today's new customers differ. That starts with an understanding of the important changes in our 21st century generations.

The process of generation aging is predictable. If one views society only from the age group perspective (i.e., 18–35), changes in attitudes and behavior seem complicated and difficult to understand. A break-out by generation can simplify understanding.

The importance of generational research is that each generation behaves differently at the same age level. A 50-year-old in the year 2000 will behave differently than a 50-year-old behaved in 1980. The difference is caused by all the things that influenced the generation and, hence, make behavior easier to predict.

Many generations of 20 to 25 years each have lived in America since 1620. Five of them are still alive, and two are most important as we move into the new century.

The "GI Generation" is defined by *American Demographics* as today's older folks, born between 1901 and 1924. They are America's rational problem solvers, the ones who have always seemed to know how to get something done. Members of the GI Generation were the original Boy and Girl Scouts. They were victorious soldiers, the creators of the space age, atomic energy, the suburbs, and highways. Today's GIs are busy senior citizens and mature consumers.

Bob Dole represents the youngest of the GI Generation. He tried to remind the country of his proud military background and offered "a bridge" to the warm and comfortable past of face-to-face relationships and innocence, but he couldn't generate interest in the ideas of his generation. The majority of Americans preferred "a bridge" to the future.

The GI Generation will have a bit of trouble understanding some of our new media. I have heard them complain about what they call the wild disorganization of editorial and graphics in publications like *Wired* and *Details*—though I suspect few members of the GI Generation will read those periodicals. Some will understand and use the Internet. We hear stories of many senior citizens using e-mail to talk with grandchildren, but it is unlikely that many will visit a marketer's Web site to buy products or services. Like each of the other generations, these consumers will respond to being treated as individuals, but the marketer who wants to reach them will have to understand the way they think.

The "Silent Generation," born 1925–1945, is next. While a few members of this generation are World War II vets, most of them were born too late for WW II and too early to feel the heat of the Vietnam Draft. They are the generation of war and depression. They are conformist, and the youngest-marrying generation in our history. They were the volunteers for President Kennedy's Peace Corps. Now they are the litigators, technocrats, and arbitrators of a society they helped make complex. Until 1992 they were the ones sitting in the Oval Office. They are still managing many of the world's largest companies.

The members of the Silent Generation were the 40- and 50-year-olds of the 80s. They were there when high inflation rates and unbounded optimism meant spend now and pay later with inflated dollars or high pay raises. They are a strong part of the consumer group with a changed perception of value. Now they are being realistic about how much they earn and how much they can afford to spend. They are among those asking, "How much is that product worth to me?"

As the 60- and 70-year-olds of the new century, many of this group will still have strong buying power but don't expect them to act as their parents did at age 60 or 70. As one writer said recently, Grandma is no longer baking pies in the kitchen. She's pitching in with the car pool to take the grandchildren to soccer practice—if she gets off work in time. Many of these folks are thinking like those much younger. They don't think of themselves as "old." As President Reagan once said, "If you didn't know how old you are, how old would you be?"

It won't be easy to sell these savvy seniors, but the marketer who takes the time to understand them and market to their interests will find success. And that won't mean picturing them as sweet, soft-spoken, elderly men and women gardening and holding grandchildren—many will be too busy dating to identify with such images.

The "Boom Generation" is one of the two generations important to understand entering the new century. Born 1946–1964, they represent the largest generational group in U.S. history. They have been the darlings of all marketers. Now, every 7 1/2 seconds (on average) for the next decade, another American will turn 50, expanding the 50-something population by 50 percent . The number of 50- to 59-year-olds will expand by 12.4 million, from 23.3 million today to 35.7 million in 2006. By then the Boomers will be a majority of those aged 50 to 74.

They have dominated American lifestyles since the 60s and will continue to be a major factor through 2020, but they are being supplanted by the 13th generation which follows them.

The Boomers are the heirs to the WW II triumphs and were born during a wave of optimism. They have been and experienced many things: flower children, advocates of free sex, hippies, draft resisters, yuppie singles, and more recently the leaders of the ecological, educational, health care, and drug prohibition crusades.

The truth is that the famous Baby Boomers are now well into middle age, and they have changed. Karen Ritchie, Senior VP, director of media services at McCann-Erickson Worldwide says:

> I for one find it extremely ironic that the generation whose anthem was
> 'Drugs, Sex, and Rock'n'Roll' has emerged, in middle age, as one of
> the most repressive and reactionary generations this country has ever

produced. The same kids who invented free love and LSD now won't let me smoke a cigarette within 25 feet of corporate headquarters.[1]

Cheryl Russell, author of *The Master Trend: How the Baby Boom Generation Is Remaking America,* makes the point that in 1950 over three-fourths of people aged 55 or older did not have a high-school diploma. Among the oldest Baby Boomers, fully 87 percent are high-school graduates. More than one in four are college graduates, and over half have some college experience. She states, "Add to that working women, divorce, individualistic attitudes, small families, and dual incomes and you've got the recipe for a new consumer market."[2]

This means marketers must change. Even though the 50-somethings are the big spenders, most marketers have been targeting the younger customer. Ms. Russell's "new consumer market" can no longer be ignored.

Ms. Russell warns businesses to prepare for radical change among mid-life consumers.[3] This well-educated, more demanding, sophisticated, highly individualistic group represents qualities not common to the more familiar 50-plus consumers. Boomers will not join the mature market. In one recent survey 70 percent of the Boomers surveyed said they looked much younger then their age. They will create a new, vibrant, midlife marketplace pushing the threshold of the traditional mature market into older and older age groups.

Russell defines three segments of this market that bear watching:

POWER PLAYERS—Boomers will come into power in the corporate world and in government. The nation will finally be run by those who understand the lifestyles necessitated by the modern economy.

FUN SEEKERS—Unlike people currently in their 50s and 60s, Boomers are not duty-bound. Starved for fun, they will be the best thing that ever happened to the travel and entertainment industries. Auto manufacturers will benefit, too—middle-aged Boomers will be a huge market for sporty, stylish vehicles.

MATRIARCHS—Baby Boom women in their 50s will turn markets upside down. They will have a fierce, new-found energy for independence. A surge in midlife divorce might result, giving way to many more women heading households of extended families. Businesses who long ignored older women should pay attention.

The Boomers have a weak instinct for social discipline and a desire to infuse new values into the institutions they inherited. Back in the 70s they were considered social misfits; today, they are setting the nation's agenda.

"The 13th Generation" which *American Demographics* recognizes is often referred to as "Generation X" or the "no brand generation" due to their lack of brand loyalty. Born 1965–1981, they are the 13th generation to live under the American flag. This is a fragmented generation, racially and ethnically diverse, a generation of four minorities: Afro-Americans, Hispanic-Americans, Asian-Americans, and Caucasian-Americans.

Born into an increasingly diverse world, they are more likely than their elders to accept differences in race, ethnicity, national origin, family structure, and lifestyle. Growing up in the age of AIDS, divorce, latchkey kids, experimental classrooms, national economic decline, and rising violence, they are well aware that stability is hard to find and danger is just around the corner. Not so long ago, it was hard to find a Boomer teenager who looked at crime, drugs, or college with blunt cynical realism. Today, it is hard to find a teenager who doesn't.

Ms. Ritchie says these younger adults are not replacing Boomers. They are turning off their televisions and their radios and turning away from magazines because there is so little that holds any real meaning for them. Media sophisticates from an early age, they are less than impressed with pundits and talking heads on news shows. One-third of these young people get at least some of their political information from comedy shows.

They are entering the workforce at a difficult time. They resent the Baby Boomers ahead of them who are blocking their advancement. Karen Ritchie, again: "In the eyes of these young adults, Boomers had a party and didn't clean up the mess." I haven't asked her but I suspect she was talking about the Boomers capturing so many well-paid jobs, expanding corporate costs causing today's downsizing and job insecurity.

Corporate downsizing has made life uncertain. This generation has diminished expectations. They feel left out of the economic advances of the Boomers and are pessimistic about their prospects. They are suspicious of companies, advertising claims, advertising in general, and the media. They are looking for more honest, straightforward information. They will not be as easy to sell as the Boomers were.

This generation's spending power may be 80 percent of what baby boomers' was at the same age level, but they do buy. The women of this generation are the primary consumers of cosmetics and fashion clothing. Since they are buying to gratify *themselves,* these young women enjoy shopping far more than Boomer women do. More than half of these young women consider shopping a form of entertainment, compared with little more than a third of Boomer-age women.

Despite their lower income, they indulge themselves. Thirty-eight percent of these young women go to the movies each month, twice as often as Boomers. And people younger than 25 spend a larger than average share of their dollars on dining out, alcoholic beverages, clothing, TVs, and stereos. They drive about 30 percent of computer sales and have had a major impact on book superstores.

The "Millennial Generation," so christened by *American Demographics,* is the last of this study, and the youngest. Born beginning in 1982, the oldest will turn 18 in the year 2000. They are targeted as being a smarter, better behaved, and more civic-minded wave of American youth.

A survey in the December 5, 1994 issue of *Advertising Age* reported that only 16 percent of 13- to 15-year-olds think that advertising is generally truthful. While it is dangerous to predict the future, the best guess is that this group will stay civic-minded and adjust well to the very different ethnic mix that is projected for the middle of the new century.

What does this generational study teach the marketer preparing for the future? The days of the self-indulgent Boomers are drawing to a close. They will tend to be much more conservative spenders for the remainder of their lifetimes. And behind them, the 13th generation and the millennial generation will be an even more realistic group who will be harder to sell.

The great opportunity lies in understanding these generations of new consumers as individuals, creating honest, open relationships with them, and changing the rules of marketing to manage customers, not just products.

In other words, mass merchandising is dead.

A mass mentality was created in the 1950s and '60s and into the '70s by the sheer number of Baby Boomers. Jack Pitney, Assistant Professor of Government, Claremont-McKenna College makes the point:

> It has been said that this was the big-unit era—big government, big business, big labor, mass production, network TV and radio, big-circulation daily newspapers. We had nowhere near the atomization that we have today.
>
> Though segregated by race, society was far more homogenized then— if separate and unequal. Most everybody listened to the radio (in 1946 only 8,000 American households had television sets); they got their news mostly from newspapers; they wrote letters rather than calling long distance; they dressed up to go to the movies and to travel because these were special events in those days.[4]

There are many reasons for the disappearance of the mass market. One is the fact that the Boomers and the group we call Generation X are marrying later, or not at all, and having fewer children. We are seeing this now in the smaller Millennial Generation; it is what we mean by "limits of growth."

We won't be a growing consumer society because there will no longer be a growing consumer group to do the consuming.

The retail industry has moved from the era of department store dominance to one characterized by stores that provide highly focused merchandise for specific, targeted customer groups. Supermarkets now focus store inventories and promotions to carefully researched neighborhoods. Packaged goods marketers have learned to create targeted products for separate age groups and hundreds of demographic splits.

Victoria's Secret, like other retailers, has always allocated merchandise to its 678 shops based on a mathematical store average. Queries to their data warehouse revealed that an average store sells an equal number of black and ivory bras, but Miami-area consumers buy the ivory more often by a margin of 10 to 1. In New York, bras with a bust size of 32 outsell the company average inventory model by 20 to 1. A Victoria's Secret executive was quoted as saying, "Our processes and systems were built around an average-shop concept, when in reality our chain has few average shops."[5]

> For the first time since the invention of the assembly line, companies now have the capability to listen carefully to what an individual customer wants, and then deliver mass-customized product or service in response to the customer's individual specifications. This gives those businesses that can efficiently link their marketing and production processes together an unprecedented opportunity to lock their current customers to them virtually forever.[6]

Motorola has re-engineered the manufacturing process flow to offer a pager with 256 options, including 11 colors with different notification choices (buzz, beep, or flash). The customer places an order. Information technology matches the order with the manufacturing process. The pager is manufactured and shipped within one hour.

Professor and industry advisor, Don E. Schultz, Agora, Inc. and Northwestern University, 1996, says:

> Technology has killed the mass market. The mass market is dead. We just refuse to bury it because it is what we know how to do.
>
> With so many marketers developing databases, the more they know about their customers the less they need to rely on mass advertising communications. The more your customer knows about your product, the less they need traditional advertising.

Another professional source agrees:

> The 21st century will bring unprecedented challenges. The United States is substantially over-stored. In this environment, marketers will grow only

by stealing market share from their competitors. Success requires an intense focus on the customer and breakthrough tools and techniques for maximizing customer relationships.

Survivors will feature the unbeatable combination of merchandising savvy, bare-bones operational efficiency and intense customer focus. Those who reinvent their business around the customer will see sales and margins reach new heights. Those who don't, won't make it into the next century.[7]

Marketers must embrace change, not run from it. It is not time to be fearful. It is time to be bold.

Marketers must learn that understanding the customer will be the business of business. Not by way of outdated concepts like age groups and zip-code clusters and demographics, but by way of profiling individual customers—their needs, their wants, their dreams; when they want something, how they want it, and how much they are willing to pay for it.

Marketers must learn to create dialogs with customers and learn from them. Keep in mind the company that held conversations with customers who replied, "Please don't clutter up our lives. We just want someone to care about us and know what we want."

Francey Smith, who developed the customer marketing approach for Bloomingdales, said it best, "We must learn to market to each of our customers as if we still knew them by name and face, like we used to."

It's just possible we can do that. IBM's original Mark I computer, unveiled in 1943, was 8 feet tall, 52 feet long, 2 feet thick, weighed 5 tons, and used 750,000 moving parts. Today, a credit-card sized piece of plastic with a microprocessor embedded in it weighs three-fourths of an ounce. Twenty years ago, a computer cost $20,000,000. Now you can buy one with 10 times the power for $500.

The wildfire spread of the computer has been called the single most important change in the knowledge system since the invention of moveable type in the fifteenth century. As Watts Wacker, Resident Futurist at SRI International, said, "We have gone from the 'TV generation' to the 'VCR generation' to the 'Download generation'."

Old Seniors, Young Seniors, Power Players, Fun Seekers, Independent Matriarchs, No-Brand Media Sophisticates, New Kinds of Teenagers—all call for intense customer focus. Averages will be meaningless. Success can only come from building relationships and marketing to the differences.

In the next chapter, we're going to begin to understand the customer differences that help us build one-to-one relationships with customers.

CHAPTER **5**

Looking for Meaningful Relationships

How customers are moving from passive status to involved participants.

You might as well know the truth. I would rather be sailing than writing this book. I love to sail. I love to be involved with anything that has to do with sailing. I have covered every America's Cup campaign since 1956, when the New York Yacht Club inquired whether the Royal Yacht Squadron would be interested in challenging for the Cup with a 12-meter yacht. The America's Cup Deed of Gift was amended then to establish a minimum waterline of 44 feet and to cancel the requirement that the challenger arrive in the United States on her own bottom. For that first post-war campaign I went to Newport, Rhode Island, in 1958 to watch Briggs Cunningham skipper the 12-meter *Columbia* and sweep four straight races from Lieutenant Commander Graham Mann, in the *British Sceptre.* So, of course I went to Perth, Australia, in 1987 to support Dennis Connor's efforts to bring the Cup home again.

The first night in Perth, a long way from home, I went out wearing a polo shirt with a facetious embroidered message: "I'm looking for a meaningful overnight relationship." In my rented car, on the way to dinner, I entered a roundabout and crashed head-on with another motorist. It was a low-speed collision. No one was hurt, but both cars were destroyed. As I started to get out of the car, I realized I had hit two Catholic nuns and that my "statement" polo shirt might be a bit embarrassing. I rushed to the trunk and, in the 100+ degree heat, put on a blazer to hide the offending shirt.

The two nuns called their Mother Superior, and she was wonderful, worrying more about me than her sisters, but that's not the point of this story.

Forget, if you will, the then acceptable attempt at humor of my embroidered shirt, but our customers in the new century will all be wearing a similar message—

I'm looking for a meaningful relationship

That means marketers must change the rules and find new paradigms of marketing communications and new models of understanding customers. With channels of distribution, perceptions of value, definitions of service, and generations all changing, the mass communications so well developed in this century will no longer serve to communicate with the New Century consumer.

At the 87th Annual Meeting of the Association of National Advertisers nearly all speakers on the conference theme of "Brand Champions" cited the consumer as the single most important factor in brand building. But marketers preoccupied with competition, price pressure, and promotion have lost touch with that constituency. "Perhaps we should think less about our brands and more about our customers," said Paul Higham, Senior Vice President of Marketing and Communications at Wal-Mart Stores.[1]

Recently, Grey Advertising surveyed US households and produced a revealing study. Customers told Grey, "Advertising is out of touch." Respondents said they don't like hype. Ninety percent of these customers told Grey they're fed up with hype and exaggeration. Seventy-two percent said today's advertising is boring. As Grey concluded, "To overcome the challenge of the 90s, marketers must turn their attention to forging solid relationships with consumers."

American Express understands this. John Hayes, Executive Vice President of Global Advertising for American Express, says, "We're reshaping the American Express brand to fit a wide variety of uses in the next century—we want to have long-term relationships with people and we're going to build them through marketing."[2]

The cover story of one marketing magazine summed this all up:

- We're moving from dealing with a faceless mass market to direct interaction with known prospects and customers.
- Consumers are moving from passive status to involved participants, often dictating what the product will look like.
- The new consumer demands to be involved, to belong, to be heard.
- Companies will have to move from mere customer satisfaction to customer astonishment—and regular doses of astonishment at that.
- Marketing dollars are being shifted from media advertising to other, more measurable forms of marketing. Companies will no longer waste money on nonprospects.
- A new dimension has been added to the sales process. What do you do to care for the customer after the sale has been made?[3]

"We just want someone to care about us and know what we want"

We can do that.

At the American Association of Advertising Agencies' 77th Annual meeting in Orlando, Florida, in May 1995, William Esrey, Chairman and CEO of the Sprint Corporation addressed the assembled marketers:

> The globalization of commercial communications does not mean reaching customers a billion at a time.
>
> It may seem like a paradox, but a global communication gives us the chance to speak intimately to each and every customer, and to actually have them talk back to us. In fact, you might say, the successful business of the future will know their customers by name or else settle for having no customers at all.

"One of the most intriguing opportunities offered by the new technologies," he said, "is quantitative measures of customer involvement and persuasion through the tracking of customer responses."

Of course, Mr. Esrey's quantitative measures of customer involvement and persuasion through the tracking of customer responses is part of what we now call database marketing.

The cat is out of the bag. The purpose of this book is to examine the expanding role of database marketing and to explore the very great differences between Direct Marketing, Database Marketing, Relationship Marketing, and Customer Management.

Surviving marketers will only be able to grow by gaining market share, and the only possible way to do this in a limited growth environment is by taking business away from someone else. As we have said, that requires:

1. Finding ways to change the rules.
2. Understanding individual target markets.
3. Making customers instead of selling things.

Thus, marketers must understand the strengths and weaknesses of these disciplines.

Come explore.

CHAPTER **6**

Popcorn, Peanuts, and Database

Database marketing is the fastest growing marketing investment in North America.

When I first got involved in catalog marketing and discovered how much catalogers knew about their individual customers, I decided there was an enormous opportunity for *every* industry to acquire such depth of knowledge about their customers. We hadn't even coined the phrase "database marketing" when I started looking for the prize that is in every box.

As I said in the preface, from the day I persuaded STS Systems to build that first Customer Profile System for marketers, I have been criss-crossing the continent as a missionary for this new customer-driven marketing. It was a tough sell. I was telling folks to change the rules. Converts came slowly.

Now, database marketing, relationship marketing, and customer management combined represent the fastest growing marketing investment in North America, in every field. It is changing everything we ever thought we knew about marketing.

We have reached the point predicted three or four years ago by Robert Blattberg, Executive Director of the Center for Retail Marketing at Northwestern University's J.L. Kellogg Graduate School of Management:

> Having a customer database is no longer a competitive advantage. Not having a customer database is now a competitive disadvantage.

Marketers who have been telling media how tight their budgets are have suddenly found a way to spend thousands of dollars, hundreds of thousands of dollars, and in some cases even millions of dollars to build and maintain a customer database.

Why? Because they have learned that customer targeting works. They learned that first with direct mail. That experience taught them to next look at the efficiency of media in new ways to achieve varying efficiencies at mass-to-microlevels of audience contact. The simple days of low cost-per-thousand are gone. As customers change, media buying efficiency changes. Low cost-per-thousand readers or viewers or listeners is not enough. We must now seek out the lowest cost-per-thousand *viable* prospects.

The advent of geographic marketing desktop software around 1985 spurred the spread of geo-target marketing, as marketers gained access to small-area demographics and began to link these to media use. Now, household data have an even greater influence. The share of media targeting that is done at the household level has been increasing every year.

As marketers learn to deal with changing channels of distribution, changing values, changing generations, and changing definitions of service, this level of targeting will be superseded by vast improvements in the ability to target and communicate at the individual level.

Most database marketing today does not target the individual. It is instead "mini-mass marketing," a term coined by Lester Wunderman. Basically, "mini-mass marketing" sends the same targeted message to a segment of people based on common, defining characteristics. Here we begin to differentiate between database marketing and relationship marketing, the targeting of selected groups of people as opposed to individuals. The new rules of marketing require a real understanding of individual customers and the capability to talk to each one-to-one.

In 1960, segmented targeting comprised 5.5 percent of total media expenditures. This share has tripled to 15 percent of today's total media expenditures. By the year 2000 it is predicted that businesses will spend more than 20 percent of their media budgets targeting individuals. And these are US total media expenditures; many retail companies have already exceeded that 20 percent mark.

Why this concentration on the individual? Very simply, we have moved beyond demographics. You don't learn individual needs from demographics. Demographics don't identify prospective buyers. Customer behavior is the key.

For years we have marketed to the averages. In the new century, we will market to the differences!

We will do that by way of database marketing. The customer database is much more than a compilation of customer names and addresses. It is a rich mine of valuable, exciting knowledge. There *is* a prize in every box.

Database marketers keep these mountains of customer information in their files because they understand successful marketing from the database must be founded on a dialog with the customer.

Think for a minute about a conversation we might share. If I listen carefully to what you say to me and take that into account when I answer you, I will make a lot more sense to you. You will find me much more charming. We will both enjoy our conversation more. God gave us two ears and only one mouth intentionally.

The advertising agency Brierley and Partners helps Hilton Hotels, Hertz, and United Airlines with their customer database marketing. Robbin Gehrke, formerly Executive Creative Director of the agency, has this to say about conversations with customers: "I look at what we do as carrying on an extensive and very personal conversation with each individual customer. If they tell us something, we need to acknowledge that in subsequent communications."

It takes a lot of information and knowledge to do that.

Database marketing can be thought of as a system for creating a central repository of all information pertaining to the relationship of your business and your customers. Data is consumers trying to tell marketers what they want. When I said that recently in a speech to a marketing group in Sydney, one member of the audience replied, in typical, understated Australian fashion, "Yes, I suspect knowing something about your customer would be a great help in getting more of them."

The driving force behind the strategic value of database marketing systems is the ability to integrate all of the information on a customer's relationship with your business and to enhance the value of the customer's lifetime value to you.

This is what we mean when we say a customer database is much more than a file of names and addresses. To develop the kind of knowledge to understand your customers well enough to maintain a dialog, to carry on conversations, to treat them as individuals, requires tracking every word you exchange with the individual customer. When did we advertise to her?

When did we mail? When did we phone? What did we offer or say each time.

When and how did she respond? Did she buy? What did she buy? How much did she spend? Did she visit a store? Which store? How far is that store from her home? How did she pay—cash, credit card (which one?), check? What size does she wear? What colors does she prefer? How did we find her in the first place? And more, and more, and more.

Added to all the information in the database is what we now call "demographic and psychographic append." This is the process of appending individual customer demographics and psychographics to the file—not just cluster codes, but specific, individual demographics and psychographics. Does this specific customer own or rent? Is that a house or a condo? What is its value? Does she have children? What ages? Pets? How many? Cats or dogs? Computer literate or not? A fisherman? A sailor? A bowler? What other hobbies? What kind of books does this customer read? All of this comes from listening to the customer. This information about the customer defines the difference between a mail file and a database, and the marketer needs it to provide the kind of personal caring and relationship building required by the new rules of marketing.

The important thing to remember, at the start, is that a customer database allows marketers to manage all customer contact, no matter what media they use. Under the new rules of marketing, customer contacts will change and be based on relevance instead of frequency and reach.

The case for database marketing has been best summed up by a marketer who captures 400,000 customer transactions a day. Speaking at a recent database marketing conference, Julia Adamsen, then in charge of the Pizza Hut customer database, said:

> Why do we use database marketing? After all, we're only selling pizza. Answer. Because we're selling a lot of pizza. $4.8 billion a year. We use database marketing to know our customers and know what they want.
>
> Customers change. Tastes and habits change. We have to keep in touch, talk to customers and listen. We're into database marketing to learn what we have to do to double our business in the next five years. Which customers are most profitable. Which customers are the biggest opportunity. How will this change.

I asked Julia, after that presentation, what Pizza Hut has learned from their customer database. She was quick to tell me,

1. The customer is an important corporate asset.

2. Not all customers are created equal.

3. Information is power.

This is what we must learn from Pizza Hut: Customers, not merchandise or services or real estate, are a company's primary asset.

Information *is* power. This is the prize that hides in every database!

CHAPTER **7**

Blame it on the Postal Person

What direct marketing *is*—and what it *isn't*.

In Chapter 5, I said we would explore the very great differences between direct marketing, database marketing, relationship marketing, and customer management. That exploration has to start with the difficult process of defining direct marketing.

The process is difficult because few folks, today, will agree on a precise definition. It used to be easy. Many people say the early mail order companies started what we now call direct marketing and use the terms "mail order" and "direct marketing" interchangeably. This is wrong. Direct marketing came from the appeal of direct mail *as a concept* and the recognition that other media and sales force activities were and are being used to generate names for the database. The importance of this distinction is that direct marketing is much different than mail order. Lester Wunderman coined the term direct marketing. It first appeared as Columbia House Direct Marketing. Then, after Pete Hoke introduced direct marketing *as a concept,* Columbia House dropped that reference.

Retail distributors, soliciting orders primarily through the mail, started with catalogs and brochures and expanded to advertising solicitations in newspapers and magazines, then on radio and television, but they always shipped the ordered goods by mail or UPS. They were retailers without stores. Over time some mail-order businesses adopted the new term, direct marketing, but their orders still came in by mail or telephone (and, now, by fax and the Internet).

Even in their latest release, the *New Grolier's Multimedia Encyclopedia* defines direct marketing as:

> In the field of advertising and selling called direct marketing, buyers place orders through the mail or some other nonstore channel—the telephone or a salesperson visiting the home, for example. Once restricted almost entirely to making customer contact through the mails, direct marketing now utilizes every advertising medium to reach its markets. The goal is always a direct response: a successful ad will persuade potential customers to return a coupon or dial a telephone number. Contributing to the success of direct marketing have been such relatively new marketing methods as the use of salesforces trained in telephone selling, or "telemarketing"; the availability of toll-free telephone numbers for buyers to call; television shopping channels, which offer merchandise that viewers can order by telephone; and mass mailings to alert customers to events such as the heavily publicized sweepstakes drawings that promote sales campaigns. Most important has been the development of computer-generated mailing lists of potential customers, pinpointed as to income, interests, occupation, or any of a number of characteristics that are used to define a market.

Well, it ain't that simple. We can't blame direct marketing on the postal service! The folks at Grolier should change their definition to fit the definition now accepted by the Direct Marketing Association.

Up until recently *Direct Marketing* magazine, the bible of the industry, ran this tagline under their logo: "Using Direct Response Advertising to Enhance Marketing Database." The inclusion of the phrase "direct response" ties back to the Grolier definition of direct marketing.

Last year, *Direct Marketing* changed its title to read:

> A Process: Databased—Measured—Integrated—Interactive—
> Media Neutral—Targeted—Response Driven—Customer
> Driven—Sale Location Neutral—Organization Neutral

No more mention of direct response or direct mail or nonstore retailing. That was the magazine's way of saying *all* marketing from the database should be considered direct marketing.

Was this just a ploy to broaden the readership of *Direct Marketing?* I don't believe it was. I see it as an honest reflection of industry trends. "Pete" Hoke, Chairman of the Board of *Direct Marketing,* writes and speaks often on this subject. It is his belief that all targeted marketing developed from a database of individual customer files is, in fact, marketing direct to the customer and is, therefore, direct marketing. Through Pete's lobbying efforts, the DMA Board finally accepted this definition of direct marketing:

> An interactive system of marketing which uses one or more media to affect a measurable response at any location with this activity stored on a marketing database.

Others agree. Donald Libey, President of the consultancy Libey Incorporated, talks of "Fusion Marketing" and calls it the new convergence of retail and direct, or "directail."

"Pete" Hoke and Donald Libey are right. We can see the convergence. With the unconscionable increases in costs of paper and postage in recent years, catalogers are now feeling the margin pressures retailers have been fighting since the 80s. L.L. Bean reported that paper increases added about $25 million to its operating costs in 1995.[1] *DM News,* in its November 6, 1995 issue, reported 10 of the 43 direct marketing companies it tracks each month—companies like Bombay, Gander Mountain, Hanover Direct, and Spiegel—had posted losses for the most recent 12 months.

Like the retail store marketers, the catalogers are hearing the clock tick closer to the moment when there is no "place," when there is no "there," when the Internet has truly leveled the playing field. Their reaction? Emulate the retailer; when in doubt, discount.

For Christmas 1995, some catalogers offered promotions such as free shipping and handling and money-off purchases to entice customers to buy and buy early. L.L. Bean gave some customers free shipping on orders placed by November 19th. Eddie Bauer paid shipping for new prospects who spent $100 or more and placed orders by October 27th. Lands' End offered to pay for the shipping and handling on second or third deliveries after customers pay standard charges on the first. Lands' End also offered free monogramming on early orders. J.C. Penney offered a percentage off or a dollar amount off merchandise. Duncan Hill Company's start-up catalog, "Kids Club," discounted from 40 to 60 percent off retail prices in exchange for an annual fee of $18.[2] L.L. Bean even had a "January Sale."

Carolyn Gould, former Editor of *Catalog Age,* founder of *Direct,* and President of Directives, a marketing and communications consulting firm that serves consumer and business catalogers, has a warning for the industry. Speaking of catalogers' repeated use of sales, buy-one-get-one-free offers, discounts on further orders, and indiscriminate implementation of incentives, she says, "Incentives cease to be inciting when they become expectations. Premiums cease to be exciting when they become expected."[3]

Taking the Hoke/Libey projection to the next level, I'd suggest that direct marketers, brand marketers, and traditional retailers are all growing more and more alike, all facing mounting pressures on margin, and all seeking new sales volume to maintain return on investment.

Recently someone remarked that advertisers had always said, "We speak. You listen. Now the customers speak. Advertisers don't listen, though; they just speak louder." The limits of growth, changing channels of distribution, changing perception of value, time poverty, and the growing importance of changing generations are forcing direct marketers, brand marketers, bank marketers, and traditional retailers to learn that loud shouts simply won't work anymore. All marketers are looking for new, more efficient ways to talk to the customer.

Most marketers now believe the future of customer communications depends on knowing more about each individual customer. We see marketers in every industry gathering the tools of database marketing.

So, we'll correct Mr. Grolier and call all marketers who target customers from a customer database direct marketers, let the post office off the hook, and get on with our subject.

CHAPTER **8**

The Check is in the Mail

How to empower your organization to increase profits.

Before we separate database marketing from relationship marketing and customer management it will be worthwhile to look at database marketing tools. While we will later separate the pure database marketers from those who are building real relationships with customers, the basic database tools are common to all disciplines.

Remember, the process of database marketing is a system for creating a central repository for all of the information pertaining to the relationship of a business and its customers. The purpose of this is not to acquire and store information but rather to drive individualized communications and generate sales. The driving force behind the strategic value of such a system is the ability to integrate all of the information on a customer's relationship with a business and to enhance the customer's lifetime value. That means keeping track of every customer contact—everything the customer "says" to us, everything we "say" to the customer, and everything we can learn about the customer's lifestyle. This central repository is often referred to as a "data warehouse."

For 40 years, computer professionals have promised senior executives that the next computer or software system would provide better management information. That promise has had about the same validity as the claim that the check is in the mail.

Now data warehousing has arrived on the scene and made the same promise. Is this time any different?

There is no more valuable resource to a business than intelligence. Critical, accurate, timely information can be directly converted into competitive advantage, and that's what it's all about. Data warehouses are nothing more than machines designed to process bits and bytes and produce knowledge for an enterprise to use as a strategic weapon to compete in the marketplace.[1]

With everyone talking about the data warehouse, just what is it and how does it differ from a marketing database?

Harte-Hanks Data Technologies has produced a data warehousing "white paper" answering that question:

A general definition for a data warehouse is a database that:

- Is organized to serve as a central data storage area.
- Is used for data-mining and other applications.
- Meets a specific set of business requirements.
- Uses data that meet a predefined set of business criteria.

In other words, a data warehouse is a process of assembling disparate data, transforming it to a consistent state for business decision making, and empowering users by providing them with access to this information from multiple applications.

A data warehouse can be simplified to include three main functions: acquisition, storage, and access.

The acquisition portion is the first step in building the data warehouse. This portion of the system includes all of the programs, applications, data-staging areas, and legacy system interfaces that are responsible for pulling the data out of the legacy system, preparing it, loading it into the warehouse itself, and exporting it out again.

The second portion of a data warehouse system is the storage area or database, which holds a vast amount of information from a variety of sources. The data within it has been organized in a way that makes it easy to find and use, and it is updated frequently from its sources.

Access is the most important component of the system because it includes all the different mining tools that make use of the information stored in the data warehouse.

A marketing database should be considered a subset of the data warehouse. A marketing database is one of many applications that can take advantage of the data collected in a data warehouse. A marketing database is specifically designed to create a "view" of customers and prospects to meet the detailed needs of the marketing function. Marketing databases provide functionality, access, and reporting unique to the needs of marketers.

The white paper makes the point that "The goal of a data warehouse is to empower an organization with the right information to flow to the right people at the right time in the correct format to *increase profits*."

The important distinction is that a marketing database is a subset of a data warehouse. Companies are now beginning to believe they don't want a giant data warehouse where data can disappear. What they really want is to be able to provide quick answers to a lot of end users and to do that as simply and inexpensively as possible. A centralized corporate warehouse can be a multiyear project costing millions of dollars. Even though the average payback for warehouse projects that averaged $2.2 million is 2.3 years, a popular option for many companies is a collection of smaller, more targeted "data marts," starter warehouses designed to prove their business value before moving to the giant, enterprisewide warehouse. The marketing database can be considered a kind of data mart.

It is not enough simply to record millions of bites of customer data. It is the functionality, access, and reporting capabilities that empower the marketer. Information is not knowledge until we analyze it and understand it. Knowledge is not power until we learn how to use it. The purpose of database power for the marketer must be to drive sales and increase profit.

In the next chapter we'll begin to see how smart marketers use critical, accurate, timely information for competitive advantage.

CHAPTER 9

Looking for Thomas Jefferson

The importance of segmentation and how it works.

OK, we have now defined direct marketing, and we have all that critical, accurate, timely data in a warehouse or mart. Now, what do we do with it? We need some tools to mine this rich vein of intelligence.

The first tool to understand is segmentation. The essence of segmentation is breaking large groups into smaller, more homogeneous ones. Segmentation is not a new concept. As far back as the 1700s catalogs were targeted; only a tiny percentage of the population was literate enough to read them and wealthy enough to buy from them. In addition, these early catalogs kept records of the buyers to insure that good customers, like Thomas Jefferson, received future mailings. (Jefferson was an inveterate mail order buyer.)[1]

Remember, the database marketer tracks all customer actions—when the customer last purchased, how often the customer purchases, how much the customer spends, what the customer buys. And he or she does this for every individual customer.

With this knowledge, the marketer can profile and identify customers with like characteristics and partition his file into segments. In simplest terms, we can think of these file segments as groups of customers whose similar characteristics make it likely they will exhibit similar purchase behavior.

We said it will no longer work to market to the *averages*. We must learn to market to the *differences*. This business of tracking customer action—when he last purchased, how often he purchases, how much he spends, what he buys—enables us to profile and identify customers with the same *differences* and segment customers into groups with common proclivities.

Profiling and identifying customers with like characteristics and grouping them into segments is what Lester Wunderman described as "mini-mass marketing." There is a lot more to it than that, of course, but clearly segmentation makes it possible for the marketer to make the right offer at the right time to the right group of customers, in order to make the most efficient and effective use of marketing dollars.

There are four major groups of segmentation variables.

Geographic	Demographic	Behavioral	Psychographic
Region	Age	Purchase occasion	Lifestyle
County size	Sex	Benefits sought	Social class
Urban/suburban	Family size	User status	Personality
Climate	Family life cycle	Usage rate	
Seasons	Income	Loyalty status	
Zip Code	Occupation	Readiness stage	
	Education	Attitude toward product	
	Religion	Actual purchase	
	Race		
	Nationality		

The geographic variable is more applicable to national advertisers such as Maxwell House, which varies its coffee strength to fit regional tastes, or Johnson & Johnson, which varies its Raid formula by season and type of bugs in an area. A retail marketer with a wide geographic distribution of stores must recognize differences in lifestyle, income, purchase behavior, product usage, and weather in each of the different geographic regions. Nordstrom has several sets of regional and local buyers to ensure that the stores respond to different geographic needs. I am told that Wal-Mart maintains a database of demographics and psychographics on the full U.S. population to enable it to merchandise individual stores to suit specific markets.

Behavioral information is the most important because it is the record of the customers' actual purchase behavior, but it still leaves the marketer reacting to what customers have done, rather than anticipating what they might do in the future. The next step, trying to understand customer motivations, can help predict future behavior.

That leads us to demographics, life stages, and psychographics. Demographics are a frequently used segmentation base. Demographics are easy to measure and important to understand. Even when market segments are first segmented by other bases, demographics are needed to determine the size and income levels of the segmented groups.

Marketers using demographics like to look at life cycles. Robert Perlstein, CEO of Lifestyle Change Communications, Inc., has trademarked the term synchographics to explain the concept of targeting consumers during important moments of change in their lives.

People at different life stages make different purchases. Just-marrieds need many things for the home. The arrival of children opens a market for life insurance. Empty-nesters are prime candidates for travel and retirement savings plans. Seklemian/Newell works with a number of electronics chain clients. We have found "new movers" to be one of these marketers' most profitable prospects.

For years marketers have been segmenting customers geographically and by demographics using zip codes. This is still valuable information for the marketer. Zip code penetration reports (Figure 9-1) are important products of the database. Here we are looking at customer penetration by zip code, which is the norm. This analysis compares household data with the company's customer data, showing market penetration.

In this example, the city of Westerly has 7,718 households, of which 22 have household members that are customers of this company, so the company has a .29 percent penetration in this zip code. The 22 customer households account for $13,389 in annual sales. Twenty-one customers are considered active, and one inactive.

A little work with a calculator exposes some big opportunities. Bristol (06010) has 231 active customers who spend $812 each, yet this company owns only 260 of the 23,533 customers in the zip. Norfolk (06058) has 6 active customers who spend $1,237 each, yet this company owns only 11 of the 614 households in the zip. Stafford Springs (06076) has 42 active customers who spend $965 each, yet the company owns only 51 of the 4,513 in the zip code. It would be easy to look at Manchester or New Britain, which have two of the greatest sales dollars, and think they are the best hunting ground but those customers spend only $620 and $604. It could well be that the bigger opportunities await in Bristol, Norfolk, and Stafford Springs

Another way to use this report is to look at zip codes where the

FIGURE 9-1

ZIP Code Penetration Report

City	State	ZIP	Census Cust	# Cust	% Penetration	Total Sales	#Active Cust	#Inactive Cust
Westerly	RI	02891	7718	22	0.29%	13389	21	1
Avon	CT	06001	5604	44	0.79%	28647	39	5
Bloomfield	CT	06002	7566	77	1.02%	37685	69	8
Bristol	CT	06010	23533	260	1.10%	187595	231	29
Burlington	CT	06013	2504	25	1.00%	15001	21	4
Broad Brook	CT	06016	2144	29	1.35%	23611	24	5
Canaan	CT	06018	1013	14	1.38%	10245	13	1
Canton	CT	06019	999	20	2.00%	16680	19	1
Collinsville	CT	06022	2082	12	0.58%	6024	11	1
E. Berlin	CT	06023	365	8	2.19%	5355	8	0
E. Granby	CT	06026	1699	20	1.18%	14296	19	1
Ellington	CT	06029	3405	36	1.06%	19457	34	2
Farmington	CT	06032	5682	44	0.77%	23467	37	7
Glastonbury	CT	06033	9349	96	1.03%	53023	86	10
Granby	CT	06035	2868	38	1.32%	22855	35	3
Kensington	CT	06037	6060	100	1.65%	49304	90	10
Lakeville	CT	06039	836	6	0.72%	4616	6	0
Manchester	CT	06040	20154	229	1.14%	126489	204	25
New Britain	CT	06051	12176	138	1.13%	87122	118	20
New Britain	CT	06052	3662	52	1.42%	19257	47	5
New Britain	CT	06053	13783	224	1.63%	128760	213	11
New Hartford	CT	06057	1967	27	1.37%	13116	23	4
Norfolk	CT	06058	614	11	1.79%	7423	6	5
N. Granby	CT	06060	496	23	4.64%	11582	20	3
Plainville	CT	06062	7064	93	1.32%	56664	85	8
Vernon Rockville	CT	06066	12325	174	1.41%	86001	148	26
Rocky Hill	CT	06067	6631	84	1.27%	46073	73	11
Simsbury	CT	06070	5152	47	0.91%	20390	42	5
Somers	CT	06071	2918	43	1.47%	17595	36	7
Somersville	CT	06072	0	6	N/A	3683	5	1
S. Glastonbury	CT	06073	1101	9	0.82%	6047	9	0
S. Windsor	CT	06074	7829	92	1.18%	50382	84	8
Stafford	CT	06075	142	6	4.23%	4523	4	2
Stafford Springs	CT	06076	4513	51	1.13%	40520	42	9
Suffield	CT	06078	3240	59	1.82%	27211	52	7
Tariffville	CT	06081	408	14	3.43%	3083	10	4
Enfield	CT	06082	15121	206	1.36%	111089	181	25
Tolland	CT	06084	3830	41	1.07%	21993	32	9
Unionville	CT	06085	2405	20	0.83%	8097	18	2

Courtesy: Harte-Hanks Data Technologies

company has above-average penetration—Canton, N. Granby, Staffior, and Tariffville—and work on the assumption that some of the 2,045 neighbors of the company's 63 customers in these towns may be very similar and therefore should like the company's products or stores.

This analysis can also be drawn by state, by market, by SCF, by block group, or even by carrier route. And for a retail report it can show the stores where customers within a certain zip code shop.

When we developed a customer database for a national department store recently, store management was overwhelmed to learn that 41 percent of all sales at one of their store units came from just one zip code. The zip code analysis provides a measure of market share, but it is not a solid predictor of customer response.

The next segmentation variable is psychographics. This starts with lifestyle, which defines how people live and what they do, plus their demographics.

To learn the lifestyles of customers, a marketer must either collect information directly from them—often a costly proposition—or purchase data from outside sources. Since the InfoBase file from Acxiom is one of the largest and most complete compilations of individual customer demographic and lifestyle data, I asked Dr. Don Hinman, an Acxiom business development executive and an expert in this field, to define "lifestyle" for us:

> In the simplest form, lifestyle may be defined as the style or type of approach that people take to living their lives and associated activities and behaviors. In many cases, the elements used to describe lifestyles are actually the *determinants* of a lifestyle. For instance, a person's demographic characteristics have often been used to describe that individual's lifestyle. A person with a high income is sometimes described as having an affluent lifestyle. A homemaker is regarded as having a lifestyle related to domestic and child-rearing activities. Younger people are generally thought to have more active lifestyles, whereas older individuals are seen in less active lifestyles.
>
> Lifestyle definitions often revolve around how an individual spends his or her leisure time. Leisure activities are *influenced* by demographic or geographic characteristics, but they are not *dictated* by them. Knowing how someone chooses to spend his or her leisure time is often indicative of how they spend disposable income.
>
> Lifestyles have a particular strength in the area of customer communication. By describing the presence (and absence) of particular lifestyle segments within a customer base, tailored communication messages can be created that speak to customers in their own "language." The offer and the

message can become more persuasive when customers are approached within the context of how they chose to spend their time.

As Don says, knowing more about the best customers' lifestyles can help the marketer relate more effectively to them in communications. Furthermore, it can help the marketer find others just like the best customers. Identifying the lifestyle characteristics of customers who purchase a given product can help a marketer comb his or her customer and prospect files for others, called look-alikes, who would make good candidates for similar offers.

Don gave us the example of a bank that used this technique to find 12,000 high-deposit prospects within its customer base, netting $6 million in incremental deposits at a cost of only 0.6 percent per deposit dollar.

A major women's magazine added the InfoBase data to its subscription files and learned the best renewal segment was suburban women, mid- to upper-income, fairly well educated, who tended to have kids in the home. The worst-performing third of the market tended to be single, urban females, women in their first career positions who were a little more blue collar, making a little less income. Actions taken with this new knowledge changed renewal performance radically.

Another source for lifestyle information about consumers is the Lifestyle Selector™ from R.L. Polk Company. The Lifestyle Selector™ provides information on interests and purchase habits compiled through product-warranty registration surveys. The 36 million household file has recently been updated with additional information including name, spouse, vehicle data, mail order buyer affinity, and consumer usage of CD ROM drives, satellite dishes, and fax modems. Polk can also identify horseback riders, cruise ship vacationers, mutual fund owners, and large or tall size clothing buyers. Marketers pay $70 per thousand names for this information.

As this is written, Club Med North America is about to test its first solo prospect mailings using this "look-alike" concept. Working with Berenson, Isham & Partners, a direct marketing agency in Boston, and using the Polk Lifestyle Selector™ database, Club Med developed three separate customer models based on 15 demographic criteria, such as income, marital status, and home value, and 60 psychographic criteria, including personal interests and sports participation. The profiles were developed by matching a test sample from Club Med's database to the Polk Lifestyle database. Twenty categories were then developed, ranking prospects from highest to lowest degree of similarity to the company's best customers—those who have gone to Club Med three or more times.[2]

Subaru of America studied the lifestyles of their owners and found a loyal base of lesbian owners. Subaru research showed they are four times as likely to own a Subaru as the general market. A targeted campaign in gay newspapers is currently running, nationwide. A Subaru spokesman said trying to be a competitor in the mainstream wasn't working, so they shifted marketing efforts to narrow but loyal segments.[3]

A number of marketing information companies help marketers to identify and segment households using census data and/or primary source data to isolate "clusters" of consumers with similar demographics and lifestyles.

One psychographic system is "VALS II,™ Values and Lifestyles." This breaks customers into eight groups, each with different attributes. While a good indicator, VALS II™ is too broad a segmentation base for many marketers. As we try to single out the Power Players, the Fun Seekers, and the Matriarchs—as we try to understand the different lifestyles of the 2001 50-year-olds—the new century will require more sophisticated tools for lifestyle segmentation.

Three new segmentation systems, all developed in the last three years, are DNA™ from Metromail, Niches™ from The Polk Company, and Cohorts II™ from Looking Glass, Inc. All of these use household level demographic and lifestyle data to categorize customers into specific groups.

Jock Bickert, who founded Looking Glass in 1993, is a seasoned veteran. He pioneered this demographic and lifestyle background capability for marketers back in 1975 when he created National Demographics & Lifestyles, Inc. (NDL). Jock says:

> The conceptual underpinning of the three approaches is that when groups of individuals are homogeneous with respect to their demographic and lifestyle characteristics, they will also be highly similar with respect to other behavioral characteristics, such as product purchases, motivations, media behavior, and direct marketing responsiveness.

As politically incorrect as it sounds, a word must be said about segmentation by social class. While most Americans reject the concept of social class, it does exist in America. The American Dream is to move up the social class ladder.

Social class can be defined as a division of society into relatively distinct and homogeneous groups with respect to attitudes, values, income, and lifestyles. It is, in effect, a means of segmentation. The general applicability of social class to marketing is product-specific. It is how the marketer positions the product.

The accepted breakdown of social class is into seven groups. They range from Upper-Uppers to Lower-Lowers. Anheuser Busch used social class to position Michelob to the Upper-Middles and Lower-Uppers. Budweiser was positioned for the Middle Class, and Busch for the Working Class.

The final psychographic is personality. This is the ability to link a characteristic with a product; Volvo for safety, Nordstrom for service, or Marlboro for masculinity.

The final, and most important, segment variable is behavioral. Some simple examples would include:

Purchase occasion	Flowers on Mother's Day
Benefits sought	Ultra Brite for white teeth
User status	Nonuser, former user, potential user
Usage rate	Light and heavy users
Loyalty status	How loyal the consumer is to the brand; amount of brand switching
Readiness stage	Unready to buy, ready to buy
Attitude	Positive, negative, indifferent

The most important behavioral pattern of all, actual purchases, is not listed above. This is the key variable for database and relationship marketing, and we're going to look at it in some detail in the next chapter.

Remember the two most important things about segmentation:

1. Geographic, demographic, and psychographic variables are all less important than behavior variables. The best segmentation base is actual purchases for existing products with an understanding of why customers buy the product and how they use it.

David Schmittlein, Professor of Marketing, The Wharton School, University of Pennsylvania, says,

> Customer transaction databases offer segmentability several times greater (at least) than that available from geodemographics. They also offer estimates of customer sales potential that are much more parsimonious, and hence more reliable, than those using geodemographics.[4]

2. Segmentation is not valid without an understanding of positioning. The classic segmentation error was made by Oldsmobile with the positioning line:

It's not your father's Oldsmobile.

Whether Oldsmobile intended it or not, the segmentation was age. The message actually caused a drop in market share. It turned off older existing customers and was not believable to the younger target segment.

"The power of these new [customer characteristic] tools in the marketplace," Jock Bickert says, "is in using them collectively. The synergy created by combining them allows us to create much smarter relationship marketing strategies—and faster bottom line improvement—with lower levels of investment."

We *are* facing a new customer. The new rules of marketing *are* changing everything we ever thought we knew about consumer marketing. Marketing to the *averages* of cluster codes and demographics alone just won't work. It all comes down to the individual customer. Mr. Esrey is right:

> "The successful businesses of the future will know their customer by name or settle for having no customers at all."

CHAPTER **10**

Three Magic Words

Recency, Frequency, and Monetary—How magic are they?

Today, the most important variable for segmenting customers is purchase behavior. We don't learn individual needs from demographics or even psychographics. Demographics and psychographics don't identify prospective buyers. Customer behavior is the key. As our old friend Tim learned, spending hours at the pond looking for frogs, or hours in the meadow hunting toads, or hours in the marshes capturing lizards, doesn't mean much if your customers are not purchasers of frogs, toads, or lizards.

With the advanced analytic capabilities available today, marketers can access their customer knowledge base to find the differences that drive customers' buying decisions. Fact-based analytics can predict propensity to buy. If Tim had access to today's database marketing software, he could save the wasted hours at the pond, in the meadow, and in the marshes. That's what database marketing is all about.

The three primary principles of purchasing behavior go all the way back to the early catalog marketers. These three principles have been called the three basic laws of database marketing:

- ◆ Recency
- ◆ Frequency
- ◆ Monetary

Recency refers to when the customer last purchased—when she last came into the store, or purchased from the catalog, or bought her last car, or bought your breakfast food at the supermarket. Here retailers and catalogers have the advantage because their direct interaction with each customer allows them to capture all of this information. Packaged goods marketers and other brand manufacturers are just beginning to find ways to add this information to their databases. Big-ticket brands learn from guarantee response cards. Packaged goods companies get some help from bar-coded coupons and will soon, I believe, create alliances with supermarkets to get even closer to the data.

Recency is relative. Meaningful measures of recency will vary by industry. Department stores and most specialty stores are primarily concerned with the last two or three years and want to know customer recency within a month or at most a few months. The electronics retailer wants to keep track of customers for at least five years and tracks in three- or six-month cycles. The auto dealer measures in years. Don Libey always likes to point out that a builder of bridges over the Mississippi might track the recency of his orders for bridges in centuries, but the supermarket and the packaged goods marketer want to be sure you shopped last week.

If a supermarket customer goes 12 weeks without a visit there is only a 10 percent chance of the supermarket seeing her again. After 24 weeks that drops to a 5 percent chance.

I like the way Professor Schmittlein states the case for recency. He says we can use the recency factor to know "when a customer is *due* versus when a customer is *done*."[1]

The most recent customer is, theoretically, a better customer and is most likely to be responsive to an offer. If we can agree that marketers in this era of limited growth will only grow by stealing market share from their competitors, and that success will require an intense focus on the customer and his or her buying behavior, then recency is the first tool the marketer should utilize. History has shown that if you can keep a customer buying (i.e., recent) he will keep on buying. That is why the 0- to 6-month customers receive more communications from the marketer than do the 31- to 36-month customers.

This process of recency is fluid and moving. On the one-month anniversary of her last purchase, a one-month recency customer becomes a two-month recency customer in the database. Conversely, the very day a three-month recency customer makes her next purchase, she becomes a one-day recency customer . . . and will probably receive a new sales offering in short order.

There is more to the recency tool than the timing of sales offerings. Marketers' recency reports monitor the health of the business. The best marketers look at the recency analysis at regular intervals for trends. A month-to-month review showing an increase in most recent (one-month recency) customers is a sign of a strong, healthy, growing company. A trend of diminishing recency (fewer one month recency customers) is the first sign of failing health.

The recency report is an important measure of customer retention. The customer who has bought your product or service or visited your store most recently is the customer most likely to purchase from you again. Moreover, it is much easier to reactivate a customer who has not purchased in a few months than one who has been absent for over a year. The marketer who accepts the strong marketing philosophy of doing business— making long-term customers instead of selling things—will win customers by keeping them recent. We will cover this in greater depth in Chapter 19, where we will be talking about relationship marketing and customer management.

The report shown in Figure 10-1 is a typical recency analysis. This kind of look at the database is commonly called a *Decile Report.* Don't get nervous—we're not going to get technical. All a decile report does is to split the total customer universe, in this case 49,596, into tenths with 4960 customers in each decile. This analysis ranks the customers in each decile by most recent date of last purchase.

The fourth column, headed "Last Purchase in # of Months," shows in one-, two-, three-month (and so on) increments the recency of each decile's last purchase. In the top (one month) decile there will be customers who shopped yesterday and customers who last shopped 29 days ago. The report can be run to measure days, weeks, or even years. This analytic has added value as a management tool, showing the total sales dollars each decile contributed in the time period measured and the percent of the total company business that decile represents. In almost every business we have studied the top decile in recency is the biggest contributor of dollar sales, so the goal of every marketer is to keep as many customers as possible as recent as possible.

Over time, as we have said, one-month customers become three-month customers and some three-month customers again become one-month customers. At issue is how many one-month customers *stay* one-month customers. At different points in time this recency analysis may seem very similar, but the internal dynamics may be very different.

It is important to remember that each of these analyses is no more

F I G U R E   10-1

Recency Decile Report—Customer Decile for Purchases Ever (Net)

Rank	Customers Number	Customers Cumulative	Last Purchase in # of Months	Customer $ Purchases	Purchase $ %	Cumulative $ Purchases	Cumul $ %	Tot/Avg $/Cust
1	4960	4960	1	2718589	21.00	2718589	21.00	548
2	4960	9920	1 to 2	1808340	13.97	4526929	34.97	365
3	4960	14880	2 to 3	1619543	12.51	6146472	47.48	327
4	4960	19840	3 to 4	1411692	10.90	7558164	58.38	285
5	4960	24800	4 to 5	1105024	8.54	8663188	66.92	223
6	4960	29760	5 to 6	1126903	8.70	9790091	75.62	227
7	4960	34720	6 to 8	993764	7.68	10783855	83.30	200
8	4960	39680	8 to 10	914846	7.06	11698701	90.36	184
9	4960	44640	10 to 12	645525	4.99	12344226	95.35	130
10	4956	49596	12 to 14	602114	4.65	12946340	100.00	121
Total	49596			12946340	100.00			261

Courtesy: STS Systems

than a snapshot in time. The analysis shown in Figure 10-1 shows only what this company's customer recency looked like on the day the analysis was run. The smart marketer will review this analysis at regular intervals to measure the trend of the business—am I increasing the recency of my customer base, or is it slipping away? It will be harder to keep the changing consumer coming back. The recency analysis gives the marketer a scorecard, and as stated, any downgrading of customer recency is an early warning sign of trouble ahead.

In addition to the recency decile report, there are many other analyses the good marketer will do based on the recency information in the database. A marketer concerned about keeping high-spending customers can query the database to find, for example, all customers who spent more than $1,000 in his store last year, or bought his brand of dog food regularly, and have not purchased in the last three months. An appropriate promotion follow-up is then initiated.

The recency report can also help the marketer avoid some of the things that make customers unhappy. If you were a furrier mailing a big discount savings offer to your customer base for example, you might be wise to eliminate from the mailing all customers who had purchased furs this year, or at least in the last few months.

We will discuss *recency* again as we progress through this database marketing process. Recency, alone, though, will not get the job done. The second measure to be addressed is *frequency*.

Frequency is the number of times the customer buys in a defined time period. It is safe to say the most frequent purchaser is the most satisfied customer. If one believes there is such a thing as brand or store loyalty, the most frequent purchaser would be the most loyal. Increasing the frequency of a customer's purchases means stealing market share from competitors; the marketer gets the sales that were going to someone else.

If the time period measured is one year, and a customer purchased three times in that year, the customer is a three-frequency customer. Like recency, this is a dynamic measurement. The day that customer purchases the fourth time within the year, the customer moves to the four-frequency file. And, like recency, customer frequency can be analyzed in decile format. In Figure 10-2, we see our same customer base of 49,596 split, again, into deciles of 4,960 customers. The report shows us that the top 10 percent of customers purchased an average of eight times. Sixty percent of the customer base purchased only once in this time frame. This is not unusual. Most marketers, seeing their customer data in this form for the first time, are shocked to learn how many one-time purchasers there are. I have had clients take a first look at these reports and tell me the reports must be wrong. They rarely are. This becomes an obvious opportunity to strengthen the business. Every time a marketer can move a one-time pur-

FIGURE 10-2

Frequency Decile Report—Customer Decile for Purchases Ever (Net)

Rank	Customers Number	Customers Cumulative	Purchases	Purchase %	Cumulative Purchases	Cumulative %	Avg Purchases	Avg $/ Purchase
1	4960	4960	37766	34.94	37766	34.94	8	120
2	4960	9920	17242	15.95	55008	50.89	3	123
3	4960	14880	11619	10.74	66627	61.63	2	124
4	4960	19840	9920	9.17	76547	70.80	2	110
5	4960	24800	6282	5.81	82829	76.61	1	124
6	4960	29760	5212	4.82	88041	81.43	1	122
7	4960	34720	5080	4.70	93121	86.13	1	146
8	4960	39680	5010	4.64	98131	90.77	1	112
9	4960	44640	4994	4.62	103125	95.40	1	106
10	4956	49596	4962	4.60	108087	100.00	1	115
Total	49596		108087	100.00				120

Courtesy: STS Systems

chaser to a two-time purchaser, he has taken business from the competition and gained market share.

If you look closely at the frequency analysis in Figure 10-2, you'll notice it shows one significant difference from the other customer decile reports. Whenever customers are ranked in a decile analysis, each decile from the top shows a lower dollars per purchase value than the decile immediately above it. If you go back to Figure 10-1, you will see that, when ranked by recency, the top 10 percent of customers spend more (and higher average per customer) than the next 10 percent, with this being a consistent pattern through most of the deciles. The monetary decile report will reflect this in exaggerated fashion. This is the pattern of all customer decile reports except the frequency decile analysis. Here, the average dollar per customer purchase is relatively consistent through all the deciles.

Many marketers are surprised, when they segment this file for promotion just on the basis of frequency, to find the group of least frequent buyers (the bottom 10 percent) often prove to be the best responders. Why is this?

The reason is the recency factor. Many of any marketer's most recent customers are first-time buyers. They have not been recorded in the database long enough to build up a frequency record.

This is even more proof of the value of recency, and a first word of caution in looking at the database, that things are not always as they seem. The tools of database marketing are like any others. Training and experience are required to use them professionally.

Think of this decile analysis as a "loyalty ladder." The trick is to move customers up the ladder. Think of the sales to be made just by moving the two-purchase customers up to three and the one-purchase customers up to two.

In Figure 10-2, we saw six deciles of customers with only a single purchase. If half of these 29,756 customers could be enticed to make just one more purchase, this marketer would add more than a million dollars in sales. More about this, too, when we consider customer management.

The frequency tool can be the early warning sign that something is going wrong with a customer. It is an important tool for customer retention.

Athletic footwear manufacturers, collectively, launch about 100 new designs a year. I'm told, the average 15- to 20-year-old male buys four pairs of these new designs a year at an average price of $120. How fast would you react if you knew 100 of those customers didn't show up to buy their third pair? Losing these third and fourth purchases from just these 100 young men would cost you $24,000 in sales . . . plus future years.

Many marketers produce three lists for sales personnel every month:

1. Customers whose recency/frequency history shows they should have bought last month.
2. Those that did buy last month.
3. Those that didn't buy.

Any customer appearing on the lapsed customer list is a candidate for immediate action.

Frequency, when combined with recency, is far more revealing and effective than recency alone. But it is still not enough because it doesn't quantify the dollars spent.

Monetary value tells us how much each customer spent in the measured time frame. It can change much of what we thought we learned from recency and frequency alone. That becomes obvious when you think about the customer who has not bought in a year (low recency), only bought once in the prior year (low frequency), but spent $10,000. One client of ours found just such a customer. We called to find out why he hadn't been back. It turned out a customer rep had not followed through with the promised after-purchase service. A bit of tender loving care brought him back as one of the company's best customers.

Looking at recency and frequency alone, the marketer would probably not send a current offer to this customer. It is the monetary value analysis that finds this valuable customer for the marketer to re-activate.

The monetary value tool can be used many ways. Figure 10-3, is called a monetary decile analysis. Here, our 49,596 customers are ranked by dollars spent. This sample report shows customer purchases for the two-year history of the file. It can just as easily be run to show purchases this year or last year or last week.

This is the big daddy of all database reports. This is the analysis that verifies Pareto's Law that suggests 80 percent of a firm's business comes from 20 percent of its customers. It shows that the top 10 percent of the total customer base spent more than twice as much as the second 10 percent and accounts for more than 40 percent of this company's business. Looking down the cumulative percent column, we see that 40 percent of the customer base accounts for more than 80 percent of all sales; 60 percent of the customers give this company more than 90 percent of its business. The last column on the right shows the average purchases for each customer in each decile. The best 10 percent of this company's customers average $1,195 each; the worst 10 percent only $18!

F I G U R E   10-3

Monetary Decile Report—Customer Decile for Purchases Ever (Net)

Rank	Customers Number	Customers Cumulative	$ Purchases	Purchase %	Cumulative $ Purchases	Cumul %	Avg Purchase
1	4960	4960	5926021	45.77	5926021	45.77	1195
2	4960	9920	2258910	17.45	8184931	63.22	455
3	4960	14880	1448198	11.19	9633129	74.41	292
4	4960	19840	1024694	7.91	10657824	82.32	207
5	4960	24800	759128	5.87	11416952	88.19	153
6	4960	29760	560472	4.33	11977424	92.52	113
7	4960	34720	409396	3.16	12386820	95.68	83
8	4960	39680	289556	2.24	12676375	97.92	58
9	4960	44640	181659	1.40	12858034	99.32	37
10	4956	49596	88305	0.68	12946339	100.00	18
Total	49596		12946339	100.00			261

Courtesy: STS Systems

If you had a small budget and could only send an offer to two or three thousand customers, would you mail to the group responsible for 40 percent of your business or the group responsible for less than 1 percent? Some of this database marketing is just that simple. Please remember that although we are looking here at a small company with less than 50,000 customers, these analyses look exactly the same when the customer base numbers in the millions. The only difference is that the savings from this marketing knowledge is much greater!

Marketers who reinvent their business around this kind of understanding of customer differences will see sales and margins reach new heights. Those who don't won't make it into the year 2000.

And, remember, our low-recency, low-frequency friend who spent $10,000 is part of that top group with the $1,195 spending average. One way to find these superspenders is to take the top decile of 4,960 customers as a separate segment of the database and run this decile analysis just for that group. This would break out to deciles of just 496 customers, showing our friend somewhere near the top.

So recency, frequency, and monetary value are the first and simplest measures of customer value. And of these we have seen that recency is the most powerful predictor. Marketers call these elements "RFM." They could, just as easily, call them FMR or MRF. Putting recency first is in recognition of its power.

As these three tools look so simple and provide so much power, a word of caution is advised for marketers new to the customer database. Because the RFM measurement is so easy to use, it is tempting to skim off the top RFM segments for promotional offers. This will probably be the first thing the new database marketer will do, and he or she will be a hero in the company, because the promotion will work. But skimming the cream of RFM deciles is like taking dope. The success of each promotion feels so good, but can't last forever. Soon these easy-to-find best customer segments will show list fatigue.

Remember, we are looking here at just the basic tools. Later chapters will explore the more sophisticated processes of understanding individual customers—what they want, when they want it, how they want it, and how much they are willing to pay for it.

RFM studies can be run to show customer purchase patterns by brand category or brand product or, for a retailer, by total store or department or class or even stock keeping unit. They can also be run, as well, to report purchase performance over the life of the database or for any selected time frame.

Another way to find the superspenders is to run the same monetary data as a purchase decile analysis. The monetary decile analysis was ranked by splitting the 49,596 customers into deciles to see how much each decile spent. The purchase decile report, Figure 10-4, is ranked by splitting the $12,946,339 sales into deciles to see how many customers account for each 10 percent of sales.

What we see here is enough to make one believe in the value of customer retention. If this company lost its top 357 customers, it would have to find more than 1,400 average customers to make up the sales loss. In other words, for every top decile customer this company loses, it must find almost 7 new customers to stay even!

Just 1,081 customers, less than 3 percent of the total customer base, are giving this company 20 percent of its sales. How much tender, loving care is enough for these folks?

Our example shows a small business. Is this unique to small companies? One Seklemian/Newell client with over a billion dollars in consumer sales gets 10 percent of its business from just 7,600 households.

Some, I am sure, will think we have loaded the dice to show these dramatic differences between customers. I assure you, that is not the case. I work with businesses of all sizes and all types in the United States and

Purchases Decile Report—Dollar Decile for Purchases Ever (Net)

Rank	Purchases Amount	Purchases Cumulative	Customers Number	Customers %	Cumulative Customers	Cumulative %	Avg Purchase
1	1293261	1293261	357	0.72	357	0.72	3623
2	1293389	2586650	724	1.46	1081	2.18	1786
3	1294026	3880676	1126	2.27	2207	4.45	1149
4	1294497	5175173	1590	3.21	3797	7.66	814
5	1294355	6469528	2132	4.29	5929	11.95	607
6	1294525	7764053	2861	5.77	8790	17.72	452
7	1294367	9058420	3894	7.85	12684	25.57	332
8	1294441	10352861	5513	11.12	18197	36.69	235
9	1294551	11647412	8450	17.04	26647	53.73	153
10	1298927	12946339	22949	46.27	49596	100.00	57
Total	12946339		49596	100.00			261

Courtesy: STS Systems

other countries. This kind of customer value segmentation holds true with startling consistency for every kind of business around the globe.

Many retailers look at customer value by profitability as well as by raw sales. In the Coca Cola study, "Measured Marketing," Brian Woolf makes the point that to the degree best customers, compared to other customers, visit their supermarkets more often per week and spend more on each visit, it can be shown they are more profitable and therefore deserve special consideration.[2] Calculating the profit contribution of each individual customer provides the economic rationale to differentiate offers among customers and opens up the opportunity to use customer category management to gain competitive advantage. He illustrates this in his study with the example shown in Figure 10-5. The example starts with the annual sales for this specific customer. After reducing the sales dollars to gross margin dollars, Brian subtracts the various promotion discounts to arrive at the realized gross profit from this customer. Finally, subtracting the variable front-end labor costs required to complete the sales shows the actual profit contribution of this customer's business.

Of course not all customers are as profitable as Mrs. H.I. Shopper. At the most recent National Center for Database Marketing conference we noted more and more sessions devoted to segmenting customers based on

F I G U R E   10-5

Customer Profit Contribution—Customer: Mrs. H.I.
Shopper

	$	%
Sales	$2500	100.0%
Gross Profit (Initial)	700	28.0%
- Markdowns ("specials")	-75	-3.0%
- Store Coupons redeemed	-10	-0.4%
- Double Coupons cost	-25	-1.0%
= Gross Profit (realized)	590	23.6%
- Variable Labor Cost*	-35	-1.4%
= Profit Contribution	**$555**	**22.2%**

* Variable Front-End Labor costs only

profit contribution. While reviewing the vendors' newest releases of database marketing software, we saw more and more vendors adding customer profit tracking to their systems. *Strengthening relationships with the most profitable* customers will be one of the new rules of marketing.

Finally, marketers can use a report that will allow them to segment customer files using combinations of recency, frequency, and monetary value. Figure 10-6 is the combination RFM index (The numbers here are different from the prior reports because this index is from a different company.) This index is built from quintile reports of recency, frequency, and monetary value. A quintile report looks just the same as a decile report except its five rows each represent 20 percent of the customers. Each of the five quintiles of a recency analysis is given a value. In this case, the top quintile is coded "A" going down to "E" for the fifth quintile. The same values are coded into quintile reports for frequency and monetary value.

The marketer can call up any of the 125 combinations available. In this sample report, the first line represents customers who earned an "A" ranking in all three reports. The second line shows customers from the second decile of the recency report and the first decile of the frequency and monetary value reports. This gives the marketer a shortcut to segmentation for testing different value combinations of recency, frequency ,and monetary value. A decile segmentation could be used this same way. Marketers choose the quintile report for this job to keep the number of combinations more manageable.

FIGURE 10-6

RFM Index

Index	Customers	Customer %	Purchases	Purchase %	Avg Purchases	Avg $/ Purchase
AAA	5962	0.84	301500	5.43	50	57.50
BAA	7979	1.12	307800	5.54	38	43.00
BBA	3210	0.45	71500	1.29	22	72.50
BCB	3210	0.45	71500	1.29	22	117.00
CAA	6490	0.91	223800	4.02	34	35.50
CBA	6493	0.91	143350	2.58	22	55.00
CCA	1441	0.20	21350	0.38	14	80.75
DAA	2118	0.29	29500	0.53	13	85.50
EAA	6420	0.90	30150	0.54	5	32.80

Courtesy: Seklemian/Newell

The marketer uses this RFM Analysis tool to pre-test promotions. Rather than mail the full house list, knowing that some of the list will prove to be unprofitable, a mailer can use Nth selection to separate out small segments of each RFM cell to test the most profitable ones to mail. If the company's list is too small to create 125 segments they can use something less than quintiles to set up the cells. Using thirds creates just 27 cells.

An analysis of the results of the test mailing will show how many of the RFM cells produced break-even or better results based on net revenue less mailing costs. For the roll-out, only the RFM cells showing a profitable percent response are mailed. Actually, most marketers discount the test response rates by about 10 percent for the roll-out because full roll-outs rarely perform exactly as well as their tests. In most cases, the marketer will lose a small amount of money on the test, a small price to pay for a powerfully successful final promotion.

The reason the index shows number of visits, average dollars per transaction, and so on is that this allows the marketer to assess the value of each cell. For example, even though the CAA cell is low on recency, those customers are high-frequency and monetary and probably worth promoting. The BCB cell, not as high on recency and not the highest on total monetary, represents customers that are valuable when they can be persuaded to buy, averaging $117 per visit.

Today marketers can grow only by stealing market share from their competitors. This will require an intense focus on the customer and breakthrough tools. We have looked at just a few of the most basic. Next we will see how companies can use database knowledge to increase market share by gaining a bigger share-of-customer—selling more of the company's products to existing customers.

If You Sell Him Suits, Why not Shirts?

The importance of Cross-Selling.

Cross-selling is another element in the marketing mix you will hear database marketers talk about. Cross-selling means enticing the customer to buy across many products within a brand family or several departments in a store.

It is an article of faith in the banking industry that the odds on keeping customers increase greatly as accounts are added to a customer's portfolio. Bank marketers have explained that to me this way.

If a customer has only a checking account, the bank's odds of retaining that customer are about 1 to 1. For the customer with only a savings account, the odds are better, but not much: 2 to 1. When the customer has both a checking account and a savings account, the odds jump to 10 to 1 in the bank's favor. Three services in the customer's portfolio jump the odds to 18 to 1. Once the bank gets a customer to use four or more services, they have winning odds of 100 to 1 that they will keep that customer.

For years, most banks didn't have any idea how many services their customers used. Checking accounts, savings accounts, CDs, and mortgages were all in separate files. Then they discovered database marketing and found ways to bring all this information together. Recently, one bank showed me how they used their database to increase the number of households with three accounts by 33 percent, the number with four by 43 percent, and the number with five by 53 percent. Given the industry odds, that represented big gains in customer retention; big gains in profit potential. This newfound ability to manage the customer file is especially important in the banking industry. Typically, 40 percent of a bank's customers are profitable, while the rest cost money to service.[1]

The cross-sell analysis in Figure 11-1 shows that this bank has 1,631 households with checking accounts. Of these, 20 also have a NOW Account, 7 own money market accounts, 199 have a line of credit, and so on. Going down the list on the left, we see the bank has 476 households holding certificates of deposit. Of these, 121 also have checking accounts, 19 have NOW accounts, 4 own money market accounts, 8 have a line of credit, and so on.

If this bank wanted to promote certificates of deposit it would probably look at the fact that 25 percent of the households with money market accounts also hold CDs and then go after the other 75 percent of money market households as prime targets.

Notice that this bank's average customer is only using 1.81 of the bank's dozen services. Identifying popular service combinations can help a bank measure the performance of the sales staff, suggest target promotional campaigns, and identify the extent of risk with changes in pricing for service combinations identified. Because the cross-shopping analysis can identify combinations that are most profitable (based on balance data) as well as most popular (based on numbers of households), it helps evaluate return on investment for product lines and sales campaigns.

All of this makes it sound like banks are in the vanguard of understanding the new rules of marketing, but are they really? Here's how banks recently rated their ability to monitor and evaluate customer relationships:

> Ability to identify all of the products, services and relationships of all members of any randomly selected household within 10 minutes. Yes 18 percent. No 82 percent.

> Ability to know when a retail customer with multiple accounts or products closes one of them, and to take action to retain the remaining accounts. Yes 32 percent. No 68 percent.

> Ability to identify the top 5 to 10 percent of retail depositors who provide the bulk of the bank's retail deposit profits. Yes 30 percent. No 70 percent.[2]

One banker who understands the new rules is Dennis Shirley, Senior VP Marketing Director, Great Western Bank. His stated goal is to move Great

FIGURE 11-1

Cross-Sell Report

Service		Checking	Now_Acct	Money Mkt	Line_Crd	Cert_dep	IRA/KEO	Savings	Loans	Mortgage	Cred Card	ATM	Safe Dep
Checking	# Households	1631	20	7	199	121	34	542	229	34	424	646	105
	% of HHs	100.0%	1.2%	0.4%	12.2%	7.4%	2.1%	33.2%	14.0%	2.1%	26.0%	39.6%	6.4%
HHS: 1631	# Accounts	1700	20	8	199	146	52	611	256	35	451	755	106
	Tot Amt (K)	$3366	$95	$186	$1364	$2128	$245	$3090	$1040	$1583	$382	$0	$2
	Amt Per HH	$2064	$4756	$26541	$6854	$17585	$7209	$5701	$4539	$46572	$902	$0	$18
Now_Acct	# Households	20	384	2	42	19	9	131	43	13	102	185	15
	% of HHs	5.2%	100.0%	0.5%	10.9%	4.9%	2.3%	34.1%	11.2%	3.4%	26.6%	48.2%	3.9%
HHS: 384	# Accounts	21	396	2	42	23	12	154	46	13	111	224	15
	Tot Amt (K)	$121	$825	$21	$292	$256	$30	$988	$278	$1104	$102	$0	$0
	Amt Per HH	$6048	$2149	$10444	$6944	$13459	$3366	$7540	$6471	$84938	$1001	$0	$18
MoneyMkt	# Households	7	2	16	1	4	0	2	0	1	0	4	2
	% of HHs	43.8%	12.5%	100.0%	6.2%	25.0%	0.0%	12.5%	0.0%	6.2%	0.0%	25.0%	12.5%
HHS: 16	# Accounts	8	2	17	1	4	0	2	0	1	0	4	2
	Tot Amt (K)	$28	$4	$293	$4	$65	$0	$2	$0	$7	$0	$0	$0
	Amt Per HH	$3977	$2088	$18282	$4087	$16212	$0	$1104	$0	$6811	$0	$0	$16
Line_Crd	# Households	199	42	1	242	8	4	28	22	11	56	65	9
	% of HHs	82.2%	17.4%	0.4%	100.0%	3.3%	1.7%	11.6%	9.1%	4.5%	23.1%	26.9%	3.7%
HHS: 242	# Accounts	205	42	1	242	10	4	32	24	12	60	79	9
	Tot Amt (K)	$261	$51	$0	$1660	$112	$9	$126	$138	$504	$54	$0	$0
	Amt Per HH	$1314	$1206	$135	$6858	$14013	$2261	$4507	$6287	$45808	$958	$0	$15
Cert_Dep	# Households	121	19	4	8	476	18	132	17	2	52	21	32
	% of HHs	25.4%	4.0%	0.8%	1.7%	100.0%	3.8%	27.7%	3.6%	0.4%	10.9%	4.4%	6.7%
HHS: 476	# Accounts	125	19	4	8	707	24	147	18	2	55	25	32
	Tot Amt (K)	$773	$133	$46	$54	$11260	$133	$1383	$102	$79	$29	$0	$1
	Amt Per HH	$6385	$7003	$11452	$6688	$23656	$7377	$10479	$6007	$39322	$562	$0	$19
IRA/KEO	# Households	34	9	0	4	18	167	31	13	3	33	17	4
	% of HHs	20.4%	5.4%	0.0%	2.4%	10.8%	100.0%	18.6%	7.8%	1.8%	19.8%	10.2%	2.4%
HHS: 167	# Accounts	37	9	0	4	27	280	34	15	3	36	20	4
	Tot Amt (K)	$120	$11	$0	$41	$315	$1120	$199	$64	$172	$21	$0	$0
	Amt Per HH	$3516	$1183	$0	$10182	$17488	$6707	$6426	$4885	$57185	$639	$0	$16
Savings	# Households	542	131	2	28	132	31	1311	154	19	243	443	55
	% of HHs	41.3%	10.0%	0.2%	2.1%	10.1%	2.4%	100.0%	11.7%	1.4%	18.5%	33.8%	4.2%
HHS: 1311	# Accounts	560	134	3	28	169	44	1526	169	20	256	510	57
	Tot Amt (K)	$983	$220	$103	$153	$2222	$187	$7224	$676	$875	$195	$0	$1
	Amt Per HH	$1814	$1676	$51298	$5456	$16831	$6026	$5510	$4392	$46026	$801	$0	$18

FIGURE 11-1

(Continued)

Service		Checking	Now_Acct	Money Mkt	Line_Crd	Cert_dep	IRA/KEO	Savings	Loans	Mortgage	Cred Card	ATM	Safe Dep
Loans	# Households	229	43	0	22	17	13	154	1156	28	304	148	14
	% of HHs	19.8%	3.7%	0.0%	1.9%	1.5%	1.1%	13.3%	100.0%	2.4%	26.3%	12.8%	1.2%
HHS:	# Accounts	242	43	0	22	19	18	172	1290	28	331	169	14
1156	Tot Amt (K)	$158	$34	$0	$100	$286	$140	$225	$6639	$869	$342	$0	$0
	Amt Per HH	$690	$787	$0	$4526	$16849	$10766	$1461	$5743	$31023	$1126	$0	$18
Mortgage	# Households	34	13	1	11	2	3	19	28	158	39	15	10
	% of HHs	21.5%	8.2%	0.6%	7.0%	1.3%	1.9%	12.0%	17.7%	100.0%	24.7%	9.5%	6.3%
HHS:	# Accounts	34	13	1	11	2	5	21	34	162	45	16	11
158	Tot Amt (K)	$63	$43	$16	$83	$3	$27	$140	$153	$7955	$41	$0	$0
	Amt Per HH	$1855	$3273	$16069	$7522	$1500	$8976	$7385	$5470	$50350	$1045	$0	$20
Cred Card	# Households	424	102	0	56	52	33	243	304	39	1621	300	47
	% of HHs	26.2%	6.3%	0.0%	3.5%	3.2%	2.0%	15.0%	18.8%	2.4%	100.0%	18.5%	2.9%
HHS:	# Accounts	440	103	0	56	60	42	264	332	39	1814	340	47
1621	Tot Amt (K)	$658	$162	$0	$260	$677	$201	$1426	$1637	$1624	$1579	$0	$1
	Amt Per HH	$1553	$1590	$0	$4649	$13025	$6104	$5868	$5385	$41651	$974	$0	$19
ATM	# Households	646	185	4	65	21	17	443	148	15	300	1163	21
	% of HHs	55.5%	15.9%	0.3%	5.6%	1.8%	1.5%	38.1%	12.7%	1.3%	25.8%	100.0%	1.8%
HHS:	# Accounts	664	187	4	65	26	23	484	155	15	316	1346	21
1163	Tot Amt (K)	$721	$207	$65	$380	$307	$77	$542	$746	$782	$293	$0	$0
	Amt Per HH	$1115	$1116	$16327	$5840	$14615	$4507	$1225	$5042	$52127	$978	$0	$17
Safe Dep	# Households	105	15	2	9	32	4	55	14	10	47	21	523
	% of HHs	20.1%	2.9%	0.4%	1.7%	6.1%	0.8%	10.5%	2.7%	1.9%	9.0%	4.0%	100.0%
HHS:	# Accounts	107	15	2	9	38	9	58	15	10	47	22	529
523	Tot Amt (K)	$712	$67	$73	$49	$516	$28	$696	$76	$327	$30	$0	$9
	Amt Per HH	$6785	$4474	$36606	$5457	$16115	$6996	$12651	$5396	$32727	$633	$0	$18
Ratios:	Services/HH	2.45	2.51	2.44	2.84	1.89	1.99	2.36	1.84	2.11	1.99	2.60	1.60
	Accounts/HH	2.66	2.76	2.56	2.98	2.45	2.81	2.65	2.03	2.25	2.18	2.84	1.65
Totals:	Services/HH	1.81											
	Accounts/HH	2.05											

Service Households 4892
Service Accounts 10009

HHs w/o Service Category 0
Accts w/o Service Category 0

Courtesy: Harte-Hanks Data Technologies

Western away from traditional bank branding ads into more retail positioning. In an effort to build a relationship with consumers, Great Western will waive fees and price products such as checking accounts on the "share of wallet" consumers have with the bank. As a start, the bank moved $3 million to $5 million of its $25 million to $30 million ad budget from sports marketing efforts to direct marketing.[3]

The importance of cross-selling is one of the new rules of marketing, and not just for banks. The odds of keeping a customer increase greatly when the customer buys more of any marketer's products or services. The trick is to use this database cross-sell analysis to make that happen. A packaged goods manufacturer would use the cross-sell analysis to ask how many customers buying a cereal brand are also buying that brand's crackers? Who are the best targets for selling more cracker brands?

A department store would use the cross-sell analysis to develop additional sales by asking questions like:

> How many customers who buy Estee Lauder foundation are not buying Estee Lauder treatment products?
>
> What percent of ready-to-wear customers are not buying cosmetics?
>
> What percent of ready-to-wear customers never shop in shoes or in the home store?
>
> How many men's customers are buying clothing but not furnishings and vice versa?

Figure 11-2 is an example of the latter. The top table on the left shows the spending patterns of the customers who buy men's clothing. The top table on the right shows how many of those customers are also buying furnishings and their dollar purchases. On the left, the 1,958 customers who spent between $501 and $750 on men's clothing in the past 12 months spent a total of $1,211,824. Looking at the top table on the right, we see that of these, 886 did not buy men's furnishings and 1,072 did. The customers that did spent $153,326 on men's furnishings.

The bottom table on the left shows the spending patterns of the customers who buy men's furnishings. The bottom table on the right shows how many of these customers are also buying clothing and their dollar purchases. On the left the 381 customers who spent between $501 and $750 on men's furnishings in the past 12 months spent a total of $227,658. On the right we see that of these, 160 did not buy men's clothing and 221 did. The customers that did spent $292,444 on men's clothing.

A total of 9,119 men's clothing customers, or 50 percent, did not buy

FIGURE 11-2

Cross-Sales Analysis—Men's Clothing vs. Men's Furnishings

Men's Clothing Buyers

Purchase $ Amount	Customers	Dollars	Average
1 to 10	21	147	7
11 to 25	284	5384	19
26 to 50	1942	78776	41
51 to 75	1209	77557	64
76 to 100	1324	118137	89
101 to 150	1686	216816	129
151 to 200	1436	255728	178
201 to 300	2097	538294	257
301 to 400	1679	596478	355
401 to 500	1513	693638	458
501 to 750	1958	1211824	619
751 to 1000	1084	938876	866
1001 to 2000	1408	1940763	1378
2001 to 3000	333	797542	2395
3001 & Over	227	1119013	4930
Total Sales	18201	8588973	472

Total Spent by Men's Clothing Buyers on Men's Furnishings

Purchase $ Amount	Customers No Sales	Customers w/Sales	Dollars	Average
1 to 10	7	14	1952	139
11 to 25	144	140	13229	94
26 to 50	1101	841	76633	91
51 to 75	696	513	50055	98
76 to 100	714	610	65654	108
101 to 150	913	773	83288	108
151 to 200	772	664	73848	111
201 to 300	1089	1008	116314	115
301 to 400	866	813	100182	123
401 to 500	782	731	91382	125
501 to 750	886	1072	153326	143
751 to 1000	453	631	103016	163
1001 to 2000	529	879	177422	202
2001 to 3000	104	229	68682	300
3001 & Over	63	164	97084	592
Total Sales	9119	9082	1272067	140

FIGURE 11-2

(Continued)

Men's Furnishings Buyers			
Purchase $ Amount	Customers	Dollars	Average
1 to 10	620	4992	8
11 to 25	6254	122315	20
26 to 50	9622	369778	38
51 to 75	6498	409984	60
76 to 100	4339	382259	88
101 to 150	4666	575123	123
151 to 200	2528	440458	174
201 to 300	2239	544582	243
301 to 400	911	314398	345
401 to 500	444	197671	445
501 to 750	381	227658	598
751 to 1000	105	89886	856
1001 to 2000	78	99741	1279
2001 to 3000	6	15248	2541
3001 & Over	6	30482	5080
Total Sales	38697	3824575	99

Total Spent by Men's Furnishings Buyers on Men's Clothing				
Purchase $ Amount	Customers No Sales	Customers w/Sales	Dollars	Average
1 to 10	512	108	26716	247
11 to 25	5313	941	263703	280
26 to 50	7948	1674	627983	375
51 to 75	5107	1391	572138	411
76 to 100	3303	1036	485960	469
101 to 150	3324	1342	649932	484
151 to 200	1635	893	471101	528
201 to 300	1347	892	557907	625
301 to 400	480	431	339670	788
401 to 500	227	217	254951	1175
501 to 750	160	221	292444	323
751 to 1000	39	66	81772	1239
1001 to 2000	26	52	131624	2531
2001 to 3000	2	4	12816	3204
3001 & Over	0	6	98394	16399
Total Sales	29423	9274	4867111	525

Courtesy: IBJ Associates

men's furnishings. What an opportunity to sell these 9,119 men's clothing customers shirts and ties and other furnishings when they are right there in the store! A smart marketer might want to concentrate on the men who spent over $750 on clothing and did not buy furnishings. They total 1,149. Of the 1,903 in this group that did buy men's furnishings, the average sale was $234—2.5 times the average men's furnishings customer.

It is more difficult to convert men's furnishings customers who do not buy clothing to clothing buyers, but it would be a worthwhile effort to try to convert at least the higher-spending men's furnishings customers who have not bought clothing.

This same analysis can be used for any combination of products or brands. The cross-sell analysis is one of the best tools to discover opportunities to generate more buying activity from existing customers.

Fresh Fields, an upscale, gourmet health-food chain, uses the information in its million customer name database to cross-sell and up-sell. People who only shop in certain departments are sent discount offers from other departments, and those who buy certain brands are offered other items in the brand line. Fresh Fields' DM agency, Insight Out of Chaos, has reported these special offers averaging a 15 percent response, with some mailings getting a 40 percent redemption rate.[4]

Later we will see how some forward-looking shopping centers have developed the skills of customer marketing. Figure 11-3 shows how a shopping center uses the cross-sell analysis.

Instead of measuring the cross-sell of products or services or store departments, the shopping center marketing manager wants to know how many different stores customers visit. The marketing director at this center was shocked to learn that 62 percent of shoppers visiting his mall shopped in only one store. Armed with cross-sell data, the marketing manager can

F I G U R E   11-3

Cross-Spending Analysis Summary—For All Stores

Total Database	1683	1 Store	2 to 3 Stores	4 to 6 Stores	7 to 10 Stores	11-19 Stores	20-49 Stores	50+ Stores
# of Customers		104900	51000	10800	1400	200	0	0
% of Customers		62%	30%	6%	1%	0%	0%	0%

Courtesy: Seklemian/Newell

put together joint tenant promotions where five or six stores will join together to send a promotion to the customers who shop at all of the participating stores. Those in charge of leasing for the center can know which kind of tenant store will bring more cross-shopping and therefore more business to the center.

This is valuable information for every kind of marketer. The customer you already have is the easiest customer to sell. If you can get the customer buying only one of your products or just one category within your brand family to try a second, or develop the customer who shops in just one department of your store to shop in just one more department, or entice the single-store shopper in your mall to visit one more store, you are doubling the business you are getting from that customer.

In the next chapter, we'll see how some database marketers are doing exactly that; but first, one more example.

Figure 11-4 shows a company's customer cross-shopping history for two years through the first quarter of 1995. It shows that 43.1 percent of this company's customers are purchasing only one category of the company's 16 categories of goods, 25.5 percent purchase only two, and 83.4

F I G U R E   11-4

Cross-Sell Summary—For First Quarter 1995 and Earlier

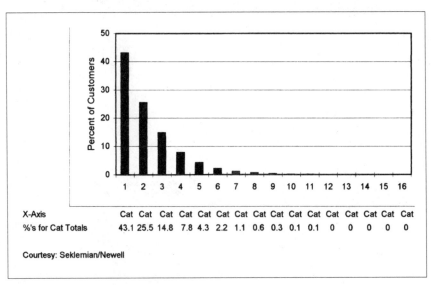

X-Axis	Cat	Cat	Cat	Cat	Cat	Cat	Cat	Cat	Cat	Cat	Cat	Cat	Cat	Cat	Cat	Cat
%'s for Cat Totals	43.1	25.5	14.8	7.8	4.3	2.2	1.1	0.6	0.3	0.1	0.1	0	0	0	0	0

Courtesy: Seklemian/Newell

percent of the customers are purchasing three or fewer of the categories offered!

Think about the opportunities presented here.

This company has more than 1,000,000 active customers. We'll call it a million. They have an average sale of $234. If just 10 percent of the customers purchasing in only one category could be persuaded to make just one more purchase in an additional category, that would mean more than $10 million in new business!

A Seklemian/Newell bank client found 43.3 percent of its customer households using only one of the bank's services, 36.3 percent using only two, 17.6 percent using three, and only 2.8 percent using four or more.

This is the kind of knowledge that opens up big opportunities for marketers. This improved understanding of individual customers will help marketers change the rules to gain market share.

Marketers are interested in the value they can develop for each customer over what they consider the lifetime of the business relationship. This process of developing a bigger share-of-customer—getting each customer to buy more of the company's products—increases the customer's value to the company.

In the next chapter we will see how marketers measure "lifetime values."

CHAPTER **12**

Will You Still Love Me Tomorrow?

Why don't more marketers use lifetime values?

All database and relationship marketing leads to creating and enhancing the lifetime value (LTV) of customers. The traditional LTV model originated in the direct-response life insurance industry. Insurance marketers measured the cancellation curve to determine what could profitably be spent on customer acquisition. But what does LTV mean to marketers, and how can it help them make better use of their marketing investments?

I cannot understand why so few marketers understand the concept of lifetime value, how few make it the core of their customer management strategy. Knowing that the customer still loves us—and just how much he or she loves us—is the key measurement for customer management.

Before starting the research for this book, I believed all of the major catalogers lived or died by the LTV calculation. The catalogers' future depends on successful prospecting for new customers to add to the house file. They spend fortunes renting lists to develop new customers, yet most if not all catalogers lose money on a prospect's initial order. The lifetime value of each new customer determines the ultimate profitability of the prospecting effort and provides a measure of the dollars that can be profitably invested in prospecting.

I was shocked to learn that about 79 percent of respondents to a recent survey of catalogers said they do not calculate the LTV of customers.[1]

LTV is a simple concept to understand.

I have lived on the same island for 20 years. God willing, I will live here another 20 years or more. My family has shopped at the same supermarket since we arrived on the island (although there are other options). We spend about $75 a week in the supermarket. That's about $3,900 a year. If 40 years is a good guess at my shopping "lifetime" with this supermarket, my lifetime value is $156,000—significant business for any supermarket! To follow the cataloger's theory, if my supermarket had spent $10 or $100 or even $500 to win my business at the beginning, they would have made a good buy. Now that they have me, I would expect them to make special, extra efforts to keep my potential $156,000 business.

They don't know who I am. Oh yes, they recognize me. Suzanne, at the check-out, says, "Hello, Fred. You must have been traveling," or "I haven't seen your wife in two weeks. Is she OK?" But I'm not treated like a $156,000 customer by the marketing management of this chain supermarket.

I have bought a Cadillac every three years for the last 25 years. I have the potential to buy them for another 20 years. At $45,000, that's an LTV of $675,000. What could the folks at Cadillac profitably have spent to get me? What should they spend to keep me? They don't know who I am. I am not treated like a $675,000 customer by Cadillac. Maybe next year I should buy a Lexus to see if I get their attention.

In the strictest definition of LTV I am not worth $156,000 to my supermarket or $675,000 to Cadillac, because a true lifetime value measures a customer's profit contribution, not just sales dollars. More about that, later.

Customer lifetime value has a number of uses It will show the marketer how much he or she can profitably spend to acquire a new customer. More than that it will provide a measure of profitable spending to retain a customer. This is the key relationship marketing question. Looking at the historic worth of new customers developed in the past, the marketer will see that some are worth much more than others. Knowing the potential worth of these better customers, the marketer can profile them and target acquisition efforts to find more customers just like them. The LTV measurement can be a more productive way to justify marketing investments than just looking at immediate sales.

LTV is a measurement of what a customer or a segment of customers is worth to a business. Of course, it's really not as simple as just measuring purchases. You can't just look at the solid customers. For every Fred Newell at my supermarket or my auto dealership there are others who switch food stores after just a few visits or choose another make of car on their very next purchase. The marketer's full customer file must be factored into any LTV equation, including inactive customers.

To understand some of the complexities of the LTV calculation it is important to understand that LTV is the net present value of expected benefits over time less the cost of acquiring those benefits, yielding the customer's worth over time. The wise marketer will use this measure of potential future profits to determine how much he or she can invest to acquire or develop a customer or customer segment.

Technically LTV is discounted by interest rates, as money today has a different value than money in the future, so the marketer will subtract from the revenue projection a time value of money discount factor to project net present value. The time value of money discount factor sounds like accountant doublespeak. It really isn't that complicated. We use it to account for the fact that revenue received one or more years from now will not be worth as much as the same revenue received today. Subtracting the discount factor from the revenue projection adds protection against uncertainty.

Most businesses establish the time value of money based on the rate of interest they seek for their investment, considering any risk involved. Discounting this factor gives them what they call net present dollars. Cutting away all the accountant talk, that means what future revenues are worth today.

So, the cataloger uses LTV to decide how much he can invest to "buy" a new customer. That's been standard practice for years. What's new is the use of LTV by marketers in every industry to add to the marketing mix a specific investment to increase the lifetime value of customers. LTV analysis can help determine the most profitable level of spending directed to each segment of the customer file. To accomplish this, the marketer creates a base LTV analysis. This is a snapshot in time. It shows the marketer's customer lifetime value the day the analysis is performed. Actually, more than one LTV analysis will be performed. The company's average customer LTV is nice to know, but is not a very precise marketing tool. (Remember the fellow who drowned in a lake that averaged one foot deep?) Different segments of the customer file will have very different LTVs. If a company does not have big differences between its high and low LTVs, it is in trouble. Moreover, the marketer will want to direct his or her efforts to increase the lifetime value of the most profitable customers.

The lifetime value of any customer segment is based on retention rate, the rate of customer spending, the profitability of the cumulative sales, and the cost of acquiring and retaining that segment. Improving one or more of these factors will increase the lifetime value of the segment.

With good customer transaction history files, these factors are easy to track. The customer file shows us how many customers have purchased in any given time frame. The only thing we don't know is the exact moment any one of these customers leaves forever. At some point some customers leave. Some move away. Some die. Some get treated poorly and go away mad. Some just no longer need our product. We have yet to find a way to get customers to tell us when they move or leave in a huff, so we look for other ways to measure retention. Some marketers have developed complex statistical models to measure LTV. Some of these detail such precise measurements they become too complicated to yield the simple answers most marketers need. It is easy to find numbers that have little or nothing to do with reality. There are shortcuts that can give the marketer all of the information needed to establish programs to increase LTV.

A brief study of Recency reports will enable most marketers to see that there is a fairly consistent period of no purchase activity that means a customer can no longer be considered an active customer. In some industries this can be counted in weeks. For most, an active customer is one who has purchased the product in the last 12 or 24 months. Once this cut-off is established to define an active customer, it is a simple matter to draw a pretty good bead on the LTV of any customer segment. If the cut-off is 12 months, we can now define lifetime value of any customer segment as the average cumulative purchases of all customers who purchase at least once a year, less the cost of goods and cost of marketing to that customer segment.

Assume a marketer's customer file contains a million households, and 600,000 of them meet the criteria of a purchase in the last 12 months and show a history of $300 annual purchases. A five-year time period is usually a good measure of LTV. The exceptions would be where transaction records clearly indicate a longer or shorter period. If we use a five year time period to track LTV with an interest hurdle of 10 percent, this marketer's customer LTV is shown in Figure 12-1.

Some businesses take a different shortcut, simply using the retention rate of a customer segment as a guide. If a given customer segment loses 20 percent of its customers a year, they say that segment has a 5-year lifetime, and they use a five year purchase history to calculate LTV. This is a satisfactory, quick- and-dirty calculation that provides some accuracy, if

FIGURE 12-1

Five-Year Projection of Net Present Value for a
Customer Spending $300 a Year

Year	Sales	Discounted Sales	Total, LTV
1	300	300	300
2	300	270	570
3	300	243	813
4	300	219	1,032
5	300	197	1,229

not precision, but it would not be my choice. Few customer segments are that linear in retention measurement.

As we said, improving the customer retention rate and keeping more customers shopping at least once every 12 months will increase a company's LTV, as will increasing the customer's dollar purchases, increasing the gross margin on the product, or reducing the marketing expense. The most effective of these is improving customer retention. If customers stay with you longer, LTV increases. If the average customer leaves earlier, LTV decreases. Smart marketers single out the attributes that define a customer who purchases more than once a year and focus acquisition resources on prospects who are similar, reducing expenditures aimed at the mass approach of gaining just any new customer. More and more marketers are moving beyond the use of LTV for acquisition strategy. They are investing more of their resources in relationship-building programs to bond customers to the brand and keep them active longer.

As marketers concentrate on customer retention, they will spend more on the high-profit potentials. If the average LTV for supermarkets is $4,680 (gross sales),[2] my $156,000 should put me in a category deserving special attention. Shouldn't my supermarket work hard at building a relationship with me, doing anything they can do to increase satisfaction?

As marketers build these relationship-building programs to increase LTV, they will need to measure results. Remember, at the start, the marketer established a base LTV analysis. Once the program is in place to increase LTV, updates of that original analysis will show the degree of increase from that base.

In the end, it is not the numbers that are important in increasing LTV—it is the relationships a company builds with its customers. The business of selling is a people business. If the people who buy your product like you enough to keep coming back, your LTV will increase. This is the qualitative side of the LTV equation. The more a company can increase customer satisfaction, the more it will increase LTV.

Dr. Paul Wang says it best when he talks about keeping lifetime value in perspective:

> After I help my students learn how to calculate lifetime value, I always try to remind them that the ultimate judge of the accuracy of the lifetime value calculation is the customer, not the CEO or CFO or anyone else inside the company.
>
> I believe that we too often take lifetime value for granted and forget to focus on what is important—our customers.
>
> The purpose of lifetime value is to achieve relevance, to create a frame of reference. In and of itself, it is meaningless. Only when we recognize it is the customer who really controls the lifetime value can we begin to attach meaning to it.
>
> Therefore, lifetime value calculation exercises should ideally be designed to stimulate a company's strategic thinking and to adjust its marketing efforts to meet its customer's future needs and wants. Lifetime value calculation is only a means to an end.[3]

Measuring lifetime value can assure the marketer that the customer romance is alive and well. LTV is one more tool database marketers use to stimulate strategic thinking and adjust marketing efforts to meet customer needs.

In the next chapter we will see how smart marketers, from auto makers to supermarkets, are putting these tools to work to develop new strategies and improve marketing efforts to increase sales and profits.

PART **TWO**

Now the fun starts. The hard stuff is behind us. If you have made it this far, we'll assume you have decided there just might be something to this business of developing a more successful growth company by understanding customer management, the importance of customer knowledge, and the new rules of marketing.

Now we'll see how some of the best marketers are playing by the new rules. We're going to look at some small businesses and some giants; from a retailer so small he doesn't even have stores, to power players like Kraft, Toyota, Samsonite, Bloomingdales, and Radio Shack. We'll even look at malls and media.

The purpose of all of this is to give you ideas. As you read these stories and case histories, try to forget about each of the specific marketer's position or his industry. Concentrate on the *concepts* and how you can apply this advantage of knowledge about the customer to your business. Most of these customer management techniques can work for any business.

Finally, in Part II we'll have a special word for the retailer, then a serious look at the issue of privacy, and a quick peek at what all this is beginning to mean in a global environment.

CHAPTER **13**

Just Because You Have a Toolkit Doesn't Mean You Can Build a House

Database marketing is much more than direct mail. You don't want to save money; you want to do more business.

At the close of Chapter 7, we agreed that all marketers who target customers from a customer database are "direct marketers." We have just examined a few of the basic tools in the direct marketer's toolbox. Now its time to take a look at how these tools can be used strategically and tactically for direct marketing.

We define direct marketing, as we will be examining it here, as a process for direct selling: transaction-driven applications that target specific segments of the customer base to solicit a sale. These are all efforts that can be measured for return on the promotion investment.

The first, obvious, and fundamental rule is that all of the customer information in the world is worthless if it is not used or used incorrectly. The large investments that companies are making in database technology are wasted dollars if the result of those investments is not added sales and profit.

The first thing most marketers think about when asked about database marketing is the direct mail opportunity. If we can target customers and mail offers only to those most likely to respond, we should be able to save a lot of direct mail advertising dollars. That's where most of us started in the database marketing business. As a matter of fact, that's how I started selling the concept to marketers many years ago. I learned an interesting thing: No one wants to save money. All they want is to do more business. One of the secrets of database marketing is to save the wasted advertising dollars and reinvest them in additional, profitable promotions.

Let me tell you a true story about a regional department store chain in the east. I have seen this same case over and over again as I have helped stores develop mailing strategies. This is just one of the more dramatic examples of results and of merchants' thinking. To understand this story, you have to understand the way most retail organizations are structured. The merchandise managers rule the roost. In most cases, they make the final decisions about how their advertising dollars are spent. Their concentration is on beating last year. Sales results mean everything.

In this case, a merchandise manager brought a direct mail promotion to the advertising department. It was a repeat of a promotion the store had mailed at the same time the year before. He asked to mail the full house file of active customers, as he had always done, about 130,000 pieces. Now it happened that over the course of those past twelve months, the store had put in place a solid database marketing system with a strong customer targeting capability. The database manager reviewed the offer and went to work on his customer file to find the customers most likely to respond. Using some of the tools we just studied, he determined there were only 30,000 customers in the file that could possibly be mailed profitably. But, as we said, the merchandisers have the clout. This merchandiser was providing the funding from his vendor for the promotion, and he insisted on mailing the full, 130,000-name file. When the promotion ended, the database manager developed a promotion analysis, reporting the results of the recommended 30,000 names separately from the results of the 100,000 names.

The offer was a simple postcard mailer that cost 18 cents apiece, printed and mailed. The targeted 30,000 names produced a 14.8 percent response, and $111,900 in sales—$3.73 for every piece mailed. The 100,000 names produced a 0.8 percent response, and $17,000 in sales—17 cents for every piece mailed. Think about that for a minute—18 cents cost, 17 cents return. It looks like the store lost $1,000 by mailing those extra names. It's worse than that. At the store's gross margin of 40 percent on this merchandise, they only had $6,800 of the $17,000 left after paying for the goods. Those 100,000 names mailed produced an out-of-pocket loss of $11,200.

Well, I couldn't wait to confront the merchandise manager to show him the mistake he had made. I couldn't believe his reply. "You don't understand, Fred," he said, "I needed that extra $17,000 in sales. I did $125,000 last year. Without those 100,000 pieces I mailed, I wouldn't have made my day."

I tried in every way I could think of to convince him of the error of his ways. He wouldn't listen, until I said. "Let's just assume, for the moment, that you didn't mail the 100,000 names. Now you have only $111,900 instead of the $128,900 which resulted from the total 130,000 mailing. You didn't make your day. But, you still have $18,000 of that vendor's money in your pocket. Let's find another offer that's right for those 100,000 customers and use the $18,000 to mail that. Would you rather have spent the $18,000 to get $17,000, or would you rather use it to get back $373,000?"

I won't bore you with the rest of this story. You can guess the happy ending. It would be hard to find a better case example to make the point. The important point here is that this example has nothing to do with retailing. The same result could come from a bank, an automaker, or a brand manufacturer. One of the secrets of database marketing is to use your customer database to save the wasted dollars and reinvest those dollars in profitable promotions.

Let's look at that promotion another way. It's just possible some of his 100,000 pieces were profitable. Again, we will turn to our workhorse, the decile report.

In Figure 13-1 the 100,000 mailed customers are split into tenths, ranked by sales results. At 18 cents per piece, each decile cost $1,800 to print and mail.

Here, we show the total sales for each decile, then multiply by the 40 percent gross margin to get margin dollars, and, finally, subtract the cost of mailing the 10,000 pieces in that decile to equal the profit dollars returned.

Ah-hah! Our merchandise manager wasn't all wrong. His database manager wasn't 100 percent right. They could have mailed 10,000 more, profitably. But how would they have known how to select this best 10,000 name segment?

The smart marketer will now do three things. First, he will go back into his customer files to look for the dependent variables that are common to these profitable responders and not to the other 90,000. Then he will go back and run the same decile promotion analysis to see if parts of the

F I G U R E 13-1

Promotion Analysis

Quantity Mailed	Customers Responding	Response %	Sales	Gross Profit @ 40%	Cost to Mail	Profit Contribution
10000	356	3.56	8366	3346	1800	1546
10000	179	1.79	3759	1503	1800	(297)
10000	104	1.04	2078	831	1800	(969)
10000	53	.53	1027	411	1800	(1389)
10000	36	.36	658	263	1800	(1537)
10000	28	.28	440	176	1800	(1624)
10000	19	.19	283	113	1800	(1687)
10000	14	.14	206	83	1800	(1717)
10000	6	.02	97	39	1800	(1761)
10000	5	.05	86	35	1800	(1765)
Total 100000	800	.8	17000	6800	18000	(11200)

Courtesy: Seklemian/Newell

30,000-name segment were, in fact, unprofitable, and, if so, repeat step one to study those customers. Finally, he will pull all of this new-found knowledge together into an historical analysis file, as a learning experience.

That's the second secret of promoting from your customer database: Every use of the file is a learning experience. The marketing power of the database continues to grow and grow. The more you use it and learn, the better it performs . . . if you do your homework.

What we just saw was a simple example from a reasonably small business. How are some of the big guys with millions of names and offices all across the country using the customer database to refine their marketing activities and target individual customer segments?

We'll look at just a few.

Subaru of America has a house database of more than a million original purchasers, and they can make segments of that big list available to individual dealers for local mailings. The program is called Flexmail. For a $250 fee, a dealer can call Subaru's 800 number, describe the customer attributes he's searching for, and choose one of many packaged mailers. Subaru gets the mailing out for the dealer in five days.

Nissan has recently instituted a database marketing program for its dealer Parts and Service programs. In the beginning, all Nissan owners got the same coupons, and dealers were retaining 16 percent of owners' scheduled maintenance. Then Nissan developed its Integrated Profit Program. Owners' mileage, captured at dealer sites, is fed to the national database, enabling Nissan to communicate to owners based on time-service rather than just discount coupons. Knowing owners' mileage allows Nissan to concentrate the program on parts and service most profitable to the auto company and its dealers.

The 775 of Nissan's 1250 dealers enrolled in the program have increased retained owners' scheduled maintenance from 16 to 30 percent. Of Infiniti's 150 dealers, 135 have brought their retention to 55 percent. Responders to the Nissan Integrated Profit Program spend an average of $135 on each dealer visit, versus $100 for off-the-street customers.[1]

Even luxury hotels are teaming up to develop one-to-one relationships with customers. The 21 members of the Preferred Hotels Association have joined together to create a Guest Information Network called Guestnet. Guest records of all the participating hotels will be pooled in the Guestnet database to help the individual properties develop better marketing and service programs. Copies of each member hotel's guest information are transmitted to Guestnet, overlaid with additional demographic information, then sent back to each hotel's Guestnet PC. The Guestnet database, still in start-up, has 175,000 names. Once all 21 hotels are fully implemented, that number should reach one million, with 50,000 to 60,000 new names added monthly.[2]

Giant retailers are database marketers, too.

One industry that needs the stimulation of customer marketing is the supermarket industry, where the national average profit margin is a razor-thin 1.4 percent. At the start of 1996, 29,700 supermarkets were operating, compared with 30,000 just two years before.

Worse yet, customers show little loyalty, patronizing one store for some of their grocery needs, but shopping around for best price. A typical customer told me, "I go to one store in my neighborhood that takes double coupons, then I go to another store where prices are lowest on other items, then I go to a healthfood store for fresh vegetables. I like working the supermarkets against each other." A recent regional customer survey confirmed this cross-shopping to be common among a majority of supermarket customers: 55.8 percent at Vons, 50.9 percent at Lucky's, and 57.6 percent at Ralphs.[3]

Vons, the nation's ninth-largest supermarket chain with 334 stores at last count, is a strong database marketing player, using a preferred customer program to try to capture more of the customer's food purchases.

Vons has been developing customer data for more than seven years through its VonsClub preferred shopper program. Growing by an average of 25 percent a year, the club now has more than 4 million members.

When a member swipes her membership card at checkout she automatically receives discounts on items Vons has chosen to promote. In the process, Vons' computer feeds each customer's detailed purchase in to the database, where it is merged with customer lifestyle information.

Each month Vons sends specific promotions to VonsClub members matching what they buy with participating vendors' coupons.

Vons is using the database information to direct its marketing efforts to increase its private-label business, now 16 percent of sales (up from 13 percent in 1993) to 20 percent of store sales, to determine which private label products offer the most promise, and learn which specific customers are the best prospects for each of the different private label items.

Vons' senior management has identified VonsClub as one of the company's most important strategic initiatives.[4]

The 1,057-store Safeway chain has had a customer database for 10 years, but just started in January 1996 to target coupon mailings with personalized offers to selected households. Safeway had been using their database to refine mailings by zip code. Now, the new program goes to the next step to target specific coupons to individual households based on prior shopping history and demographic segmentation.

Safeway sells space in these mailings to packaged goods brand manufacturers. Participating vendors receive detailed response analysis reports, but not names and addresses of customers.[5]

But, what about a really small company?

Here is another example that makes the point we often need to drive home to marketers who think their "mailing list" is a database.

Vitamin Health Centers is a small company headquartered in Marlton, New Jersey. They are so small, they don't even have stores. They operate kiosks in major malls in the Northeast and in Florida, selling vitamins, weight-loss regimens, and other health products, and they had a marketing problem.

With low-volume outlets in more than a dozen major markets, they couldn't afford any meaningful mass media advertising. They were spending their small advertising budget on price-offer mailings to their mailing list. Sounds like a wise decision, but there are mailing lists and then there are mailing lists—all mailing lists are *not* created equal. VHC's mailing lists represented customers who, over the years, had signed up to be on the list. Since the company couldn't track customer purchases, they had no idea how much these folks were buying or even if they were still shopping at the VHC kiosks. The mailings called for customers to bring in coupons for special offers, so at least they could track response. Response to these mailings averaged 1 to 2 percent, not enough to drive the business. Chainwide sales were slipping.

We talked about building a customer database and tracking sales. Would it be worthwhile to track purchases of all customers and establish a database of customers that could be evaluated? The owners said, "No way. That would be too expensive for us." We talked some more. We finally agreed to develop an inexpensive test at four malls to learn what database marketing could do for this small firm.

We started tracking all customer purchases in the four markets in January. It was September before we had enough customer history to test a first mailing.

The last price-offer mailing to the old list had been August 1st. They had mailed 20,000 pieces and gotten a 2.3 percent response with total sales of $19,564.

In September, we analyzed the new database to select customers for our first test. Using the RFM tools and product purchase information, we found just 8,755 customers whose records showed a probable propensity to respond to our offer. The response to this first test was 8.4 percent, with sales of $37,177. Almost four times their best previous response at less than half the expense of names mailed. Almost double the sales. We went on through December with mailings that produced 8.5 percent, 6.6 percent, and 5.3 percent.

The company has now rolled this program out to all of their markets, and the high rate of response and profitability continues. A recent gift-with-purchase offer produced a 9.5 percent response. A free gift offer produced a 29.7 percent response and brought in $13.27 for every name mailed! That is the power of good database marketing.

There are two lessons here:

1. You are not too small to play in this league. There are ways to make it work to fit your budget. You will hear about the giants spending hundreds of thousands of dollars, even millions of dollars to license software and build databases, and that's OK . . . for them. The VHC program was built with one smart programmer, working from his home with an off-the-shelf software product. Now Vitamin Health Centers is outgrowing this first system and will be licensing one of the "big guy"

products. That's OK, too, because now they can afford it. At the end of last year, their best profit year ever, the owners told me at least 25 percent of the annual profit was directly attributable to this database marketing.

2. *All mailing lists are not created equal*—I can't say it often enough or loud enough. If you can't track customer response against the list, don't keep the list. It gets old, tired, and expensive, real fast!

If direct mail promotion was the only use of the customer database, we could close this book right now. But there's much more to cover. In the next chapter we'll look at packaged goods marketers, see which ones are the most committed to database marketing, and learn why the experts predict even more manufacturer activity.

CHAPTER **14**

From Homunculi to Giants

Why 10 leading packaged goods companies have 3,246 programs.

From the smallest businesses to the largest, database marketing is working for predictive marketing, and they're not just retailers. The giant packaged goods marketers are into this big time. From the second quarter of 1992 to the second quarter of 1995, the number of packaged goods companies using database marketing rose from 235 to 791.[1]

A 1996 survey by Carol Wright Promotions, Inc. reports that 65 percent of packaged goods manufacturers contacted have or will build a consumer database in the coming year. The two most popular methods of building a database are premium offers/rebates (100 percent of manufacturers) and contests/sweepstakes (86 percent of manufacturers).

At the Direct Marketing Association's fall conference in 1996 in New Orleans, Ryan Direct and Donnelley Marketing announced the creation of a Packaged Goods Consortium Database combining manufacturers' nonproprietary customer data for shared use predictive marketing. The goal is for the database to have 40 million records all enhanced by household data, psychographic data, and demographic overlays from Donnelley's DQI database, which lists nearly every household in the country. Cross-tabulations with retailer databases will also be possible.

And packaged goods manufacturers are using their databases more. Seventy-three percent use it for promotion evaluation, up from 55 percent. For customer communication, 73 percent use it, up from 45 percent. For cross-selling and up-selling, 55 percent use it, up from 36 percent. Half the manufacturers surveyed report they will use their databases more in the coming year.[2]

In the coming year, they will have another way to use database marketing. The companies that produce co-ops—those multi-insert or card pack mailers—are finding that targeting using a consumer database is essential in order to get attention. Toronto-based Target Dimensions is helping packaged goods manufacturers use database marketing. Harvey Beck, President of Target Dimensions, says that each of this year's 2 million recipients of his co-op received a different envelope depending on their response to Target's behavioral survey. The survey results allow companies to send different coupons or samples to various segments of the list. For example, the makers of Wisk detergent might want to send one offer to current users of Tide liquid and another offer to users of Tide powder.[3]

John Cummings & Partners DBM/SCAN® in Armonk, New York monitors the database marketing programs of almost 2,000 brands in the United States. Speaking at a recent industry conference, Cummings reported a 26 percent increase in the database marketing activities of packaged goods companies for the 12 months ended September 30, 1996, over the previous year. The top 10 companies combined for 3,246 activities. Ranking the companies by the number of database efforts his firm tracked in the year, Kraft led the list.

Leading Companies

Rank	Company	# of Efforts
1	Kraft Foods	725
2	Procter & Gamble	506
3	Perrier Group	330
4	Nestle	270
5	Johnson & Johnson	256
6	Philip Morris	250
7	Ralston Purina	241
8	Campbell Soup	240
9	R. J. Reynolds	219
10	Quaker Oats	209

He then scored each company's commitment to database marketing on the basis of: loyalty programs, incidence of direct mail promotions versus others, new products, in-coupon data collection, household coded coupons,

name/address/plus data collection, size of database marketing staff, and
each company's database marketing program trend. The ranking of highly
committed database marketers changed.

The Highly Committed Database Marketers

Rank	Company	# of Efforts
1	Kraft Foods	86
2	Ralston Purina	79
3	Phillip Morris	77
3	SmithKline Beecham	77
5	Kimberly-Clark	76
6	Nestle	74
7	Bristol-Meyers Squib	73
8	R.J. Reynolds	72
8	Sandoz Consumer	72
8	Sara Lee	72

Notice that 5 of the leaders in terms of number of efforts did not qualify for
the top 10 in commitment. Procter & Gamble, #2 in number of database
marketing efforts, didn't make the top ten of those highly committed.

While loyalty programs accounted for only 10 percent of the file,
with new programs started in the last year up 24 percent, the list of other
activities was impressive: action marketing, contact marketing, dialog
marketing, involvement marketing, one-to-one marketing, personal marketing, relationship marketing, and stealth marketing. Applications included: targeted direct mail, continuity programs, newsletters, catalogs,
custom magazines, and interactive.

Cummings says, "The Internet is in high gear." He reported 176 companies with Websites, many multiple-brand; total activity up six times versus prior year; 90 companies mentioning Websites in their magazine ads;
and 30 companies mentioning sites in their freestanding inserts.

His predictions for the next 12 to 24 months: Brands driving consumers to Internet sites via mass advertising, drug companies launching symp-
tom-specific loyalty programs, and more retail partnering programs.

He listed six key, emerging trends for packaged goods database marketing:

1. 800 # usage increasing dramatically each year.
2. More tie-in programs to reduce cost.
3. Increasing use of multimedia data collection.
4. Shared name-generation programs possibly leading to shared
databases.

5. Focus on critical data (e.g., product usage).

6. DBM means different things to different companies.

He also listed four reasons for a promising outlook for database marketing in the packaged goods industry:

1. The inevitable fragmentation of audiences persists.

2. The computer will continue to have an increased impact on all business practices.

3. Younger managers are more favorably disposed to new technologies (they are computer literate and less tied to past approaches).

4. The growing interest in testing new media.

He concluded by pointing out that it's not just the small brands that can't afford mass marketing that are leading the way. Rather, it's the super brands—the giants—that are paving the way, creating a dialog with customers to build brand loyalty.

Phone companies, airlines, automakers, and retailers have an easy time of it. They have, or can get, customer names and addresses, and they can track transactions. But what about the packaged goods marketer, or the luggage manufacturers, or the makers of dinnerware whose only direct customers are the retailers—or, another step removed, the distributors who sell to the retailers? Or, more difficult yet, the fabric suppliers who sell to the manufacturers, who sell to the distributors, who sell to the retailers, who finally get to meet the customer?

We'll start with the packaged goods company that John Cummings rated number one in database marketing experience. Kraft maintains a customer database of more than 25 million names. They mail over 100 million target mailings a year, but they use the database for a lot more than direct mail. Kraft's consumer penetration is near 100 percent, with almost all households in America buying at least one of their products. They have learned that heavy users are worth 30 times more than light users.

On average, a household spends about $375 a year on Kraft products, or about 10 percent of their grocery dollars, but 20 percent of all households account for the biggest percentage of Kraft volume. The average heavy-user household buys 33 Kraft categories. These heavy-user households are worth over $600 a year to Kraft. And yet because Kraft has traditionally spent most of their $1.6 billion in advertising and consumer promotion on mass programs, they spent the same amount on the light-user households as they spent on the heavy-users—until they built the database.

Direct marketing techniques and a powerful database, coupled with the knowledge that the customer base is made up of heavy users, average users, and light users, allow Kraft to get to the profit-pay-off step that identifies and targets heavy-user households in ways that are both efficient and effective.

As a successful mass marketer, why is Kraft attracted to database marketing? Kraft is trying to use database marketing as an alternative to off-price promotion and coupons. Earlier, we saw the dramatic growth of coupon distribution in the packaged goods industry. Even with that proliferation, coupons still work, but 1) the baseline is not increasing, and 2) the industry is killing brand equity by over discounting. Kraft is trying to use database marketing to build more regular price business and brand equity.

As we have reviewed, the marketing challenge lies in the fact that price has become the consumer's point of difference. Product differences are quickly eliminated by the competition. Maxwell House has a basic coffee that competes with Folgers. Kraft introduces a Rich French Roast, so does P&G. Maxwell House introduces a Colombian Supreme, so does Folgers. So, the database marketing role at Kraft is to market and exploit differences: differences in brands, differences in people, and differences in communications.

Kraft believes that by adding value, reinforcing the equity, and creating a unique interaction between the consumer and the brand, they can increase share-of-mind and increase profitable volume.

The objectives for direct marketing at Kraft are to deliver the right message to the right people via the right medium at the right time. By marketing to the differences, Kraft elevates the brand from competing just on price and creates a true competitive advantage.

Like any other database, Kraft's begins with names and addresses. The second piece of information is that these households are promotionally sensitive, and the third is the brand they purchased. That's just the start.

Through proprietary survey programs, Kraft learns about the Kraft brands and the competitive brands used in each household. They go to outside sources to learn more about the individuals in each household— demographic information like age, number and ages of children, income, and psychographic specifics like hobbies and magazine preferences. They use all of this information to identify current users, to profile for high-potential users, and to create communications that will be relevant and interesting to each household.

Of course, Kraft also goes to syndicated sources like IRI and Nielsen to obtain volumetric information. For example, does the brand have a heavy-user skew? Are there issues with penetration (difficulty getting new users or loss of current users)? Using all this, they can create usage and demographic/psychographic profiles for buyers of each of their brands and use this data for modeling. Then they create special communications to fit the separate models.

Miracle Whip Cooks! is a relationship marketing program specially designed for heavier users of Miracle Whip. The program, utilizing a newsletter format, centers on food preparation needs and offers recipes and ideas featuring Miracle Whip as a helper and friend. The program is a recipe strategy and has proven effective due to the highly receptive audience and the large usage per serving occasion. The program has proven highly effective over several years in building incremental volume and nurturing brand loyalty.

Another Kraft brand is Kool-Aid, whose direct competition is Coke and Pepsi. Against the two giants' massive ad budgets, Kool-Aid had to create a point of difference—something unique and ownable. Since kids and fun are synonymous, Kraft made Kool-Aid fun with the Wacky Warehouse. A direct mail piece to database households with kids was an important element in the introduction of the program. Kids could interact with the brand by obtaining merchandise in exchange for proofs of purchase, reading the Kool-Aid Man comic book, and working through activities, all fun and involving.

For every use of the database, Kraft starts by establishing direct marketing objectives and strategies. Actually, the direct marketing creative must satisfy two gods. First, the god of brand equity. Every direct marketing communication must compliment and build the image and statement the brand conveys in its advertising. Second, the god of strategy. Creative executions must meet the specific direct marketing strategic need. There must be only one message. It must be interpreted by the customer as being a one-to-one communication, and the offer must be well presented. Kraft understands the unique disciplines of customer database marketing.[4]

Ralston Purina is another company that understands the value of customer database marketing. A case study developed by Case-in-Point reported that since 1990, when they began building a database of superpremium pet food customers, they have developed a multimillion-name customer file. In addition to the fact that Purina O.N.E. dog and cat food sales have grown at a 25 to 30 percent rate for three years running, Ralston credits its database efforts for a strong shift in the user base from infrequent users to occasional and loyal users with those who satisfy over half of their pet food requirements with Purina O.N.E. growing at double digit rates. Ralston is spending about 70 percent less to keep these customers in the franchise than it would without the database.[5]

The luggage manufacturer, Samsonite, is a market share leader with a 40 percent sales growth over the last four years. Samsonite sells through catalogs, department stores, chains, mass merchandisers, warehouse stores, and their own factory outlets.

According to *Case-in-Point,* they are database marketing leaders, using their large database for cultivating existing customers and acquisition marketing. In August 1990, they instituted registration cards to capture information about their luggage buyers. The cards ask 25 questions that establish each customer's demographic profile and travel habits. Samsonite gets back 25,000 to 35,000 cards a month and now has a very rich database of over 1 million Samsonite buyers.

The database has enabled Samsonite to target product types to specific customer and prospect groups by age, income, sex, and business or leisure travel. Customer and prospect knowledge from the database helps select focused print and media, including direct mail and selective binding, and guides creative to target customers with pinpoint accuracy.

In March 1992, Samsonite initiated toll-free telephone numbers to handle product questions and problems. This has become a prospect source from which the company collects names and addresses, sends product brochures, conducts basic market research, and refers consumers to nearest dealers. From the hundreds of thousands of calls, 29 percent purchased luggage and 60 percent of those purchased within one month of their call—25 percent within seven days—forcing Samsonite to change brochure postage to first class. Almost 70 percent of those purchasing luggage bought Samsonite.

Samsonite uses the customer database to contact consumers to check overall satisfaction semi-annually and specific products quarterly. Immediately after the introduction of a new product, 200 consumers are asked detailed questions to uncover any product problems. The demographic profile and travel pattern knowledge from the database is a key tool for new product development. Beyond that, the customer database has become a strong force to gain distribution. The salesforce can say, "We know your customer. We know why your customers buy Samsonite. We know how to help you attract the consumers you want."

Finally, Samsonite has developed a customer loyalty program. Consumers returning four or more registration cards receive a letter from the president with a travel alarm-clock gift. Follow-up research shows increased brand equity with loyalty program customers. Seventy-one percent of those receiving the letter called Samsonite "A company you can trust," while of those not receiving the letter, only 40 percent agreed with the statement. Of those receiving the president's letter, 69 percent called Samsonite "A leader in the industry" versus 40 percent of nonrecipients. The statement "Products are good value" rated similarly: 77 percent versus 57 percent.[6]

Another manufacturer, Lenox, is building a customer loyalty program because they know that exclusivity, privilege, and preferred access lead to increased purchases, customer bonding and commitment, and long-term, profitable relationships. They have created a Lenox membership program with these benefits:

- Members' only merchandise
- Gift for joining
- Quarterly newsletter
- Birthday remembrance
- Special events
- Members' materials

Their goal was to build a strong relationship with their most enthusiastic customers. They wanted to create a "special connection" with frequent purchasers and develop a two-way flow of information (i.e., the dialog we have been talking about).

A Lenox representative reported at a recent direct marketing conference that club members are purchasing twice as much as they did before the program started.

It pays to trust your database. I have been told the story of a bicycle manufacturer who learned a very large segment of bike owners in the company's database liked outdoor activities. Marketing suggested the need for "off-trail" bikes. The company didn't trust the data and rejected the idea. That was in the early 80s. The company missed a big marketing opportunity. Most mountain bikes may never climb as much as a molehill, but two out of every three bikes sold in western Europe and the United States are now of that type.[7]

Skil Twist trusted its database and opened up new markets. Skil Twist markets a cordless, electric screwdriver primarily to the do-it-yourself market. The database demonstrated a secondary market of older women. Research showed the cordless drill solved a problem for arthritis sufferers. Skil Twist redirected some of its media efforts to gain this new market.

We have seen enough of what some packaged goods marketers and other manufacturers are doing to realize there are numerous ways to use the database to grow the business. But what if your business is several steps removed from the end user? How can you use customer knowledge for more profitable selling?

Read on.

CHAPTER **15**

Three Steps Removed— A Whole New Way to Sell

What if your business is three steps removed from the end customer—what is purchase-after-purchase?

Gore-Tex manufactures a breathable, weatherproof material. Not only do they not have direct contact with the consumer; they don't even have direct contact with the retailer who sells to the consumer. Gore-Tex is sold to value-added resellers who manufacture clothing. Through a registration card procedure (like Samsonite's), Gore-Tex has built a database of households representing purchasers of some item of clothing made of Gore-Tex fabric. They developed a catalog of products using Gore-Tex, then used their customer database to score prospects that "looked like" Gore-Tex buyers.

Targeted prospects received invitations to local stores and were offered free headbands with proof of purchase. Gore-Tex got a 10 percent redemption rate on the gift with purchase.

As we've emphasized throughout, there is a lot more to database marketing than direct mail. Here's a quick case history.

A regional department store group with a solid database capability asked the question, "Now that we know the shopping behavior of our customers, can we find a way to use that information to save some mark-downs?"

The objective of this test was to see if the store could use database knowledge to improve gross margin performance in the women's better, branded sportswear departments. Remember, one purpose of database marketing is to use the study of past shopping patterns to group customers together in segments that share some behavior. The procedure was fairly simple. The company started by identifying customers who bought in these departments but only bought on sale. They used the purchase history database to segment customers who, over three fashion seasons, had shopped only during prime markdown periods in four merchandise classifications, only in one store. Remember, this was a one-store test. They isolated first-markdown-only shoppers, second-markdown-only shoppers, and both-markdown shoppers, together with dollars spent. Using these data, they calculated total markdown dollars given up to these customers at the different stages of the markdown process.

Of the total $14,500 in markdowns, they found only $4,500 went to first-markdown shoppers. The big hit of $10,000 went to the smaller group who bought later. Every shopper who waited for the second markdown cost the store $75.

The objective of the test was to move second-markdown shoppers to first markdown shoppers and save the $75 per customer. Having identified the target customers, the store set two measurable objectives for the test:

1. To stage an event to increase sales volume 50 percent over the prior year for the same days.
2. To make five times the cost of the event in markdown dollars saved.

A direct mail promotion went to the second-markdown customers to tell them the store had marked down their favorite brands (first markdown) and they should hurry in for best selections. This was a two-day event, a one-store test, just 1,400 customers, just $850 cost.

The store increased sales 97 percent over the two days.

That extra business at the 25 percent markdown cost $9,000 to move the goods. Had these customers waited for the second markdown, the store would have given up twice that amount, $18,300.

This store spent $850 to save over $9,000 by moving these sales to the earlier part of the markdown cycle and achieved both of its goals. Next season, rolled out to include all 30 of the company's stores, the potential profit increment is $300,000.

Every time I present the case for direct marketing to an audience, I am asked if this is really changing the focus of major marketers. What the questioner really means is, are these marketers actually moving dollar investments from general advertising to database marketing? The answer is yes.

There are many examples. For the first time this year, Hyatt Hotels spent more on direct marketing media than on conventional advertising. For their "Nights After Nights" campaign in the Fall of '95, Hyatt spent $4 in direct marketing for every $1 in general advertising. Of the $4 million spent on the campaign, less than $1 million went for print ads. The hotel chain reports that approximately two-thirds of its 1996 advertising budget will be spent on direct and database marketing, with the rest going to general advertising.[1]

Hyatt has a robust database of 2 million Gold Passport members who are frequent guests, a 13-million member general transaction database, and an 8-million name joint database with American Express.[2]

While advertising dollars are shifting from general advertising to direct marketing, they are also being conserved. Marketers who used to mail full customer lists are learning to mail only the best prospects. Carson Pirie Scott, the major midwest department store chain, has been a pioneer in customer database marketing. While they mail some promotions to their entire customer list, they increasingly rely on smaller and more targeted mailings, which account for 80 percent of their mail volume.

Mail volumes that used to range between 500,000 and 1.3 million pieces per campaign a few years ago have been curtailed, often by as much as 40 to 50 percent, many slashed to as few as 500 pieces for targeting selected market segments.

That kind of pinpoint targeting is a winning strategy for the best database marketers today.

United Audio Centers, a strong regional chain of upscale audio-video stores headquartered in Chicago, uses advanced targeting to beat the fierce price competition in their industry. They call their target selling program "Purchase-After-Purchase." They use their computerized database marketing system to search the complete customer database—every household that has bought something at any United Audio store within the past few years. The search shows the audio-video products each customer currently owns, enabling United Audio to send warm, personal, interesting offers of complimentary products or upgrade possibilities. The program has been a huge success.

Al Copland, United Audio Center's Director of Marketing and Advertising, says:

This is a whole new way to sell that makes the most of our strengths . . . and our competitors' weaknesses.

This is a completely different plan than trying to attract new customers we don't know anything about, or sending "junk mail" to our current customers. Thanks to the incredibly powerful database marketing system we have right in our offices, we're able to communicate with each of our customers on an individual basis about products we know they are qualified to buy.

That means when they come into one of our stores, a successful sale to them has already begun. They don't just know what they want, they know we have it for them and what it costs. When you add our expert personal advice and service, that's a value and quality combination that no mass retailer can ever match.

These offers are sent every 30 days to qualified prospects to communicate with customers over time instead of overloading them. This generates steady business and allows United Audio to monitor results and fine-tune the program. Most of the offers do not include special financing or discounts and are primarily educational in nature, all relating categories of goods to customers' previous purchases. And they are producing profitable results!

A 12-page mailer to customers who owned quality receivers but had not bought speakers recently explained that speakers are the most important part of any sound system and showed all the different choices for upgrading the customer's existing sound system. Just 38,320 pieces mailed produced almost a million dollars in speaker sales without a special price offer!

A mailing of less than 10,000 pieces to customers who had always bought top-line products was headlined "Quality is naturally a part of your lifestyle," and offered United Audio's most expensive exclusive brand. Results were more than $55 in sales for every name mailed.

Gore-Tex, the regional department store, Hyatt, Carsons, and United Audio Centers have each found more profitable ways to sell, and these discoveries have changed their marketing investments.

Next, a case history from an unlikely direct marketer, an eye-opening surprise—how a company found a whole new market within their customer file—and a new way to look at the customer database.

CHAPTER 16

Malls, Northern Lights, and Constellations

The customer database as an observatory.

It's not just the retail chains that are moving marketing dollars to pinpoint customer targeting. Even the big, regional shopping centers think they are database marketers. They have "Customer Club" cards. They ask members to swipe their club cards at mall kiosks to win prizes. The trouble is, they are not learning the most important things they need to know about their shoppers.

They are learning that these customers "visited" the center. That's a good start, but it falls far short of database marketing. Did these customers spend any money? How much? Where? They might just be mall walkers. Do they shop a single store or many? Which combinations of different stores do different clusters of customers cross-shop? How much is each customer worth to the center? What share of the center's business do individual segments of the customer file represent? How much of the center's marketing budget should be spent to talk to each of the different segments of the customer file?

These are tough questions, but they must be answered for effective database marketing. You can sign up customers all day long and append all the demographics you can afford and still not be a database marketer. As we have learned, demographics alone will not predict the future shopping behavior of specific customers. Only past behavior will give a sound prediction. We must know what the customer buys.

It wasn't until 1995 that any regional shopping centers developed the capability to actually track customers' buying behavior in a center's tenant stores. In January of that year, Trizec Hahn Centers, one of the largest U.S. shopping center developers, asked us to help them develop a true database marketing program for their properties. The development started in test at two of its centers, The Oaks in Ventura County, California, and North County Fair in San Diego.

Like any other shopping centers, these two had done enough research to know their median-age shopper was 39.1 years, with 40.2 percent between 25 and 44, 67.6 percent female shoppers 18–65, and 35 percent with children 17 and under. Now they know which specific customers are 18 or 25 or 44 or have children.

More than that, they now know from the customer database when each of these individual customers shop, which store or combination of stores each customer shops at, how often each visits the center, and how much each spends on each visit, in each store.

The customers tell them their shopping preferences by swiping a "Shopping Advantage" membership card at the time of purchase in each of the participating stores. A dedicated VeriFone card reader, located in each store, records every customer's transaction immediately after a purchase is made. Information, stored until the close of business each evening, is automatically downloaded by the Verifone software to the marketing office computer.

The software is flexible enough to allow the mall marketing manager to implement many types of incentive programs to generate traffic and sales, including first-time shopper, senior, and "off-peak" purchase bonuses.

The mall marketing manager generates reports and makes customer selections based on the total center's database, by store category, or by individual store. Some of the data the centers are using for target marketing includes total customer purchase dollars, recency and frequency of individual customer visits, which stores customers cross-shop, how many stores each customer cross-shops, which customers respond to each promotion, and specific customer penetration and dollar sales by zip code. The centers also track "absentee customers" to increase customer retention.

As a major added benefit, the system automatically tracks customer purchases made on behalf of schools and charitable causes, saving the customer a trip to the mall service desk and saving the centers the expense of manually entering sales checks for these events.

Participating stores are able to request reports and mailing labels for their own customers in the database, and groups of stores can get together to create mailings for their joint customers. But the success of the program has meant much more than just the value of this direct mail capability. The knowledge gained from the customer database has given Trizec Hahn Centers an X-ray of its business; knowledge that is just as important to those responsible for leasing as for the individual center's marketing managers.

Based on the success of the Oaks and North County Fair test, the program was rolled out to three more Hahn centers in 1996.

Because the Hahn Company implemented this program to make sure they take special care of their best customers, they chose not to build membership with a "points" or "discount" program, generally referred to as a "hard benefits" program. Instead, they are rewarding customers with myriad "soft benefits" that have included such things as free valet parking, free strollers and wheelchairs, free cellular phones with purchase, birthday gift certificates, theater tickets and special movie showings, gifts with purchase, special store discount offers, and extra values from third-party partners. The very best customers can even get up-front reserved parking on the days they plan to shop.

This is such a classic case of smarter marketing with the database, it is worth the time to examine the centers' original objectives and first six months' results.

THE OBJECTIVES

- ◆ To capture market share and create a point of difference against competition by building a loyalty program for The Oaks and North County Fair customers.
- ◆ To develop a program that determines customer behavior by tracking daily customer spending, both at the individual store level and throughout the mall.
- ◆ To empower mall marketing managers and merchants to maximize the efficiency of their marketing dollars and increase sales by selecting their best customers for each promotional offer.
- ◆ To develop one-on-one relationships and increase sales from members through timely direct mail correspondence that would generate immediate response.

- To secure third-party sponsorships of at least $75,000 that would increase customer interest, add value to the Shopping Advantage Program, and cover the expense of the program.
- To generate a minimum of $1 million in receipts from Shopping Advantage members participating in the schools' fundraising program.
- To generate an additional $75,000 in overage income from participating merchants.

THE RESULTS

- Membership drives at both centers have resulted in over 12,000 customers joining the program within the first six months.
- Since the inception of the program, over 135 merchants, including Nordstrom, have installed dedicated Verifones in their stores and are participating in the program.
- Individual store promotions by Ben Bridge Jewelers, The Body Shop, El Portal Luggage, and McClaves Jewelers that targeted a select group of their best customers achieved 10 to 30 percent responses and generated important sales increases.
- Direct mail postcards and letters to Shopping Advantage customers resulted in 10 to 25 percent returns and generated an additional $190,000 in sales. A personalized letter inviting customers to receive a free cellular phone with purchase resulted in 2,900 responses and generated $150,000 in additional sales. A direct mail postcard offering a gift with purchase and free mocha resulted in a 25 percent response and realized an additional $40,000 in sales.
- Sponsorships were secured with a local entertainment company, local newspapers, a cellular telephone distributor, and center merchants generating $368,270—4.5 times the goal.
- The schools' fund raising programs exceeded all expectations, generating $4.1 million in verified receipts, over 4 times the goal.
- Participating merchants realized over $237,000 in overage income and all posted increases.

That's using the database the right way!

According to Alberta Davidson, Vice President of Marketing at The Trizec Hahn Centers, "Our best programs are indeed those that are driven by the database they create. A marketing direction that can precisely motivate a customer in a fashion that equates directly to the customer's past behavior has a better chance of successful conversion than those typically shooting in the dark."

We have talked quite a bit about the importance of knowing the customer's cross-shopping habits. We'll end the chapter with my favorite cross-shopping story. Remember, we said one use of the cross-shopping analysis was to find nonbuyers most likely to purchase a specific product.

When Bloomingdale's first began tracking customer purchases and established a customer database, they discovered that some of their prior assumptions about customers were not necessarily true. Today Bloomingdale's fur department, Maximilian, features a trendsetting collection of designer furs. In those early days of the store's database development, the fur department was called "Northern Lights" and represented more moderately priced furs. Even so, since a fur purchase represented a major investment for the customer, the merchants in "Northern Lights" believed that the designer fashion customer was the best prospect for buying a fur. As a result, all sales promotion efforts were directed to this marketing segment. As Bloomingdale's marketing executives began to examine the sales data flowing into their customer database, they began to suspect that this conclusion was not true.

They analyzed cross-shopping reports to find the other Bloomingdales departments that fur buyers shopped most frequently and found these to be the Liz Claiborne, Better Sportswear, Juniors, and Men's departments. Subsequent fur offers were tailored to frequent shoppers in these four departments who had not previously purchased a fur.

Bloomingdale's learned two important lessons. Reduced mail quantities carefully targeted to most likely prospects produced significant increases in sales, and the store had a much broader market for furs right within their customer file.

So we have seen that the customer database can refine the marketing process to help marketers identify best customers, develop new customers, earn more business from existing customers, deliver a message consistent with product usage, cross-sell and complimentary-sell products, improve delivery of sales promotion efforts, personalize customer service, and establish new management resources . . . all based on customer segmentation.

My friend Stephen Shaw, a respected Canadian database marketing consultant, has written:

> If you think of the customer database as an observatory, where the actual behavior of customers can be closely observed, segmentation analysis can be compared to studying the constellations.

To the untrained eye, that mass of celestial lights seems amorphous; but, to an astronomy expert, the patterns of stars are clearly visible. The same might be said of the customer universe.

By relating the demographic and socioeconomic characteristics of customers to their buying habits, and then probing for their underlying motivations through traditional research methods, the database may be partitioned into unique groups for whom different strategies may be deployed.

Understanding what makes each group different may inspire adjustments in product positioning and help to strike the right emotional chords in advertising. Those marketing strategies can then be validated by analyzing the subsequent transaction activity on the database.

It is time to see just how we do that validation. Marketers have always known that some portion of their advertising was wasted. They have always believed the magic bullet would be the ability to find those wasted portions. Let us now see how the new rules of marketing are developing that magic bullet.

CHAPTER **17**

If It Can't be Measured, It Can't be Improved
Finally: Which half *is* wasted.

Generations of marketers have quoted John Wanamaker saying, "I know half my advertising is wasted. I just don't know which half." It took my first trip to speak in London to learn that the same generations of marketers in the United Kingdom attribute that sage quotation to Lord Leverhulme.

No matter who deserves the credit, the conclusion was all too accurate. Since the development of mass media, marketers have used general advertising to transmit news to consumers about their products and services. If the consumer responded to the advertiser's message, that purchase action took place in a manner and venue that was difficult, if not impossible, to measure.

Historically, the results from a newspaper or television advertising expenditure could be measured only through the sales of the advertised offering or the increase in traffic at a retail store. Even positive results could not help the marketer define which purchasers came in specific response to the advertised offer, and in no case could the marketer address the Wanamaker/Leverhulme question of which segment of the purchased audience was a waste. The unprecedented challenges ahead of us make that unacceptable. We must find ways to change the rules.

Direct marketing, as we have defined it here, begins to change the rules. It brings us to serious methods of measurement. The catalogers learned the science of response measurement early through the magic of the key number or source code, that strange alpha/numeric gibberish like G3373-LG or 88HR just above or to the right of your name on the catalog address panel. Today, when you call that 800 number to order from an ad or a catalog, the first thing the order taker asks for is that magic number. That code provides the measurement of how many responses came from each rented list or each separate advertising investment. And, now, with the power of computers and optical scanning devices, the magic number tells the marketer not just how many responses the investment produced, but also who responded and who did not. Mr. Wanamaker and/or Lord Leverhulme would be thrilled.

It was the cataloger's key-code knowledge of customer response that led me to try to develop this opportunity for other marketers to know as much about their customers as the catalogers did. With the customer database and purchase tracking capability, every marketer can measure virtually every element of his marketing investment. That starts, of course, with the measurement of customers: which ones are the most valuable, which ones can be made more valuable, and which ones are not worth much marketing investment. More than that, the new direct marketing can measure which creative approach or printing technique, or offer, or timing is most productive (with which audience), or which medium actually delivers the most acceptable selling cost.

In database marketing today, banks and insurance companies have the names, addresses, phone numbers, and purchase details of their customers. Most retailers started developing customer databases from their proprietary charge account records. This was a good start, but fell short of the full knowledge needed for true marketing analysis. Rarely was the house charge card base responsible for more than 40 percent of sales volume, and charge card activity tracking missed even the charge customers' bank card, check, and cash transactions. Stores I work with that are capturing all customer transactions find that one-third or more of all cash and third-party card purchases are made by customers who have the store's proprietary charge card but are not using it. Tracking only proprietary card purchases gives a false picture of the cardholder/customer's purchase activity. A retailer tracking only proprietary card sales could place me in a low recency decile and a low monetary decile, even though I was in the store yesterday and spent $1,000 on my bank card.

If you shop in any Radio Shack store, you know it is virtually impossible to buy even a 45-cent fuse without giving the sales associate your name and address. Many businesses use the customer's telephone number as the customer ID. Entering the phone number along with the sales information at point-of-purchase ties the transaction data to the customer's record in the company's database, providing date and amount of the purchase, method of payment and product information down to the stock-keeping unit definition. Companies always ask me, "Won't most of our customers refuse to give out their phone numbers?" The answer is no. I have only worked with one company where we had difficulty getting the customers to give us phone numbers. When we checked the problem out we found the interaction with the customer went something like this.

> "May I have your phone number, please."
> "Why do you need my phone number?"
> "I don't know. It's just another damn thing management makes us do!"

A bit of sales associate training solved the problem quickly. As soon as the sales associate was able to tell customers how this would help the company give them better service, the problem disappeared.

Some companies ask their customers to provide name and address at the time of their first purchase. Others send the phone numbers to a service bureau that matches the number to the name and address. Because of unlisted numbers, of course, this does not provide 100 percent capture. The capture rate varies from a low of about 40 percent to a high of 70 percent, with Californians showing the lowest capture rate.

Many businesses—retailers, manufacturers, credit card companies and, as we have seen, even shopping centers—have developed customer club programs. When the club membership card is swiped at point-of-purchase, all of the transaction data flows to the customer's file. Of course, manufacturers gain a lot of customer data from warranty cards. Marketers with a high percentage of bank card and/or travel card sales develop customer transaction history by what is called *reverse append*. The marketer sends his register tapes to a third-party source and gets the name and address for each card transaction.

If it *can* be measured it *can* be improved. The analysis of each marketing investment helps make the next investment more profitable. No matter how the marketer captures the customer identification, once he can tie that ID to customer transactions he can measure very specific results. The total marketing cost per delivered household is the new behavioral standard.

The process of measurement must start with clearly defined objectives. Here are some rules one marketer has adopted for its promotion analysis:

1. SET THE GOALS

Is the goal of this marketing expenditure to achieve sales? How many? Is our goal to acquire new customers? How many? Of what quality? Are we trying to get more sales from existing customers, increase our average sale, sell specific products, increase cross-sell, or simply reduce expenses?

2. DEFINE DESIRED RESPONSE BEHAVIOR

Are we looking for a specific product inquiry? Will we measure based on any purchase, purchase of a specific product, or purchase of specific products plus other purchases? Will coupon redemption be the test?

3. DETERMINE THE TIME FRAME FOR ANALYSIS

Will we measure just the time limits of the promotion, or will we look at the pre-promotion and post-promotion period as well? (If a mailer was in the customers' home a week before the event, did that have an effect on our sales pre-promotion? Were some of the purchases driven by the promotion simply planned purchases that would have been made later, causing our post-promotion sales to fall below the norm?)

4. ESTABLISH KEY BASELINE MEASUREMENTS AGAINST WHICH THE PROMOTION WILL BE RATED

What elements will we score? Percent response, cost per response, average sale per responder, non-promoted sales levels during the event, profit per response, sales or profit per name mailed, and return-on-investment are the most common. But if the promotion was to obtain sales leads, the marketer must measure conversion. If we were selling subscriptions, we must go forward to measure renewals for the true evaluation, or if we are signing up "club" members or selling a continuity program, we must measure attrition.

5. DEFINE THE ANALYTICS

What kinds of analysis reports will be generated?

1. Analysis during the promotion?
2. Historical analysis at the conclusion of the event?
3. Executive management summary?

6. LOOK FOR WAYS TO ADD TO OUR KNOWLEDGE AND IMPROVE OUR EFFICIENCY

How will we establish the most important variables? There are so many things we can measure, it is important to separate the "nice to know" from the "need to know." There is an old saying among database marketers, "The food begets the appetite." The more we learn about our customers, the more we want to know. The problem is that we can now generate so many reports and so much information that we can be overwhelmed. Data has no value until it becomes usable knowledge.

Some obvious answers that will add to the marketers' knowledge and improve their efficiency are cost effectiveness, lift analysis, trend analysis, sales volume distribution, and response composition.

We have talked about finding new paradigms of marketing communication and new models of understanding customers. We have said the mass communications we have grown up with will no longer serve to communicate with the new customer. As we search for the best of the new paradigms, we will still need the capability to measure and improve.

In the next chapter, we'll look at how direct marketers are using some sophisticated measurements to improve their marketing skills with the new rules of marketing.

CHAPTER 18

The Importance of the Incremental
Beware the incidental buyer!

The basic measurements marketers look for in their evaluations are all incremental. It is never enough to look at the raw sales results. In many cases, other advertising and possibly even other promotions are in place that may have attracted buyers for the product or to the store. If the marketer is attempting to measure the influence (and therefore the success) of a mailed promotion, other media may have been used to promote the product or the event. In comparing annual events, there may have been promotional changes this year versus last year. Current sales trends will always have an effect.

To measure incremental results—the sales provably generated by the promotion—the marketer must eliminate the impact of the incidental buyer. Enter the *control group*. The control group is a randomly selected subset of the targeted customer segment that does not receive the offer. It is important to understand the process of selecting a control group. I have had marketers tell me some strange things. One said recently, "Oh sure we use control groups. I select the customer segment I want to mail and that always leaves me some customers that didn't qualify for that selection. I just take a few thousands of those and set them up as control."

Of course, that marketer is heading for trouble. The point is, this is such a new science for some marketers that there are folks in every industry using their customer data in naive ways, getting bad answers and not always knowing they are providing faulty reports.

An honest control group must be a carefully controlled sample of the exact customer segment that is being given the offer. The purest of all control groups would be customers who never receive any offer—the thinking here being that even a prior offer may affect their buying decision at the time we consider them part of a control group. Most marketers, retailers in particular, will never make control groups that pure because they are not willing to eliminate any of their best customers from all offers. This is probably a wise decision, and one that will not destroy the basic credibility of their control groups. It is important to remember that even though database marketing is a science, it is not a 100 percent exact science. There will always be some buyers whose purchases were not captured. There will always be some pieces of any mailing that were misaddressed. Still, marketers measuring incremental sales by comparing the purchase behavior of the promoted group to the purchase behavior of the control group are getting valid measurements of success.

Figure 18-1 shows a typical incremental sales analysis. This is a typical incremental sales analysis report. Some of the details reported here will differ from industry to industry, but the process of measuring incremental sales is basic. The marketer measures specific purchase activities of the promoted group and compares those results to the same specific purchase activities of the control group for the same time period.

This analysis is used by a marketer to evaluate a mailed offer. Each line represents a customer segment selection from the database. At the time the separate segments are defined and selected for the mailing, a control group is defined and selected for each segment. The customer names in each of the segments (mailed and control) are flagged in the file so they can be analyzed after the event purchase tracking has been completed.

The first segment represents customers with purchases of $1,000 or more in the trailing 12 months. Of the 100,000 who were mailed the offer, 14 percent responded. Those responding to the offer purchased $640,000 of the advertised product, plus $260,000 of other merchandise for a total of $900,000. The average responder in this segment purchased $64.28. Many marketers will also calculate sales per name mailed.

Enough of the same information is reported for the control group of the segment. Of this selected customer segment, 10,000 did not receive the offer. One thousand of these customers, 10 percent, came in and purchased

Promotion Analysis-Incremental Sales Analysis

Segment Descript	# Mailed	# of Resp	% Resp	Mailed Group Sales of Advt'd	Sales of Non-Advt'd	Total Sales	Avg Sale/ Resp	# in Cntrl Group	# of Resp	% Resp	Control Group Sales of Advt'd	Sales of Non-Advt'd	Total $ Sales	Avg Sale/ Resp
>$1000	100000	14000	14.0	640000	260000	900000	64.28	10000	1000	10	42800	17200	60000	60.00
$500-$999	75000	6150	8.2	285000	72700	356700	58.00	7500	345	4.6	11834	5071	16905	49.00
$50-$499	50000	1250	2.5	48000	9500	57500	46.00	5000	120	2.4	4224	1056	5280	44.00
Total	225000	21400	9.5	973000	341200	1314200	61.41	22500	1465	6.5	58858	23327	82185	56.00

Courtesy: Seklemian/Newell

the offered product even though they did not receive the offer. They spent a total of $60,000, or an average of $60.00 each.

Now we have the information we need to calculate incremental sales.

Since the folks in the control group, who did not receive the offer, had exactly the same attributes as those in the mailed group, it is logical to believe the purchase actions of the mailed group would be very much the same as discovered in the control group. This, of course, suggests that if some of the members of the control group were incidental purchasers, then some within the mailed group must also have been incidental purchasers who would have purchased even without receiving the mailer. We must eliminate the purchases of these probable incidental purchasers to get a measure of the incremental sales produced from this marketing effort.

A simple formula gives us our answer. Total sales (minus the number of names mailed, times the control group percent response, times the control group average sales per responder) = incremental sales, or:

$$\$900,000 - (100,000 \times .10 \times \$60.00) = \$300,000 \text{ incremental sales}$$
from the first segment: customers who had spent more than $1,000.

With this information in hand, the marketer can drill deeper into the data to learn even more about the effectiveness of the promotion and to measure incremental profit. Figure 18-2 shows the incremental sales for each segment that was mailed the offer. On the incremental sales side of the report, we see two new measures; incremental sales per name mailed and percent lift. The first segment, our customers with purchases of $1,000 or more in the trailing 12 months, produced a lift of 4 percent (percent response of the mailed group minus percent response of the control group).

FIGURE 18-2

Incremental Lift and Incremental Profit Analysis

Segment Descript	# Mailed	Total Incr Sales $	% Resp	Avg $/ Resp	Incr Sales Name Mailed	% Lift	GM %	GM $	Promo Cost	Cost/ Piece	$ Profit
>$1000	100000	300000	14.0	64.28	3.00	4.0	36	108000	50000	.50	58000
$500-$999	75000	187650	8.2	58.00	2.50	3.6	36	67554	37500	.50	30059
$50-$499	50000	4700	2.5	46.00	.09	0.1	36	1692	25000	.50	(23308)
Total	225000	492350	9.5	61.41	2.19	3.0	36	177246	112500	.50	64746

Courtesy: Seklemian/Newell

Finally, we can measure the profitability of this effort. On the incremental profit side of the report, we multiply the incremental sales by the gross margin percent to produce total gross margin dollars, then subtract the promotion cost to get the total dollar profit. This report also gives us the chance to look at cost per piece mailed versus incremental sales per piece mailed. Some marketers divide gross margin dollars by total promotion costs to get a measure of the return on our promotion investment.

Even a quick look at this report makes the case for analyzing marketing investments by segment. Looking only at the total results of the promotion could be misleading: It shows an incremental profit of $64,746, but doesn't show that the promotion would have produced $88,054 in incremental profit if the $50-$499 spenders had not been mailed. Only when you look at the productivity and the profitability of each segment of the mailing list does the learning experience begin.

Sometimes real data isn't pretty. Sometimes marketers get answers they don't like. That's all a part of the learning experience.

I remember being called in to review the promotion efforts of a client. They were concerned that their mailings were not showing enough lift to prove their effectiveness. They had been looking only at promotion totals. By separating the mailing lists into many segments, we could show that some segments of the lists were, in fact, producing powerful, double-digit percent lift, with other segments drawing down the average to make the total look weak. Summaries always cover up facts.

The fact is that the very best customers, high dollar spenders, or the most recent, or the most frequent purchasers, are going to purchase whether they receive a special offer or not. They are coming to the store or buying the brand on a regular and consistent basis. The truth is, we don't have to mail to this group to keep them coming. One school of thought is, "Save the money. We don't have to promote to these folks." The other is, "They are our best customers. We must send them everything." We should be sure to communicate with them, but they rarely produce incremental sales.

Incremental sales produced by a promotion effort gives the only true picture of the value of a promotion investment. I have had clients tell me, "We mailed 150,000 pieces of that offer and our sales were flat to last year. We shouldn't repeat it." What they failed to realize was that their total business compared to last year had been trending down seriously prior to the event. We were able to show them that the offering did generate significant incremental sales. Without the promotion, their business would have continued in decline.

In another case, a company had mailed a million pieces and showed a 3 percent sales increase during the event. The client wanted to repeat the event the next year. In this case, there had been a significant amount of other advertising during the event time frame. We could show them that the million pieces mailed generated virtually no incremental sales. They were able to re-invest these dollars in more profitable offers.

One client historically mailed almost two million pieces for an offer, using only the customer monetary index for list selection. The kind of segmentation analysis we have just reviewed showed them that the greatest gain in incremental sales came from customers with a strong purchase history for the category, not from the big spenders. This marketer resegmented the list selection based on product purchase history and reduced the quantity mailed by 20 percent. Total sales in the period increased almost 20 percent, and incremental sales for the mailer increased 50 percent!

This analysis process can also tell the marketer incremental sales and incremental profit results by state or zip-code or store location, by employee versus nonemployee, or by customer type, customer income, or any other customer description in the database.

Figure 18-3 analyzes a "new mover" program over six months. This company rents names of new movers in three categories: new prospects (new to the city), previous prospects (lived in the city before but not a current customer), and previous customers (moved from one area of the city to another). Two mailings are done to each resident, one month apart, offering them a discount on merchandise within the next 45 days.

From February through July approximately 33,000 names were mailed, twice each, generating 66,000 pieces of mail for a total promotion cost of approximately $55,000. Of the individuals mailed, 1,586 made a total of 4,590 purchases, which was a 5 percent response. The total amount purchased by these customers during the period was $999,391. The company was able to show that 90 percent were new customer relationships.

The important fact developed from this analysis was that this single promotion accounted for 3 to 5 percent of total company sales in the period.

We learn from this that a company with a solid database marketing capability to track and analyze sales responses can use that capability to attract new customers as well as develop more business from existing customers, and they can measure the results of such efforts.

One more example. Hi Fi Buys, a regional chain of electronics stores based in Atlanta, is a dedicated database marketer. Over the years, their agency, Meisner Direct, has helped them develop a strong base of cus-

FIGURE 18-3

Total Store Sales vs. New Mover Promotional Sales

Month	Store 1	Store 2	Store 3	Store 4	Store 5	Store 6	Store 7	Store 8	Store 9	Store 10	Store 11	Store 12	Total
Feb	510552	297712	585337	489628	248213	167077	440252	399081	2795	208588	426099	213443	3988776
March	532139	250849	523019	426071	218723	129355	475847	356852	1818	192736	479600	186610	3771383
April	557790	237198	445859	426644	212527	121007	469555	298589	-0-	185026	378795	168581	3503408
May	587144	245335	568117	370114	230542	129704	471841	363528	-0-	167266	382164	171285	3687039
June	612273	263916	502724	431831	203696	156778	463179	391540	-0-	195808	401298	185224	3808267
July	612273	257092	574562	546587	178902	195427	506145	450072	-0-	228691	503967	243867	4297585
Store Sales	3412171	1552102	3199618	2690895	1292603	899348	2826819	2259662	4613	1178115	2571923	1169010	23056458
Promo Sales	105436	56575	155286	137071	-0-	-0-	138541	90102	1897	60592	118865	51768	999391
% Generated by Program	3.0	3.6	4.8	5.0	-0-	-0-	4.9	3.9	N/A	5.1	4.6	4.4	4.3

Courtesy: Meisner Direct

tomer data, which they use strategically to analyze their business and implement their marketing programs. They wanted to educate potential customers about Surround Sound Home Theater and to drive new and existing customers into the stores to generate new sales of Surround Sound components (audio and video).

They selected customers from the Hi Fi Buys database, based on past purchase history, to target those most likely to be ready to trade up to Surround Sound Home Theater, then reviewed outside lists to find prospects with the same propensity to buy, "deduping" all lists to ensure one mailing per household. The promotion was an outstanding success, and their careful list selection proved it is possible to rent outside lists that will be almost as productive as the house file. A CD club and a video club continuity buyers list ranked a very close (and profitable) second to the house file, proving, once again, demographics alone do not identify prospective purchasers. Customer behavior is the key.

We have looked at a lot of reports and a lot of data and have seen how marketers are measuring incremental sales. All this crunching of numbers is fine for the marketing database manager, but we can't expect senior management to take the time to comb through all of this detail.

At the same time, it is vital to get senior executives involved. The more they are able to see that the marketing database drives sales and profits and makes the company's marketing investments more effective, the stronger support they will give to the database marketing team . . . including the all-important funding for marketing database staff and state-of-the-art computer technology—but bringing a long computer printout to the CEO is a career-ending move. Thus the need for a concise executive summary for each measured event.

The management report, Figure 18-4, brings the most important elements of the promotion analysis together on one page. Senior executives, who may have had little or no involvement in the marketing effort, can see at a glance all of the information the marketing department has judged most vital.

The "Objective" states the case for the effort: what the marketing department set out to accomplish. The "Description" covers a description of the offer, including pricing, promotion dates, and both gross and net cost. The gross and net cost is a major factor for most retail promotions. Department stores, specialty stores, supermarket operators, appliance dealers, and others are often working with significant vendor dollar contributions to their marketing efforts.

The "Summary of Results" highlights the incremental sales and the

FIGURE 18-4

Management Report

Objective

- Achieve a 12% October sales increase for department 123
- Test 33 segments of the house file

Description

- 4-page flyer mailed to 225,000 customers
- In-home date, October 12, 1995
- Total Cost $112,500 = .50/piece
- Vendor contribution $38,000
  (All profit calculations based on gross cost)

Summary of Results

- Sales of merchandise advertised $973,000
- Sales total department 123 $1,314,200
- Incremental sales $492,350
- Incremental sales per name mailed 2.19
- Lift = 3.0%
- Low spenders not profitable
- The incremental sales from this promotion resulted in a
  14% increase in department 123 sales for the month of October.

Results by customer segment

| | Incremental | | | | Incremental Profit Analysis | | | |
List	Sales	Sales/ Name Mailed	Lift %		GM$	Promo Cost	Cost/ Piece	Profit
#1	300000	3.00	4.0		108000	50000	.50	58000
#2	187650	2.50	3.6		67554	37500	.50	30054
#3	4700	.09	0.1		1692	25000	.50	(23308)

Courtesy: Seklemian/Newell

incremental profit on both a gross cost and a net cost basis. This part of the report also highlights results based on original objectives. In the case of the report in Figure 18-4, objectives included the testing of three different segments of the store's house file. The "Results Summary" answers the question of which segments were the most profitable.

Finally, the results "By Customer Segment" give the bare bones results in just three lines.

The purposes of this book are to examine the roll of database marketing, and explore the very great differences between direct marketing, database marketing, relationship marketing, and customer management. We have been looking at marketers' activities in direct Marketing and database marketing—what Lester Wunderman called "mini-mass marketing."

Now it's time to look at the other side, relationship marketing and customer management, which views the customer as an individual.

CHAPTER **19**

Finally, the Customer

How a 1 percent increase in best customers equaled a 20 percent profit improvement for a multibillion-dollar business.

The direct marketing, database marketing, and "mini-mass marketing" we have been looking at are strictly transaction-driven applications of technology to aim a company's communications toward the best segments of the target audience. In every case, the purpose of the communication is to solicit an immediate sale. Relationship marketing, on the other hand, is an attempt to modify people's behavior over time. It may be called loyalty marketing or retention marketing or relationship marketing or customer management. By any name, its goal is to strengthen the bond between the customer and the company or the brand. Database marketing is what psychologists would call classical conditioning. Relationship marketing is instrumental conditioning.

Let me remind you of the difference. Pavlov's conditioning was classical. It paired stimuli and response. You'll remember he gave meat powder to the harnessed dog every time a tuning fork was struck. As the episodes progressed, the dog reached the point at which the ringing of the tone, alone, would cause the dog to salivate. B.F. Skinner's conditioning was instrumental. It depended on reinforcement. Since reinforcement is the key to learning, Skinner taught us that the rat, the pigeon, or the human had to learn which response produced the reinforcement.

The lesson for us is that classical conditioning depends primarily on the stimuli that comes before the response. Instrumental conditioning—real learning—depends primarily on the reinforcements that come after the response. Off-price offers are no more than stimuli. Too many marketers have been teaching today's consumer to salivate at the mention of price. Genuine customer development requires reinforcement.

How important is this issue of customer development, customer relationships, customer loyalty, and customer retention? Don Libey likes to suggest, "There is another company hiding inside your existing company and it may even be bigger." That other company consists of all the existing customers who can be retained and persuaded to buy again. Don believes attrition rates, as a rule of thumb, are around 50 percent the first year and 20 percent of the balance every year after. He says, "If you obtain 100 new customers today, at the end of six years only 16 of those 100 new customers will remain. If you only kept 16 additional customers at the end of six years, your company would double in size."[1]

The Coca-Cola study, "Measured Marketing," which we reviewed earlier, reported that supermarkets tracking customer purchases learned to their great surprise that their customer defection rate ranged from 25 to 50 percent, showing just how easy and penalty-free it is for customers to change shopping frequencies at different food stores, or stop shopping at one supermarket.[2]

In any transactional activity between a seller and a buyer there is always some kind of emotional response. Satisfaction makes the buyer feel good. We all know a "satisfied" customer will be a better customer and, at the extreme, will become an advocate. Dissatisfaction is unpleasant. A "dissatisfied" customer will cost the seller future sales and probably result in negative word of mouth.

Psychologists refer to dissatisfaction following a choice as *cognitive dissonance*. Some years ago Leon Festinger, a Stanford Psychology professor, labeled personal beliefs (cognitions) "consonant" meaning positive, or "dissonant," meaning negative. His theory proposes that dissonance is likely to occur after a choice has been made, and the more cognitive dissonance a person has about the choice, the higher the dissonance will be. His theory suggests people will take action to relieve the unpleasant feelings of dissonance. In our case of buyer and seller, the action the buyer with cognitive dissonance will take will be to purchase a different brand or shop elsewhere. On the other hand, cognitive consonance reinforces the buyer's decision and supports the repeat choice.

The marketing implication, of course, is that if the marketer can keep the customer feeling good about the purchase decision, that customer will continue to buy the brand or shop at the store. One way to assure this cognitive consonance is to attempt to influence all aspects of the customer's decision process—prepurchase, time-of-purchase, and post—always getting across the idea that when you buy this brand you get something extra you don't get from anyone else.

The fact is that customers want to believe their purchase decision was a good one. They will pay more attention to communications about the brand they purchased as a means of reducing dissonance. Some marketers believe that consumers actually read more ads for the brand they have purchased after the purchase. This suggests that continuing post-purchase communications will be well received by a company's customers.

We talked earlier about the importance of creating a dialog with customers. Dialog is the essence of relationship marketing. If the only time your customers hear from you is when you are trying to sell them something, and the only time you hear from them is when they have complaints, that's not dialog.

Simon Anholt, one of the best writers I know, talks about relationship marketing as "Friendship Marketing . . . the kind of dialog which enriches your relationship and shows you can give without expecting to receive." "This is essential," he says, "if your customers are to believe in your brand."[3]

Anholt reminds us socializing with clients is almost more important than pitching to them, and nonselling customer communications are the mass-market equivalent of the after-work drink. He writes:

> Anyone with whom you've managed to build a broader and deeper relationship, with whom you can meet socially and talk about things other than business is the one easiest to sell to. They feel they know you and trust you.
>   Then the selling dialog, when it happens, is simple and direct. If they want or need your product, they'll buy it, and if they don't want it or need it, they know they can tell you why.
>   The honesty of their response becomes a valuable and constructive feedback channel for your product development cycle.[4]

It has been proven that the longer a company can keep a customer, the more the customer comes to depend on the company and the less chance there is for the competition to take that customer away. The nonselling communications Simon Anholt talks about help customers reaffirm their purchase decisions, and the dialog helps the seller to maintain a measure of the customer's satisfaction.

All of this brings us back to the theory of cognitive dissonance. That's a good start but, actually, the marketer has to do more than just reduce dissonance. True relationship marketing requires more than satisfying the customer. Too many satisfied customers change brands or suppliers every business day. Customer satisfaction is not a surrogate for customer retention. While it may seem intuitive that increasing customer satisfaction will increase retention and therefore profits, the facts are contrary. Between 65 and 85 percent of customers who defect say they were satisfied or very satisfied with their former supplier. In the auto industry, satisfaction scores average 85 to 95 percent, while re-purchase rates average only 40 percent.[5]

Don Hudler, President of Saturn Corporation says, "Eleven years ago when we first started to think about building the Saturn we knew that customer satisfaction wouldn't cut it. We knew we had to have customer enthusiasm so customers would be advocates." Don told me the Saturn marketing plan looks like this:

+ Product 25 percent.
+ Price-promotion-place 25 percent.
+ Shopping, buying and the ownership experience 50 percent.

It has worked so well that Saturn owner customers actually volunteer to work auto shows to help sell the car to others, and Saturn has never used a price incentive.

Relationship marketing with the aim of customer retention requires the development of a loyalty program that goes far beyond customer satisfaction and has the capability of measuring results.

Whenever I first talk to marketers about relationship marketing and loyalty programs, the first response is almost always, "Yes, we'll start a frequent buyer program." They are not one and the same. Giving up gross margin to bribe customers is not building relationships! Nor do frequent buyer programs assure customer retention. There are now about 6,000 reward-based credit cards available. They are offering everything from cash rebates, to frequent flyer miles, merchandise discounts, giveaways, and donations to your favorite charity.[6] The minute a competitor offers a bigger "bribe," the customer is gone.

One marketer told me, "Loyalty is what's left after the bribery stops." I must admit I have a real bias about this. I have lost potentially profitable clients for our company because I refused to build their loyalty programs based on reward points and discounts. A frequent buyer program can be worthwhile for some brands and some industries. The airlines and hotels present a unique opportunity, as we have discussed, but these are rare opportunities. And, now, even the airlines are becoming more frugal with benefits.

It has been reported that General Motors Corp. will soon announce changes in its GM Card loyalty program as it faces a potential $2 billion liability on new vehicle rebates for its gold Master Card customers who have been collecting points in the rewards program since September 1992.[7]

One major North American retail chain with a long-running frequent buyer club has told me it is the worst thing they ever got into. The member record keeping and rewards are now chewing up their entire marketing budget. They wish they could get out of the program, but they can't figure out how to do that without upsetting the entrenched customer-member base.

I said at the start that customer management, customer development, and responding to the needs of individual customers is now the only successful marketing formula for most businesses. (Of course there will be some exceptions.) Customer management cannot mean going to the expense of building a customer database and managing all that data just to give away profit margin.

Database relationship marketing is the only alternative to off-price discounting, coupon discounting, and rebate discounting. If we can bind the customer to our brand or our bank or our store or our dealership with caring treatment, unique service, and helpful knowledge of individual customer needs, price becomes a nonstarter, and we can sell at full profit . . . a nice change.

I don't mean to get on a soap box about this, but it's that important. Pavlovian marketers in every field have destroyed the profitable selling opportunities we once enjoyed by training the customer to buy off-price or with coupons or rebates. Now that the smart marketers are investing significant time and money and manpower to gain knowledge about customers, there is just no sense in investing these big bucks to continue to give the product or the store away at discount prices.

Now, having boldly stated that customer management, customer development, and responding to the needs of individual customers will be the only successful marketing formula for most businesses, I must back up a step and state the obvious. No marketer will ever be able to create this kind of bonding relationship with all of a company's customers. That's OK, because no marketer should want to do that.

Successful relationship marketing forces us to look at a new marketing fact of life. The buyer-seller relationship is not a democracy. All customers are not created equal. All customers are not entitled to the same inalienable rights, privileges, and benefits. All customers should be treated equally; that's just good business. But customers should be rewarded differently; that leads to good profit. If you treat your very best customers like everybody else, they will treat your store or your brand like any other. To treat all customers equally is wasteful management.

Bob Nelson, author of *1001 Ways to Reward Employees,* has a theory about companies who give turkeys to all their employees at Christmas time. He says the practice makes no sense. He makes the point that whenever you give everyone the same reward, you are not differentiating performance. Since the smart marketer wants to use rewards in the instrumental conditioning sense to change or support performance, Nelson's analogy applies to customers just as well as employees. When top performers get the same reward as average performers, it causes one of two things to occur: 1) You lose the top performers—they leave to find a company that better appreciates them, or 2) you lose the top performance. Nelson says when top performers and average performers receive the same reward the top performers stop giving the same effort because no one seems to care, and the average performers get the message that it's OK to be only average.

Some marketers have trouble with this concept. More than one client has said to me, "I don't want anyone in my company to think one customer is better or more important than another." This makes a good platitude and it certainly sounds like good old country-store friendliness, but is it really good business? Is it really even good for the customer?

I believe it is reasonable to suggest that a customer who gives a brand or a firm all of his or her business is giving up something, some flexibility of choice in package size or taste or selection or convenience or, certainly, savings opportunities. Relationship marketing must be collaborative. Both the seller and the buyer must benefit from the effort of developing and maintaining the relationship. That means some customers must earn "better treatment," than others, whatever that means.

If you can't accept this undemocratic fact, quit reading and close the book, right now. Database relationship marketing is not for you.

For those brave and foresighted enough to continue reading, before we look at how some marketers are building relationship marketing programs, let's recap a few reasons why "best" customers are more valuable.

As Kraft Foods showed us, a heavy user of Kraft products is 30 times more profitable than a light user. At one of our women's specialty store clients, the top 10 percent of customers average $791 per year per household; the average customer $162. A large chain department store tells us their top-decile customers average $3,500 a year versus the average customer's $275.

The average supermarket customer spends $7.50 per week, which means $390 per year in her favorite supermarket; for the best customer those numbers jump to $71 per week and $3,674 per year.[8]

Garth Hallberg, Worldwide Director of Differential Marketing at Ogilvy and Mather, reports that of the 95 million households in the United States, about 36 million buy Folger's coffee at least once in a year, but just 4 million households account for nearly half of the brand's annual volume. Five percent of households buy 85 percent of Levi's blue jeans, and 3 percent buy 82 percent of L'eggs pantyhose.[9]

Hallberg makes the point that the marketer should be able to target such a small number of high-profit buyers without severely crimping the rest of the marketing budget. He says incremental profit can be earned by relatively modest changes in share of customer; going from a 20 percent to a 30 percent share of customer increases the profitability of the household by 50 percent.[10]

One Seklemian/Newell client has average annual sales per customer of $67.05 and average annual number of transactions of 1.64. For this chain, the average annual sales of the top 10 percent of all customers is $273.63 with 4.62 transactions and ... the top 10 percent of customers involved in the company's relationship marketing effort average $2,017.32 in annual sales and 36.13 transactions!

Those dramatic numbers lead us to the retention factor in the relationship marketing equation. For that study, it is important to look at why companies lose customers:[11]

Deceased	1 percent
Moved	5 percent
Lured by friends	7 percent
Competition	9 percent
Quality problem	15 percent
Customer ignored	63 percent

This suggests that almost 80 percent of lost customers could have been saved by improved relationships.

What do we lose when one of these best customers defects? Immediate future sales and immediate future profits, of course. Then we have the expense of replacing each lost customer. Experts tell us it costs 7 to 10 times as much to replace a customer as it does to retain a customer, but that's not the worst of it. The typical industry sales comparisons above show that for every best customer a company loses, they must recruit many more average customers to make up the sales and profit loss.

Recall the company where best customers average $3,500 a year versus the average customer's $275. Every time this company loses a best customer, they must find 13 average customers to make up the $3,500. Of course, some of the recruits may grow to be best customers, but even that requires time and investment.

This company has 3 million active customers. The top decile (300,000 customers) has an attrition rate of 5 percent. That means 15,000 of those $3,500 customers disappear every year. If this company could develop a relationship marketing program just for this top 10 percent of their customers, and if that program only reduced the attrition rate by 10 percent, the 1,500 customers saved would mean $5,250,000 in plus sales. This is true in every industry.

If we agree that a best customer is usually an advocate for the company, then we lose that valuable advocacy as well—perhaps have even traded that positive for negative word-of-mouth

How about the positive side of increasing customer retention through relationship marketing?

A bank reported that increasing customer retention by just 5 percentage points generated balance growth sufficient to raise annual after tax profits over 30 percent, from $33.8 million to $44 million within 5 years.[12] An increase of just 5 percent in the customer retention rate can increase profit 25 percent for an auto service chain, 60 percent for an industrial laundry, and 120 percent for a credit card business.[13] For banks, improving deposit retention rates 5 percent to 10 percent can grow annual branch profits 250 percent to 400 percent over 5 years.[14] In the life insurance business, a 5 percent increase in customer retention lowers cost per policy by 18 percent.[15] Sears reports that in test stores an increase in the base of best customers by just 1 percent equals a 20 percent profit improvement.[16]

So we see that long-term customers buy more, require less of a price premium, reduce operating costs, and even bring referrals.

To accomplish this retention and loyalty, the relationship marketing program shifts the marketer's emphasis from inducement to reward. When price was the only inducement, we were, in effect, rewarding promiscuity. Relationship marketing rewards loyalty. This represents a profound change in the way we will market in the near future.

Some will now think that by using the word "reward" I am changing my position and advocating the frequent buyer points program. Let me stress, again, rewards do not have to be economic to be effective. Brian Woolf makes the point: "Satisfying customers' ego needs is as important as satisfying their economic needs, especially when it comes to building long-term loyalty. Providing customers with various forms of recognition through your program provides an added reason for them to drive past competitors to shop with you and acts as a barrier against their defecting."[17]

As a 3-million-mile American Airlines AAdvantage Platinum member, I like the miles that earn free flights for my family, but that's not the reason I remain loyal to American. Much more important to me is the special at-the-gate and on-board recognition, the upgrades and other "ego" perks.

As one writer said, "The loyalty of customers cannot be bought—it can only be given to you if you really deserve it."[18]

Don Peppers and Martha Rogers, in their excellent book *Enterprise One-to-One,* take this one step further by proposing that enterprises that can establish "relationship quality," building a learning relationship with a customer, remembering that customer's preferences, and always picking up in the customer dialog where they left off the last time will make the relationship so convenient for the customer that the customer will resist the entreaties of competitors who do not already know his specific needs. They suggest this will build "a barrier of inconvenience"—a reason for that customer never to want to deal with your competitor again.[19]

Building relationships from the customer point of view, we will now be building brand equity from the customer up. We will be making every customer contact more meaningful and more profitable than the last. Every point of contact with the customer will help to create brand value.

CHAPTER **20**

Don't Put All Your Faith in Vilfredo

Why your best customer may not be your biggest opportunity.

I suppose it would be impossible to write a book about database marketing without quoting the *Pareto Principle*. The world knows Vilfredo Pareto as the Italian economist and sociologist who studied mass action and believed that mathematics made a genuine study of society possible. Through these studies, he gave us the now famous 80/20 rule we know as the Pareto Principle. Marketers apply the principle to say that 80 percent of a brand's business comes from 20 percent of the company's customers.

It isn't always 80 percent, but it's always close. In Chapter 10, our look at one company's monetary decile analysis showed the company's top 20 percent of customers responsible for 63 percent of sales, and the top 40 percent of customers delivering more than 80 percent. The Coca-Cola Study showed us the top 20 percent of supermarket customers account for 66 percent of sales; the top 30 percent equal 77 percent of total sales. I saw a study once that said just 15 percent of beer patrons account for 65 percent of beer sales. In all of the companies I work with, the top 20 percent of customers account for a minimum of 43 percent and a maximum of 83 percent.

Pareto wasn't wrong, but there is more to maximizing sales than just making a friend of Vilfredo.

In Chapter 19, we talked about the importance of retaining and building relationships with customers. Most of that discussion centered on the fact that not all customers are created equal. We said to treat all customers equally is wasted management and made the point that a customer who gives a brand or a firm all of his or her business is giving up some flexibility of choice and, therefore, should be rewarded with some form of better treatment.

We talked also about the importance of retaining those best customers: i.e., the 10 percent of customers that give Kraft $791 per year, per household; the top-decile customers who spend an average of $3,500 a year at the department store; and the top customers who spend an average of $3,674 at their favorite supermarket. We *do* want to be sure those customers do not defect. Remember, we showed the company that would have to recruit 13 new, average customers to make up the $3,500 that would be lost each time a best customer leaves. We showed how that company could *save* over $5 million by retaining just 10 percent of the best customers it was losing.

Retention of best customers is a big opportunity to save sales volume that might otherwise be lost to competition, but it is not the only opportunity and perhaps not even the biggest. Special programs designed to hold on to these customers are important to *maintain* existing market share. The next question is where can the marketer look in the customer file to find the biggest opportunity to *gain* market share.

A customer marketing database is an expensive tool with high fixed cost and a low variable cost. The more it is used, the lower cost per use. That suggests that this valuable knowledge of customer buying activity should be used for more than just maintaining market share. Every marketer is looking for ways to *increase sales* and gain market share.

It is important to remember that the customer purchase history contained in the database shows a snapshot of each customer's buying activity based only on that customer's purchases of the company's brand or purchases within the company's stores. It does not show the customer's purchases of *other* brands within the category or his or her purchases at *other* stores.

Looking back at Figure 10-3, the basic monetary decile analysis, we see that the median average purchase for this company was $133. The third-, fourth-, and fifth-decile customers spend from $153 to $292. This 30 percent of the customer base represents the big opportunity. These customers should be the easiest to develop into bigger spenders; they are, in fact, serious customers the marketer would not want to lose even though they seem to be giving some of their shopping dollars to the competition. They have shown they like the company, which means it should be easier for the company to get more of their business than to find new customers. Most importantly, these customers represent the company's biggest opportunity to steal market share from the competition.

Garth Hallberg tells us brand-purchasing households may spread their buying over as many as six brands each year. We know the retail store customer spreads his or her purchases across many stores. We know the key to increased market share and greater profits is to change individual customer buying behavior, and it is best to start with these second- and third-decile customers. In my work with marketers, we have found greater gains in bottom-line profit can be earned from these lower rungs on the "loyalty ladder" than from the top tier.

By taking each of these customer segments and analyzing individual customers' specific buying patterns of recency, frequency, cross-shopping, and response to promotions, or by factoring in demographics, the marketer can discover the special opportunities for changing buying behavior.

Marketers are accomplishing this by sending different communications to different segments of the customer database. One fast-food operator sends a two-for-one offer to families with children and a price-only offer to single males. A dishwashing liquid manufacturer sends a $1 coupon to frequent coupon users and a $2 coupon to nonfrequent users.

Jennifer MacLean, Vice President Marketing, Metromail Corporation, tells how Metromail helps Service Merchandise fully customize direct mail pieces to send individualized messages to consumers mere days after they shop in any one of the 400 stores in the $4 billion chain. The Service Merchandise marketing department partnered with merchandise buyers to develop a list of conditions recognizable in the company's database that could serve as a trigger for a highly targeted and personalized direct mail piece. They have developed 150 such situations, using existing inventory and frequently purchased items as the trigger.

Metromail and commercial printer R.R. Donnelley & Sons built a delivery system geared to provide the retailer a high-speed means of developing this dialog with customers. At the end of each week, Service Merchandise downloads customer files based on the purchase of one or more of the 150 pre-determined items to Metromail's computers. There the data files are matched to corresponding direct mail pieces with individualized texts, illustrations, and offers in a process that takes only several hours. Jennifer reports Service Merchandise is enjoying double-digit response rates.[1]

Another retailer sends more valuable offers to the lower segments of its customer purchase file than it does to the top group to stimulate additional purchasing. In one case they sent top-decile women's buyers coupons for a 10 percent discount in the women's departments and a 15 percent discount coupon good only in the men's departments. The next two deciles of customers received a coupon for a *20 percent* discount in the women's departments and a second coupon good for a 15 percent discount *anywhere in the store.*

My friend Ray Jutkins tells of more than a dozen restaurant chains that know how to build additional sales from the middle ranks of their customer base. Examples include:

- A birthday offer to a chain's 450,000 guests generating a 33 percent redemption, more than 400,000 guest visits, and $3.1 million in sales for a cost of about $630,000.
- A holiday offer to 12,500 guests, producing 9,391 visits and $76,400 in sales.
- A simple card mailing to 457,871 prior guests asked them to return. Of these, 109,096 made return visits, for a total of 259,661 guest visits and more than $1.5 million in sales.[2]

Ray makes the point that if your average customer buys from you twice a month, 24 times a year, and you can get that total up to 27 times a year—an increase of only three more sales in 12 months—you are increasing your sales by 12.5 percent.

But what if the marketer doesn't want to build plus business with discounts? The cross-shopping analysis we studied in Chapter 11 can identify department store customers who are buying shoes, hosiery, and cosmetics, but not those buying sportswear or dresses. It's a pretty safe bet this customer is not walking around town or going to work wearing nothing but shoes, hosiery, and a pretty face. She's buying her clothing from the competition. The supermarket can identify the customer buying only soft drinks, dog food, canned goods, and cereal and woo her to some of the higher profit perimeter departments. Brian Woolf calls this "customer category management" and suggests that it allows an even more accurate profit contribution figure per customer and provides the platform for the inter-relationship between product category management and customer category management.[3]

There are two lessons here. To *maintain* existing market share it is important to give tender loving care not only to the top customers, but to all of those who spend more than average customers. To *gain* market share, the best opportunity presents itself not in the top decile but in the second, third and, in some businesses, even lower groups.

Someone once made the wise observation that it is more profitable to have 100 percent of 10 percent of a market than to have 10 percent of 100 percent. The number of customers is the same, but the costs are far different. This business of developing mid-range customers into top-range customers goes back to the objective of gaining share-of-wallet. Getting that 100 percent of a market means getting the customers who spread their buying over six brands to remain loyal to just one. That's the surest way to *increase* sales and *gain* market share. That starts with cultivating the customers on the lower steps of the loyalty ladder.

Pareto wasn't wrong, but there is more to maximizing sales and getting the best return on your marketing investment than making him your only friend.

Let's see how some big-league marketers, from airlines to packaged goods to McDonalds, are using their customer files to maximize sales and improve return on investment.

CHAPTER 21

"Just Do It!"

The "Nike Method" of database marketing.

Francey Smith, Director, Direct Marketing Resource Center, Knight Ridder, Inc., tells me that whenever she talks to a company about relationship marketing, the senior executives tell her they haven't started a program yet because they feel they should wait until they rework their system to link 90 to100 percent of their transactions with a customer name and address, or because they are working on the best way to find an even more advanced customer marketing database. Then they ask her for her recommendations on best methods.

That's when she tells them, "In my opinion, the best method is the Nike method." She tells me their brows may furrow, sometimes there's a brief quizzical look, but either is always followed by a smile of understanding. The Nike method, of course, is to "Just Do It." What Francey is telling them is not to wait for the perfect solution—start with whatever you have. Make it into a database and then add to it as time, money, and staff support become available.

Let's look at some folks who decided to "Just Do It."

First, a handful of simple but wonderful relationship marketing efforts. United Airlines has several levels of recognition: Mileage Plus, Mileage Plus Premier, Mileage Plus Premier Executive, and the 1K card for fliers who travel on United more than 100,000 miles a year. If you are a 1K flier, chances are, sometime during your flight, the flight attendant will hand you a business card from the captain of the plane with a hand written note, thanking you for flying United. Mine always says, "Thank you, Mr. Newell, for being one of our best customers." The customer's reaction to these captain's notes is always impressive. Captains even receive letters from appreciative customers.

The Neiman Marcus InCircle reward program for best customers offers things as exotic as a round the world trip, but I am told the most popular perk is the invitation to have lunch with the store manager.

As I said, earlier, I appreciate the free miles and the upgrades I earn on American Airlines, but I was most impressed when Michael Gunn, American's Senior Vice President, Marketing, sent me a giftwrapped box of the chocolate, strawberry, and butterscotch ice cream sundae toppings they serve in first class, with a personally signed thank you note.

Some automakers are leading the way in relationship marketing to build owner retention because they have learned that for every 5 percent improvement in customer loyalty, profits grow 10 to 15 percent. A Ford VP says, "One point of loyalty is worth $100 million in profits."

Just a few days after taking delivery of our new Cadillac, we received a thank-you note and a beautiful plant from the owner of the dealership. (We call it our $45,000 plant.) Then about three months later came a nice note with a year's worth of fertilizer for the plant. Along with the gift was the suggestion that the complimentary fertilizer will feed the plant for a year, but the dealership service staff will keep our car running at its best a lot longer than that. This dealer continues to get our service business.

My favorite is a relationship campaign from Jack Daniels. I have only heard about this. I was not on their mailing list, but I believe the story is true. As I heard it, the folks at Jack Daniels managed to compile a list of heavy brand buyers then sent them the following: First, a framed deed to one square inch of land in Lynchburg, Tennessee (population 361) where the distillery is located. Think about that for a minute. I suspect a loyal Jack Daniels customer is a lot like a Harley customer. That property deed would be a pretty neat thing to hang on the wall. Some weeks later, the deed recipients received in the mail an authentic bill from the city of Lynchburg for the annual taxes on the "property." Clipped to the top of the tax bill was a note that said, "Your friends at Jack Daniels have taken care of this for you." Then, in another month or so, there came in the mail a small rumpled scrap of paper with a hand scrawled note, "Went by your property this week, and saw it was covered with weeds, so I cleared it for you. Don't worry about this, your friends at Jack Daniels took care of me."

I hope this story is true, because it just doesn't get any better.

Richard Weber is the Director of Differential Marketing at Rapp Collins Worldwide. He developed the concept of differential marketing during his 30-year career with the Dow Chemical Company. He used his concept of household programs using differential marketing to manage double-digit impact on consumer behavior. Having proved that differential marketing works at the household level, he went on to prove it could be used in a mass advertising and promotion setting, delivering a 9 percent increase in sales while decreasing spending by 15 percent. Under Rich's leadership, Rapp Collins Worldwide has embraced differential marketing as one of the new ways to reach consumers. Rich was kind enough to allow us to include this case history to tell the story.

The case study involves the practice of differential marketing at the household level. The packaged goods company from which these case studies are drawn saw a great deal of external market place change occurring which affected its business performance. This company realized that its marketing practices were not providing the same financial returns they once enjoyed. Beyond the diverse and changing consumer base we discussed in Chapter 2, this company saw, as did others in the industry, that the dollars allocated to supporting trade promotion as reduced price features meant reduced consumer franchise-building marketing activities— less money for enhancing brand equity. They began to investigate direct consumer household communication to see if there was a better way to more effectively and efficiently market to their consumers. Their objectives were:

- To differentiate the brand by service and attributes.
- To develop a relationship with the consumer.
- To differentiate between consumers.
- To use multiple marketing strategies.
- To determine effectiveness and efficiency vs. alternative methods.
- To measure the impact of these procedures.

The focus was on those consumers giving the most value to the brand—the heavy category customers. They hold the key to producing the greatest return per dollar invested. Their value is 5 to 10 times that of a light customer. They are few in number. They have long-term value. They are the brand's core and most valuable asset. They represent the most ready source of significant volume opportunity.

The company developed a strategic framework that drove the communication strategy, which was to deliver the relevant message and the relevant incentive, working in concert to achieve the desired purchase behavior with the target consuming household. A sophisticated research plan was designed that would measure attitudes, usage shifts, loyalty changes, and consumption. Three relationship programs were tested:

Product Categories	Vehicle	Providing
Food protection	Newsletter and special mailings	Busy person's guide to household management.
Laundry care	Newsletter and special mailings	20 years of laundry knowledge for your clothing care.
Bathroom care	Newsletter	Bathroom cleaning, maintenance, and decorating tips.

Each program had a variety of editorial content. The newsletters provided a platform for communicating product benefits, help in selecting related products for specific applications (i.e., mold- and mildew-resistant paint for your bathroom), and added incentive opportunities. All three programs focused on creating a mutually beneficial relationship between the brand and the consumer, resulting in consumer household retention. New buying households increased consumer sales demand.

Opportunities for interaction were created to attempt to establish a dialog with these consumers, thereby personalizing the relationships. Every communication was viewed as an occasion to enhance the knowledge of the consumer—through surveys, letters of acknowledgment, and even the promotion incentive programs.

The program research results:

- Event recall, 70 to 95 percent.
- Read all or part, 70 to 91 percent.
- Validated editorial, 20 to 30 percent.
- Passed along, 50 to 53 percent.
- Wanted to continue to receive, 90 percent.
- Brand volume impacted sales growth, 26 to 213 percent.

As Rich says, these programs work. Loyalty programs are no fad.

In addition to tracking and monitoring the database marketing programs of national brand companies, John Cummings & Partners DBM/SCAN® provides analysis of database marketing trends. They report this trend in the growth of database marketing programs of packaged goods companies:

Year End	Total Efforts	Percent Change
9/30/92	1,511	—
9/30/93	2,222	+47 percent
9/30/94	2,655	+19 percent
9/30/95	3.331	+25 percent
9/30/96	4,200	+26 percent

At the National Center for 79th Annual DMA Conference in New Orleans, October 1996, he listed these new loyalty programs started in 1996:

- Pepsi Stuff Merchandise Continuity Program
- Salads Love Kraft Newsletter
- Eye Openers from Filly and Lender's Newsletter
- Kellogg's Best to Your Family Notes Newsletter
- Tropicana Perfect Breakfast Club
- All Things Equal Newsletter
- Hellmann's Planet Sandwich Club (Internet)
- EnFamil Family Beginnings Program
- FLONASE On the Nose Newsletter
- Glaxo Wellcome Air Currents Magazine
- Seldane AllerDays Newsletter
- Searle SHUTEYE News Newsletter
- Tampax Teen Advisory Committee/Pen Pal Club (Internet)
- Alpha Hydrox SkinSations Newsletter
- Iams Eukanuba Canine Collectibles Club
- Bailey's Best New Chefs Club

Miracle Whip Cooks and the Triaminic Parents Club are now in their fourth year. I repeat: Loyalty programs are no fad.

Building relationships with brands goes far beyond newsletters. The Camel Company catalog is now 40 pages and offers 120 Camel brand items. Purchases require no proof of purchase, just cash or a credit card. Coca-Cola has a catalog, as do Anheuser-Busch and Lipton Tea. The Jack Daniels Lynchburg General Store catalog has been ongoing for 40 years.

In October 1996, Philip Morris launched a quarterly lifestyle magazine targeted to young adults from its database of Marlboro smokers—about 2 million customers it thought would be interested in the magazine.

Unlimited: Action, Adventure, Good Times, a glossy magazine that won't be available on newsstands, was mailed to Marlboro smokers aged 21 and over. Philip Morris called the effort a move to provide value-added promotions that will cultivate brand loyalty.

Unlimited's first issue contained articles on rock climbing, a road trip on Highway 61, poker, America's best poolhalls, and winter cybersports. No articles discussed smoking.[1]

Now Volkswagen has a "Drivers Wanted" catalog of nearly 40 items from $31.95 denim logo shirts to $125 Swiss Army brand watches, all designed to reconnect customers and dealers with the VW brand; "Land Rover Gear" is also now available. Even The Discovery Channel is getting into the catalog game with 600,000 copies of a brand equity-builder catalog mailed in spring '96.[2]

When Pepsi-Cola faced the daunting marketing challenge of keeping sales up in the face of Coca-Cola's powerful Olympic tie-in in the summer of '96, they launched their biggest promotion ever. Pepsi printed and distributed 500 million catalogs via Pepsi delivery trucks to outlets across America, which displayed them on store counters. The catalogs, called "Pepsi Stuff," are filled with apparel, sports bags and equipment, phone cards, caps, bikes, and more featuring the Pepsi label. Kids earn free points to buy "stuff" by purchasing Pepsi soft drinks. The program swamped Pepsi's fulfillment center.[3] Pepsi is doing more than building relationships—it's selling product and building a strong kids database. When customers order they are asked to give their names and addresses, household information, credit card data, and family soft drink preferences.

And, guess who—McDonald's—will soon have a catalog. It is reported they are putting together a multipurpose, brand-building, direct marketing database and have already captured more than a third of their 500,000-name target. Merchandise offered will include collectible plates, ornaments and porcelain dolls commemorating past McDonald's ads, a line of children's clothing, and McDonald's jewelry.[4]

We have talked about creating a dialog with customers and getting them to talk back to us. Now we are beginning to see marketers finding ways to get customers to talk to each other to strengthen ties to the brand. Harley-Davidson started it all in 1993 when they invited bikers to Milwaukee to help celebrate their anniversary. I happened to be in Milwaukee on business when more than 60,000 Harley bikers took command of the city. Almost that many Saturn owners (44,000) came to the Spring Hill Saturn factory for the "Saturn Homecoming," paying a $36 admission fee to spend time with the men and women who built their cars and share the experience with other owners. At the same time, 130,000 owners celebrated the Homecoming in local area events. One of every six Saturn owners participated. Ten thousand members of the Saturn Car Club pay a $30 annual fee for access to events and premiums. Holiday Inn has two family gatherings a year where Priority Club members can use their points for a weekend to hear well-known speakers and meet other club members, and now Chrysler Corporation has a "Jeep Camp" for its off-road driver owners.

Does it make sense to think customers will actually develop a relationship with a brand or a bank or a store? Perhaps not, but is it possible? Absolutely. It just takes care and understanding and time. Four case histories will show us how.

CHAPTER 22

The $85 Yen, The 1-Peso Gift Check, The $400 Suit, and The 45-Cent Fuse

Four case histories.

THE TOYOTA STORY

When it comes to marketing, Toyota Motor Sales, USA is one of the best. In 1996, the five-year-old Camry model crept close behind Ford Taurus and Honda Accord for the number-one seller spot in the United States. Camry ranks at the top in owner loyalty among Toyota models with 43 percent of Camry owners buying another Toyota. With the new 1997 Camry, Toyota officials have been quoted as saying they think they can raise that in a few years to nearly 60 percent.[1]

Most industry analysts agree that if the production capacity can be made available, the Camry will take over the top seller spot in 1997. The folks at Toyota credit this to the excellence of the product. While product excellence is certainly a factor, one would have to give credit to Toyota's superb marketing skills, and that certainly includes their skill at direct marketing and the use of the customer database.

Toyota has a unique way of looking at integration and has a totally integrated approach to direct marketing. This starts with the sources of the data it captures and flows through to the outbound communication—the transaction and informational data they tie in as source material for communication outbound—for both conquesting and loyalty. A focus on the individual drives much of the marketing at Toyota.

Why are they so intense about direct marketing? The answer I got from Jim Pisz, National Direct Response Manager, was a simple one:

> When I started with Toyota in 1986, the yen was about 220. We have seen it dip down below 85. If you think about that, you can understand there is always a lot of pressure on your ad budget and great urgency to be more efficient and cut costs. Those are real items I live with every day, and I think I have been able to prove to our management that database marketing is the most economical way to accomplish some of our marketing objectives. The cost of sales from conquests is three to five times higher than the cost of a loyalty sale. To obtain those loyalty sales (and to make conquesting more efficient) you need a basic component, and that's a database.

Toyota has 14 different products and a very targeted buyer for each. Toyota considers its need to hone in on each target very critical. In the auto industry, the acquisition process is becoming much more complicated; the marketer must understand the hot buttons for the different customer segments. It may be that the Tercel buyer is most interested in zero payment down. The Camry buyer may be more interested in low payments. Avalon or 4-Runner buyers may be looking for attractive leases. The database helps Toyota find these clues.

Toyota believes that the fact that consumers are both becoming information-laden and requiring more information is another reason for the need for database-driven communications. Most consumers going into the dealership today are better prepared, perhaps, than some of the auto showroom salesmen. They have in their hands more raw data from all kinds of sources, probably even including the dealer's cost for the car. The database allows Toyota to provide more of the information each customer wants, thus making the customer more comfortable with the purchase decision.

Jim says the database is really Toyota's foundation. At Toyota they have multiple databases they use for direct marketing. They focus in on two areas: prospects and owners. They have three mission critical guiding principles for utilizing the databases:

1. Inbound centralization and consistency.
2. Outbound targeted communications.
3. Continuous improvement.

The Toyota owner database houses about 10 million owner names, representing approximately 80 percent of the Toyotas on the road today. The prospect file consists of people who, in one way or another, have raised their hands to say, "I am interested in becoming one of those owners." In 1997 the prospect file will be 700,000. This is what they accumulate in 12 months. Although some individuals state that they will be in the market in 0 to 3, 3 to 6, 6 to 9, 9 to 12, or more than 12 months, only prospects with less than a year in purchase horizon are considered bonafide prospects. Because the prospects are considering other makes as well as Toyota, the prospects are considered as a rolling 12 months versus a cumulative file like Toyota's owner database.

The owner database can be a challenge. Since the average car is sold often in its lifetime, there are many owners to try to track. While registry information can help track all new owners, there are 16 states with privacy laws that prohibit giving unencumbered registry information. To develop all possible owner information, Toyota focuses in on its in-house legacy systems for one of the operational databases, capturing warrantee information, sales information, and information gained from customers calling the 800 line.

On the prospect side, Toyota takes a totally integrated approach to inbound sources of data. They are constantly looking for new ways to make the multimillion-dollar mass media expenditures pay. They take the market driven variables and put them into a prospect database. They do promotional events. They are active on the Internet and on-line services. The general advertising infomercials all have a response mechanism built into them. Toyota captures prospect data from the thousands of consumers who attend the big auto shows and local sales events in smaller markets. All of this feeds back into the system and onto the Toyota database.

I was most impressed with the consistency of the consumer data Toyota collects. When we talk, later, about some of the important things to achieve in building a customer database, we will talk about the difference between "need to know" and "nice to know." Many companies are asking customers for more information than they will ever be able to use. Toyota knows specifically what they need to know about the what, where, who, when, and how of those interested in Toyota. They collect this information through registrations on-line, inbound telemarketing scripting, business reply cards, and point-of-purchase surveys. Toyota excels at this information-gathering process because they always ask the same six questions:

1. When will you be in the market for your next vehicle?
2. Do you plan to purchase or lease your next vehicle?
3. For which model would you like to receive information (14 choices)?

4. What age range do you fall within?

5. What is your annual estimated household income?

6. In which of the following ways would you like to receive information in the future—brochure, CD-ROM, video, telephone, or e-mail?

One of the things that impressed me the most as I listened to the folks at Toyota was their dedication to respecting the customer. Question number six is an example of that. Toyota's marketing team will only contact a prospect or owner by e-mail or telephone if the individual has requested that method of communication, and then they will only send information in which the prospect or owner has expressed interest.

They do use their Website (@ Toyota) to gather consumer data. The home page shows four areas. In "The Hub," Toyota publishes lifestyle demographic information focused at Toyota owner demographics. Areas like *Living Homes* are focused at the Camry/Avalon buyer, covering the kinds of things they are likely to do at home. Toyota also considers this a branding area for people not necessarily interested in Toyota today but who may be a year from now. Toyota is trying to give them a reason to continually come back to the Website, in the hope that when they are ready to consider purchase they will move to the "Vehicle" section under the pickup truck icon.

Clicking on the pickup truck, a prospect can learn about different Toyota vehicles, dealer services, and means for locating dealers or products, and communicate with the corporation. There is also a section where prospects can use the Website to find the best deal on a specific Toyota model anywhere in the nation.

Clicking on the area that relates to direct response brings up a page that focuses in on communication, including but not limited to these three:

"E-mail infrastructure" is one of Toyota's tools for two-way communications with consumers and is one of the sources in broadcast e-mail for outbound communications.

"Talk to Toyota" is a questionnaire area, where Toyota solicits feedback on the Website or on specific products. During the Website's first week, 1,000 people asked for information, and Toyota was able to capture the names to pass on to their dealers for contact. Toyota considers this a key source of inbound information for direct marketing for the future.

The "On-line registration form" is where the consumer is asked the six questions listed above.

Again, we see the same questions centralized, as they are in all lines of in-bound, general advertising media. When consumers call the 800 number from a TV commercial or infomercial, or click on a ski promotion on-line, they will get the same six questions. This is one of the ways the prospect database is filled.

Toyota uses this prospect database for conquest communications. Jim tells me they have found general conquest mailings to be very ineffective, but when people raise their hands—when someone says, "I'm interested in that 4-Runner"—even if they drive an Explorer, chances are they really are interested in the 4-Runner. Mailings to prospects that "have raised their hand" actually exceed response rates from the loyalty database.

Toyota focuses communications to the prospect database via e-mail, direct mail, and teleservices outbound, and they use these for all of the different automotive strategies: launching a vehicle, sales events, special promotions, or localizing an event.

The prospect database tells Toyota what model the prospect wants to lease or buy and when; where the prospect lives; and where each household came from as a source. By determining the success rate of each offer, the marketing team uses the database to enhance their ability to continuously learn from the data.

For the owner database, Toyota focuses in on all of the characteristics that can help them make a marketing decision: behavioral, transactional, demographic, lifestyle, geographic, vehicle ownership, and so on—120 variables for each household. They use Harte-Hanks P/CIS software to analyze the owner file in order to better customize communications to individual owners.

What does all this mean for Toyota in terms of applying these principles? For a good example, we can go back to the launch of the '97 Camry. One million Camry owners were targeted to preview the new model at a special event during Premier Week, the third week of September. The mailer asked recipients to request additional information on video or CD ROM, or in a brochure. I visited with Jim just after the first partial mail drop, and they had already received 42,000 responses.

Following their dedication to total integration of direct mail and Internet activities for two weeks of the launch, including offering a sweepstakes opportunity to win a new Camry, they bought the Yahoo! Home Page, a leading search engine. The Yahoo! banner produced 20,000,000 consumer impressions, and 130,000 people clicked onto the sweepstakes icon to go into the elaborate application site. At the application site, Toyota offered a free MCI phonecard to those who would download a coupon to take into the dealer for a test drive. More than 10,000 consumers responded.

Currently the Toyota direct marketing team uses the prospect database and the owner database to produce more than one major marketing project a day. These can range from 10,000-piece mailings, where a dealer or group of dealers go through their regional office to request a list from headquarters, to corporate mailings of 10,000,000 pieces.

The information in the database is so complete, Toyota has now developed a matrix of 100 different offers for conquesting. The X axis might be model preference—this prospect is interested in a sport utility vehicle. The Y axis might be income—here's what the prospect can spend. Adding things like vehicle ownership and lifestyle data can lead to very individualized offers.

For example, the general $500 rebate can be personalized to fit individual cases. To the Toyota owner, the offer might say, "We want to keep you in the family and here's $500 to show you we mean it." To the Ford owner, the offer might say, "The Camry trunk has twice as much space as the Ford, and here's $500 to let us prove it to you." Or knowing the income and lifestyle of a prospect, the offer might be to bring the car to the prospect's home or office for a test drive, instead of offering any rebate. One of the things the company hopes to accomplish with this sophisticated understanding of its customers is to find creative ways to move away from expensive, rebate-type incentives. Given a pro like Jim Pisz, who leads the direct marketing team, and everything we have learned about the positive effects of building relationships with customers, don't be surprised to see the Toyota Camry at the top in 1997.

A SMALL CASE HISTORY

The giant Safeway chain has been in the database business for the last 10 years, and the VonsClub preferred shopper program has 4 million members. Lest those examples lead readers to think database marketing in the supermarket industry is only for the giants, this is a case history of a small company doing everything right.

I don't know which supermarket chain was the first in America to begin database marketing, but I do know which was the first in Argentina. Seklemian/Newell works with Tecnologia Telecomunicaciones & Informatica SA, the largest outsource systems solutions company and a database software provider, and with Mario Ascher y Asociados, a retail marketing consultancy, to develop customer management programs for Latin American companies. One of these clients is Quijote Supermercados, a local supermarket chain located in Rafaela, a delightful, small city about 500 km north of Buenos Aires.

Quijote management made the decision to invest in the development of a customer marketing database to gain a competitive advantage. Their largest competitor had just announced a new affinity MasterCard. Quijote wanted to start a preferred customer program as quickly as possible to keep its customers from defecting to the competitor's new card. They called the program "QUIJOTE PLUS—un sistema para comprar bien" (a system for good buying). It launched in January 1996, making Quijote the first Argentine supermarket (perhaps the first Argentine retailer of any kind) to have a database marketing system.

Customer transaction data is householded, but each member of the household (including children aged 12 and over) has his or her own coded QUIJOTE PLUS card so the company can track individual preferences. It is important to know that many Argentine households represent three-generation families, a big difference from the household marketing we know in the United States.

QUIJOTE PLUS is not a points program. Management believes that customers become more excited and interested by frequent, immediate-gratification offers and delightful surprises than by the concept of year-long points accumulation. There are many benefits for members. They receive special recognition in the stores. There are special "Members Only" savings on selected items throughout the store every week, and members are offered surprise gifts and opportunities to earn special rewards on a regular basis. Knowing customers' purchase habits, the stores make special offers on items specific customers buy regularly and on their favorite brands.

The program was announced with a full-page newspaper ad, a radio campaign, and a private delivery flyer to every household in Rafaela. All of the advertising featured the program benefits plus a special opening offer: Get your card immediately and shop with the card the first two weeks of the program and earn a 1-peso gift check for every 30 pesos spent in the period. The gift checks were valid for merchandise from Quijote's higher margin departments. They wanted to be sure customers started shopping with the card right away. At sign up, each new member was welcomed with the offer of a gift tray of bakery goodies for the first shopping trip with the card—"Because we care about you and want you to feel special."

This company is taking swift action to bring in customers who have not yet shopped with their card, and they are not afraid to be interesting, arresting, and fresh in their communications. The envelope teaser for this effort says, "Lamentamos informarle que Ud. perido" [We're sorry to inform you that you have lost]. Inside, the copy says, "Pero tiene todavia mucho para ganar" [But you still have much to win], offering a basket of basic food supplies greatly discounted to just 10 pesos.

As soon as they collected enough transaction history to identify the very best customers, they sent the 3.13 percent of them who account for 20 percent of the supermarkets total sales a bottle of champagne in a colorful box with the message, "Estamos tan contentos de tenerlo de cliente que nos dieron ganas de festejar" [We are so happy to have you as a customer that we feel like we want to celebrate]. This is good stuff, and it's working. By the end of the first few months they were capturing 60 percent of sales pesos and 40 percent of store transactions and gaining valuable knowledge about their customer base.

Even these folks aren't perfect. They started well, then missed opportunities to communicate with customers while they refined the transaction collection process. They got back on track quickly.

Argentina is emerging from a deep recession. Unemployment is 17.7 percent. That's the official figure. My friends tell me the real figure is more like 30 percent unemployed and underemployed people. Supermarket industry sales, I'm told, are off 15 to 20 percent. The first two months of this supermarket's customer recognition program showed *"exceptional sales gains."* Even the few months the program was coasting and catching up produced small gains. In recent customer research, the membership card "was especially perceived as a very good initiative. It was seen as a sign of distinction and modernism. It attracted new customers."

The point this case history makes is that customers do want to be recognized, do want special treatment, do want to know a company cares, and will respond by giving the caring company more business. Customer management cannot be just a series of promotions. Customer management is not another add-on to the promotion schedule: It is the development of relationships to build customer loyalty. Quijote Supermercados is a company doing that very well.

DEVELOPING MEN'S BUSINESS FROM MEN

This is a case study from a national specialty department store. While the name is omitted, all of the facts and figures are real. It is a most complete marketing case history, involving the use of the customer database.

This store's decision to invest in the men's business was the result of a well-thought-out subpositioning strategy to achieve a very narrowly defined objective, and it all came from the database.

The company did a great business in men's clothing, furnishings, and sportswear. However, an analysis of the database indicated that significant sales were to women buying for husbands or boyfriends or as gifts.

The objective was simple—to increase their men's business from men. The only thing that men have to buy for themselves is clothing, due to the alterations required. If a man becomes a clothing customer, the odds are that he will also buy furnishings and sportswear from the store.

A close look at the objective revealed a number of marketing issues that had to be dealt with to achieve the objective:

1. The first issue was how good the assortments were in each store and whether more open-to-buy was needed.
2. Next, how did their men's area sales associates stack up against the competition? Did they need to hire additional help from competitive men's stores?
3. What type of sales training program had to be developed? Sales training for new salespeople? Retraining of existing staff? Merchandise information when new lines of clothing were added to existing stocks?
4. How good and how fast were alterations? If there were problems, how could they be fixed?
5. Did any stores need more selling space, fitting rooms, repainting, or new carpet in the men's area?
6. In the marketing communications area, who were the target customer groups? What media and copy platform should be used? Did the store need new garment bags or packaging?
7. Finally, could the store afford all of this? How long would it take to execute? What would be the measures of success?

The simple objective of getting more men's business from men required the resources of the total organization to execute the strategies needed for success. These strategies were:

1. The personnel area analyzed staff needs and training.
2. The director of stores and the operations management team examined the ambiance of each store and developed a capital budget.

3. The merchandise group reevaluated assortments and additional open-to-buy that might be required.
4. Operations management reviewed the quality level and speed of alterations.
5. Marketing communications determined the target markets, packaging needs, and standards and methods of measuring success.

At a final conference with the CEO, it was decided to implement the plan in half the store markets and, if successful, to roll it out to the remaining markets. Due to the complexity of the program, the target date for execution was nine months hence. Three target markets were identified:

1. Current men shoppers. The objective was to move light users to heavy users.
2. Existing store households that had not shopped in the men's area in the past three years. The objective was to get them to shop in the men's area.
3. New, nonstore customers.

For each of the target markets, the company developed the following measures of success. This is an important step. It forms the benchmarks against which the campaign can be objectively measured.
   1. Moving light to heavy users. The agreed upon desired result was to increase sales from existing men's customers by over 10 percent.
   2. Sales from existing store households who had not shopped in the men's area. The agreed upon measurement was a 20 percent internal market share increase. Internal market share is the number of customers buying men's items as a percent of total customers. For example, if a store had 1,000 customers who bought men's items out of 10,000 total customers, the internal market share would be 10 percent. If the store started with a 10 percent internal market share, the goal of a 20 percent increase would raise the internal market share to 12 percent. It is important to realize that the sum of a store's internal market shares will exceed 100 percent because customers buy in more than one area of the store.
   3. Measuring new customers. New, nonexisting store shoppers would show up in the database. The goal was 7,000 new men's customers.
   The marketing department decided that a six-month, multimedia campaign was required. Direct mail was used to reposition the men's area to existing men's customers and attract current store customers who did not shop in the men's area. Through the use of segmentation technology

and their database they also used direct marketing to create new men's customers. TV was used to support the positioning statement in multistore markets, and radio in single store markets. Newspaper advertising consisted of a series of small space item ads in the target markets.

A look at the direct mail program that was designed to get new customers is insightful because the segmentation technique used shows the importance of targeting a narrow range of potential customers and a customer database.

Since the key to developing a loyal men's customer is men's clothing, the store created a twice-yearly men's clothing catalog. It was distributed to existing men's clothing customers, selected current store households that were not currently buying in the men's area, and to nonstore households. Current men's shoppers were identified from the database, as were selected potential customers from the store's file that were not buying in the men's area. The database became a key factor in identifying the potential nonstore shoppers targeted for the catalog.

Mass distribution of catalogs is the most expensive form of customer communications, but catalogs are the least expensive when highly targeted. The store decided to distribute 400,000 catalogs to nonstore households. The risk lay in how to select the right consumers as targets.

Out of the large universe of men in the areas where this company had stores, how to select the right 400,000 to target? By knowing your customers. Knowing best customer attributes enabled the store to target potential new customers from three basic sources.

An analysis of their database of current men's customers indicated that the store should target professionals, such as doctors, lawyers, members of Boards of Directors, CEOs, and CFOs.

Next they selected a group of magazine subscribers that came close to matching their target profile and included those magazines in the campaign. They chose six magazines: *Business Week, Fortune, Forbes,* and three men's magazines. Finally, a group of mail order customers was chosen from a select group of lists. They specified which type of doctors they wanted: Only those with high-income medical specialties, such as cardiovascular surgery, as opposed to general medicine. Lawyers were limited to senior partners with law firms at prestigious addresses. The CEOs, CFOs, and members of Boards were restricted by company size.

The mail order lists included mail order buyers of companies like Britches, Brooks Brothers, and the Custom Shop. One would think that these requirements were pretty strict, but they were not good enough.

All of these groups represent men, but no psychographic qualification had yet been applied to the resulting names. The firm had lifestyle data appended to their database. When they ran their existing men's accounts through the lifestyle cluster groups, they found that over 60 percent of their men's customers fell into only six lifestyle clusters.

The next step was to screen all the lists through the cluster groups after eliminating duplication with each other and the store's existing accounts, and then to mail only to the remaining names that fell into the six cluster groups and did not have an existing store account. This gave the store a pinpointed male audience with the same psychographics as the typical existing male customer, and gave the final mailing list a high probability of success. None of this would have been possible without the database.

Remember the three strategies:

1. To move light users to heavy users.
2. To get new men's business from existing store households who had not bought in the men's area in the past three years.
3. To get new, nonstore customers for the men's area.

Let's see how this retailer did.

The first strategy of moving light men's users to heavy users had a goal of a 10 percent increase in sales from light users. The result was a 15 percent increase in sales from this group.

The second strategy was to get sales from existing store customers who had not bought in the men's department in the past three years. The goal was to increase the men's internal market share by 20 percent. The result was a 30 percent increase. Remember, this means if the store started with a 10 percent share, the 30 percent increase brought the internal market share up to 13 percent.

The third strategy was to gain 7,000 new customers for the men's area. The result was 9,554 new customers.

The 400,000 direct mail catalogs sent to nonstore households got a 1.5 percent response or 6,000 new customers. These folks spent $2 million over the next year. Their five-year lifetime value was projected at $9 million. In addition to the 6,000 new customers generated from the catalogs, the media campaign plus the better assortments and service resulted in the net addition of 3,554 new customers. The men's business continued to grow in the following three years at a faster rate than the total store's business, despite a substantial reduction in communication expenditures in years two and three.

The point of this case history is not to dwell on this national specialty department store's marketing, but to illustrate how the database tool was used across many different marketing functions.

1. While the original objective was to increase men's business, the database revealed a more narrowly targeted opportunity of getting more men's business from men.

2. The database enabled the firm to hold focus groups with light users, heavy users, existing store non-men's customers, and prospective non-store customers to determine how they felt about assortments, service, and the appearance of the men's department.

3. The database allowed the store to audit existing client books and update them.

4. The database was the key to the ability to measure results versus goals.

5. The database allowed them to write to new and existing customers, thanking them for their purchases, and to develop outbound telemarketing for calls to customers.

6. The database was essential for selecting the right nonstore customers for the catalog mailing.

This is a classic case because the database was used by store management, market research, merchants, sales associates, and marketing communications. The CEO and CFO used the database to audit the return on investment versus the plan.

The database enabled the store to develop strategies and measure the results of their objective of getting more men's business from men.

THE RADIOSHACK STORY

RadioShack is the largest consumer electronics retailer in the United States, with 6,800 stores, $3.2 billion in annual sales, and plans to add 500 new stores. Ninety-four percent of all Americans live or work within five minutes of a RadioShack store. They are one of the most effective and most efficient database marketers in North America.

We said earlier that it is virtually impossible to shop at RadioShack without giving them your name and address. David Edmondson, Senior Vice President Marketing and Advertising, verifies this and says, "People do talk a lot about our requests for name and address. Though they tease us about it, the fact is that it has become such a part of the buying experience at RadioShack that very few customers are bothered by it. We will try to capture your name and address whether you are buying a 45-cent fuse or a $4,000 computer."

David is responsible for managing research, strategic planning, and all marketing and advertising functions necessary to promote RadioShack as a retail service concept. Under his leadership the marketing database has come to center stage as a marketing tool, and new strategic marketing positions have been identified that will be at the heart of RadioShack's future growth. David must be right when he tells us the name and address request has become such a part of the RadioShack buying experience that it doesn't bother folks, because they have captured what he calls "a few good facts":

119 million customers (last three years)

89 million customer households (last three years)

80 percent male

20 percent female

Flat profile

The profile is so flat that there is no more than a 15 percent variance from segment to segment when they overlay demographic and psychographic cluster codes on the big database. The reason for that, of course, is that 99 percent of all American households have made at least one purchase in a RadioShack store in the last three years.

RadioShack's five-year strategic business objective is consistent, profitable sales. Their goal is a 10 percent increase in revenue and a 20 percent increase in profit. They use the customer database to enhance the consumer perception of the value provided by RadioShack. That includes these specific objectives:

- Increase the frequency at which America shops with RadioShack.
- Increase the average transaction of the consumer base.
- Increase the number of departments shopped.
- Increase the number of shoppers per household, specifically women and teens.

They don't need new customers. Their objectives all aim at developing more business from the customers they already have.

There are three businesses RadioShack wants to own: the parts and accessories business, the telephone business, and the repair business. They are so serious about the telephone business they have just announced an exclusive deal with Sprint, whereby each of the 6,800 stores will feature a store within a store called the "American Telephone Store" offering phone equipment and services exclusively from the nation's third largest long distance company. The repair business will also be expanded to a store within a store called the "Repair Shop at RadioShack."

In addition to other media investments, RadioShack plans to use the customer database for 62 million dollars worth of direct mail in 1997. The campaign will be built around RadioShack's 30 most important products and will involve different programs for different segments of the list. Instead of creating programs and then looking for the best target customers, RadioShack will be selecting customers and developing programs with special relevance for each. Certainly one of those groups will be the 4 percent of all customers responsible for 30 percent of the RadioShack business. To show they "care enough" about these customers, they are already sending them Hallmark cards. The company recently sent 6,000 cards at a cost of $2,500. It generated $102,000 in sales and prompted 3,400 store visits over the year. We can expect to see even more tender loving care in 1997.

CHAPTER **23**

I Feel Like I Have a Sister in the Company
Measuring profitability one customer at a time.

Only businesses that identify the right kind of customers and retain more of them than their competitors will survive into the millennium[1]

The customer database has taught us that greater customer understanding leads to greater profits. Companies that are loyalty-focused will outperform their competition when measured against revenue growth and profitability.[2] There are a great many good reasons for this. The longer a business can keep a customer, the more that customer comes to rely on the business. Moreover, when you keep more of your best customers, you leave only the leftovers for your competitors to fight over. Keeping more loyal customers can help marketers break out of margin-depleting price discounting.

In Chapter 12, we examined lifetime value and saw that catalogers, and now other marketers, use the LTV measurement to decide how much they can profitably invest to "buy" a new customer. Beyond that, we suggested that more and more marketers will be making new marketing investments to increase customer lifetime value. We identified one of the important elements of customer lifetime value as retention. Now it is time to review why customer retention is so important to every marketer, look at some current trends of retention/defection, and find some answers.

The dictum at the start of this chapter holds true for every kind of business. Some examples:

- The 3,500,000 loyal customers in Hallmark's "The Very Best" program develop a 25 percent increase in purchases over average customers. These are the loyal buyers Hallmark fights to keep with continuing contacts, including new product news, free product samples, gift certificates, and inside information like special notes from the artists. Through quarterly personalized newsletters and customer replies, Hallmark builds a dialog with its "Very Best" customers. One customer, commenting on the program, told Hallmark, "I feel like I have a sister in the company."

- For the packaged goods industry, Garth Hallberg makes the point that often less than 15 percent of households—the "high-profit buyers" in the category—produce the overwhelming majority of current or potential brand volume and profits and that winning over and building the loyalty of these high-profit consumers is the most productive path for profitable growth for most brands.[3]

- Bain & Company reports that a 5 percent increase in customer retention produces a 25 to 55 percent increase in profitability in business-to-business marketing.

- In the supermarket industry the top 30 percent of customers account for 75 percent of sales, the bottom 30 percent just 3 percent. It becomes obvious that the supermarket's profit must come from the top-tier customers.[4]

Sears has developed a profitable program to increase the loyalty of best customers. "Sears Best Customer Program" was tested in the Harrisburg market in 1991 and has now been rolled out to reach four and a half million customers Sears wants to be sure to keep. Sears defines a "best customer" as having a profitable "market basket margin," meaning a heavy share of regular price purchases, being creditworthy, cross-shopping more than four departments, shopping at least seven times a year, and spending at least $1,000 a year.

Al Malony, who led the development of the Sears program, reports that every 1 percent of retention improvement in this customer group delivers "several million dollars" in net profit. Al says each of these best customers is worth five average customers. While it costs Sears about $5 a year for each customer in the program, they consider this a good investment compared to the $113.72 they have learned it costs them to gain five new customers.[5]

This is a company that maintains a direct customer relationship with more than two-thirds of America's 97 million households. Sears' database contains information on 77 million families.

To create the customer dialog, they include some customer survey questions in every communication tool. While Sears offers its best customers some hard benefits, like 0 percent financing and savings certificates, the thing customers tell Sears they like best about its program is the recognition. Al likes to say, "The program substitutes relevance for discounts." Sears has learned that recognition translates to loyalty.

The loyalty-retention specialists, Bain & Company, define three second-order effects of customer loyalty:

1. Revenue growth as a result of repeat purchases and referrals.
2. Cost decline as a result of lower acquisition expense and efficiencies of serving experienced customers.
3. Increased employee retention because job pride and satisfaction increase, in turn creating a loop that reinforces customer loyalty and further reduces costs as hiring and training costs shrink and productivity rises.[6]

This makes the point that loyal employees are just as important as loyal customers and can, in fact, help to create customer loyalty. Because loyal employees know more about the business and its customers, they can provide better service.

Given these powerful arguments for the commercial value of customer loyalty, one would expect to see most marketers so loyalty-based, so focused on keeping customers that brand switching and customer defection would be reduced to the minimum. Surprisingly, all marketers will agree when customer loyalty goes up profits go up, yet only a few companies have achieved first-class loyalty programs. The promiscuous customer persists.

Terry Vavra, President, Marketing Metrics Inc., and Associate Professor of Marketing, Pace University, calls the cumulative impact of customer defection staggering. He estimates that over 180 million customer affiliations are at risk or are broken in the U.S. every year.[7]

Consumer purchase promiscuity not only persists, it appears to be growing.

Packaged goods marketers rely on MRCA data to monitor brand loyalty. MRCA Information Services provides a proprietary data file that captures household purchases by brand for the packaged goods industry. A special analysis that MRCA undertook for Garth Hallberg showed substantial declines in brand loyalty for 26 major brands from 1977 to 1992, with the declines among heavy category buyers outpacing those of the lower-profit segments. The heavy category, high-profit consumers who once gave 50 percent of their category purchases to one brand, declined by more than a third from 17 to 11 percent of category heavy buyers buying the brand. Almost 90 percent of the high-profit buyers of a brand give it less than half their business.[8]

In the supermarket industry, 80 percent of customers shop at the same market less than once a week and shop somewhere else the rest of the time. The average supermarket loses 25 to 50 percent of its customers every year.[9]

One Seklemian/Newell client learned that 16 percent of its proprietary credit card customers and 34.3 percent of its third-party bank card customers who spent more than $100 in twelve months a year ago had not made any purchases in the most recent 12 months.

Another client analyzed retention of most profitable customers and found a giant sales opportunity. In fiscal 1994, 656,960 customers spent more than $1,000, with more than 80 percent of their purchases made at regular price. Of these, 73,708 (11.2 percent) made no purchases in fiscal 1995. The average annual spending of these customers, when active, was $5,013. Total sales lost from these customer defections equaled $369,458,000. If this company had a customer retention program that could have saved just 10 percent of this lost business, they would have added almost $37 million in fiscal '95 sales.

In order to boost sales and profits by increasing customer retention, it is important to go back to Nicholas Poulos' quote, "Only businesses that identify *the right kind of customers* and retain more of them than their competitors will survive into the millennium." Profitable retention efforts must start with the identification of the "right kind" of customers. Sears identified their right kind of customer as one providing profitable margin, being creditworthy, cross-shopping more than four departments, shopping at least seven times a year, and spending at least $1,000. The Seklemian/Newell client example defined the right kind of customer as one who spends more than $1,000 a year with more than 80 percent of their purchases made at regular price. The definition will be different for each different business. The important thing is that the marketer make the decision and identify his or her "right kind of customer."

Marketers must qualify the financial impact of loyalty and realize that some customers will never stay loyal. Knowing which ones will tells us which ones won't. With this knowledge we can move marketing dollars away from the losers to spend more on the potential winners.

This shift in marketing dollars is the simple starting point many marketers miss when they set a strategy for building brand loyalty. As a result, many build their loyalty programs on the wrong platform. The problem we see most frequently is companies rushing to emulate the airlines, to grab the "frequent buyer" solution and try to force it into a business solution where it is often a very bad fit. Most marketers don't need a high-tech, point-counting solution; they need to know enough about their customers to invest loyalty-building dollars against customer segments that will deliver the best long-term return, and they need to monitor these investments.

B. G. Yovovich, in a four-part series on "Info-Driven Marketing" in *Advertising Age,* quotes W. H. Grant, founder of the Boston-based consultants Exchange Partners:

> Today, using information and technology tools currently available, companies can link their investments in customer relationships directly to the returns those customers generate. That means companies can more easily identify the customers who have the highest profit-improvement potential and use databases to understand the specific needs of those subsegments. This ability moves marketplace competition to a new playing field where it becomes crucial to use information to closely manage the relationships between the financial investments a company makes in particular customer relationships and the return that customers generate by the specific way they choose to respond to the company's offering.[10]

Bruce Wood is Database Marketing Manager for Canadian Tire Acceptance Ltd. and a new rules marketer. He believes database marketing is the critical enabler to developing a holistic view of the profit values of different customers and determining the appropriate marketing spend intensity against each.

Believing that a portion of the marketing mix must embrace the concept of potential profit by customer segment, and agreeing with me that this must be monitored, he has developed a "corporate scorecard." It focuses on a detailed view of investment versus revenue from the different segments of the customer base. He believes this top-level scorecard is a quick way to track the health of an organization's customer database at each point in time and to keep score on the marketing investments for each segment.

That's the key to this scorecard—it keeps the score of how much is invested against each segment of the customer file. It delivers an early warning notice that too many dollars are being thrown at low-profit customers and not enough spent to develop the loyalty of those who will assure the company's survival.

Here is the scorecard Bruce Wood suggests:

	High-Profit Customers			Medium-Profit Customers			Low-Profit Customers		
Top-level indicators	'95	'96	% change	'95	'96	% change	'95	'96	% change
# of customers									
Revenue/customer									
Investment/customer									
Contribution/customer									

Bruce believes the results of this methodology can have wide-ranging implications for traditional marketing functions. He envisions the organization of the marketing department into strategic groups focused on key customer segments based on profit contribution per customer.

The only addition I would make to Bruce's scorecard would be a fourth column to show the "No-Profit Customer" who never buys products or services but still receives a significant portion of advertising and marketing investments. When we add in those marketing investments and subtract the total from gross profit, it quickly reveals that our net profit would be higher if we could only eliminate, or at least reduce, the investment against the no-profit segment.

Profitable investments in customer retention require a dedicated, separate strategy. They can't be accomplished as an add-on. They must be a basic corporate business strategy. Increased customer retention is not a quick fix that will drive sales for this quarter's report to Wall Street. Relationship building is not an event. It is a process.

That creates problems within some organizations. The typical brand management systems work against marketing investments to retain best customers. Dan Davidson, Director of Database and Target Marketing for Ralston Purina's Check Mark Division, has been quoted as pointing out that fact: "Brand managers are typically goaled to build market share for one or more brands, and often move on to new positions within one or two years. This advancement tradition does not serve the interests of loyalty marketing."[11]

Wolfgang Berndt, President of Procter & Gamble North America, says, "P&G is moving back toward fewer people on our brands, in most cases, back to one brand manager. Further, P&G is refocusing on the brand manager as the primary expert on the consumer."[12]

Developing a loyalty-based focus and concentrating on customer retention in any company requires a serious change from traditional market share thinking. That means loyalty marketing is not for everyone.

There is no magic to loyalty marketing. It requires a lot of hard work and well-planned, meaningful, friendly communications and recognition and caring that, together, become a web of connections between the marketer and the customer. It cannot be just another series of promotions based on our new-found customer information. True loyalty marketing is finding out what the customer wants, delivering it, and, in the process, developing relationships with that customer.

Richard Dunn summed this up at a recent NCDM Conference:

A company guided by loyalty marketing . . .

- Creates value through bond building with customers.
- Does not deliver what the market wants, but what a specific customer wants.
- Knows the people to whom it sells, and the products and services needed.
- Recognizes that its greatest asset is its customers' loyalty.
- Does not pursue transactions, but cultivates relationships.
- Is adept at giving the customer more than she expects.[13]

Remember well the lessons of this chapter. The longer a business can keep a customer, the more that customer comes to rely on the business. Keeping more of the right customers means leaving only the leftovers for competitors to fight over. And only businesses that identify the right kind of customers and retain more of them than their competitors will survive.

CHAPTER 24

From Frequency and Reach to Relevance

Media are marketers, too. Why their challenge is compounded.

Media are marketers, too. Certainly, everything we have learned about the new customer will affect the ways newspapers, and magazines, and radio, and television stations and networks market to their readers, listeners, and viewers. The media challenge is compounded: While the media face the same challenges as consumer-marketers—to understand, and communicate with, and sell to the changed consumer—they must also find new ways to serve their second customer, the advertiser.

Marketers are telling me it comes down to this. Media that want their business must know as much about their readers, viewers, and listeners as the advertisers know about their customers and must find ways to cross-feed this information to support advertisers' objectives.

Advertisers have always considered the mass media efficient because they offered a nice, low cost per thousand impressions made. Today those same advertisers realize that true efficiency lies in getting the lowest cost per thousand *viable prospects*. Marketers' goals are changing from frequency and reach to *relevance*.

This fact is changing the playing field, with mass media well on their way to becoming a minority share of media expenditures unless they find ways to help their advertisers increase the level of efficiency of their space and time buys.

In the words of the president of the Newspaper Precision Marketing Group at Claritas:

> In the face of today's increasing competition—for readers' attention and advertisers' dollars—publishers have only two choices: either use the technology to expand and protect your existing business or open the door for somebody else to skim it or to take it over entirely.
>
> The stakes are too high, particularly in light of the unbelievable (some say unconscionable) newsprint price increases, for publishers to ignore the power of the new desktop marketing technologies. These tools, used in thoughtfully designed programs, can have a tremendous impact on the bottom line.

Media use is changing. When folks talk about interactive media, they usually mean TV or the Internet. Now, however, we're hearing about what some folks are calling *interactive radio.*

Starting in 1994 direct marketers discovered radio. In most major markets, spot sales for direct response advertising have been surging. Why? The cellular phone. According to the Cellular Telecommunications Industry Association 17,000 Americans sign up for new cellular service *each day.* Cellular phone users now number 40 million and are expected to grow to 70 million by 2002.

More and more of these wonderful, captive customers listening to their car radios can now respond to promotions by phone without missing a stoplight. Tests have shown that 70 percent of calls are made within 10 minutes of a radio spot airing. And advertisers have been surprised to learn that there are listeners at other times than just the morning and evening drive—some of their best response results came between 11 a.m. and 3 p.m. Of all the New Yorkers that tune to the radio Monday through Friday 6 a.m. to 3 p.m., only 23 percent don't stay tuned in at midday.[1] Interestingly, while 53 percent of the morning drive (6 to 10 a.m.) radio audience is in an automobile, almost as many—51 percent— of the midday (10 to 3 p.m.) radio listening takes place in a car.[2]

Radio executives believe shopping by phone while driving will continue to grow now that new technology allows cellular callers to respond immediately to direct response radio appeals by dialing 800 numbers at no charge, from wherever they are. Previously, people using cell phones had been reluctant to dial 800 numbers because of high phone charges. The new technology enables companies with 800 numbers to change a 1-800 call to a #-800 call, making the call free for cell phone users.[3]

The introduction of personal communications services (PCS) in late 1996 will make things even more interesting. PCS devices, broadcasting in the two-gigahertz frequency range, can be miniaturized to a size where they are likely to be worn like a watch or jewelry. Users will be able to communicate by voice, video, data, fax, and even wireless electronic messages to computers. "There's no reason for phones to have cords. It's just that that was what was possible when they were invented."[4]

The IDS Financial Services Division of American Express was the first advertiser I know to use radio for a national direct response push. They reported that 40 percent of the callers were converted to requests for consultations. Their direct response radio was 2.5 times more profitable than the direct mail campaign they had been using.

But other major marketers say that's not good enough. One direct marketer looked at this growth and told me he won't consider radio a direct marketing vehicle unless radio stations have established databases they can provide advertisers to qualify listeners. He wants to know who owns Chevrolets in the audience. He complains there are only a handful of stations doing database marketing to the degree they could be doing it: "Either use the technology to expand and protect your existing business or open the door for somebody else to skim it or to take it over entirely."

The media giant, Time Inc., is using this technology. They are leveraging their 52-million-name database to help advertisers sharpen their targeting. Recently, they helped Chevrolet create a prospect database for the launch of its new four-wheel drive Chevy Blazer. The publisher identified owners of Ford Explorers, Grand Cherokees, and Chevy Blazers in its subscription base. They then conducted surveys of Explorer and Cherokee owners to determine what they would like to improve in their vehicles. That knowledge drove the creative for each subscriber segment. Personalized messages were ink-jet printed on reply cards bound into the subscriber's magazine next to a Chevy Blazer ad.[5]

This is known as the "big event" in media database marketing. When media can identify the best prospects in their audience for an individual advertiser, they have added value that can't compare. This is what database marketing is all about for the media.

Does it work?

In the case of Time/Chevrolet the promotion generated five times the response rate compared to cards that ran in competitive magazines, and that was with no premium offered—just a simple request to call for more information.[6]

Database marketing is still a fuzzy concept for many people in the media world. They hear a lot about it and read all the articles, but few understand the challenge. Simply put, database marketing represents a more sophisticated way for newspapers, magazines, radio, and television stations to do what they have been doing for many years—working to increase audience and advertising revenue.

To put this in the perspective of the new rules of marketing, let's look at media database marketing from two important perspectives:

- ◆ As a cost-effective way for media to target consumers and build circulation and audience.

- ◆ As a way to identify specific members of that audience who are the best prospects to receive the messages of specific advertisers.

Recently, I was fortunate enough to meet a very bright fellow, named Tony Coad, the Development Director for the Telegraph group of newspapers in the United Kingdom. Tony understands the challenge and the media opportunities inherent in the new rules of marketing. He told me to think of the strengths of a newspaper, or a magazine, or a radio or TV station as "Two databases and a brand." That is, a potentially powerful consumer database of subscribers, or readers, or listeners, or viewers *and* an unbeatable editorial database of news, and information and entertainment *and* a strong, well-accepted, trusted *brand identity.*

Gary Young, Executive Vice President, N.W. Ayer, Chicago, also explains the newspaper as a brand:

> Developing a newspaper brand starts with defining the paper's personality. If you think of newspapers as products, many of them are alike, and you're never going to change that, but every paper has an individual personality born of the people who are the driving force.
>
> My advertising experience proves that any brand that clearly defines itself in the marketplace will always beat out a product that does not. Unfortunately, that is something newspapers have neglected.[7]

Cathleen Black, when President and CEO, Newspaper Association of America, agreed:

> I see newspapers, both individually and collectively, as powerful brands that can identify who we are and what we do. Yet the world's view of our industry is often confusing and contradictory. Building brand awareness for individual papers and the industry as a whole can change that perception and enhance our franchises.[8]

Another media executive sees strength in the newspaper brand. Peter Levitan, President, New Jersey Online and Journal Square Interactive, com-

mented on why Microsoft won't send newspapers running and screaming
into the night:

> When push comes to shove, we know that our greatest asset is our brand
> and its power to provide trusted, compelling information and news, the
> power to link our Web services with our newspapers and broadcast proper-
> ties.[9]

This is not just true for newspapers. Any medium can use the power of its
consumer database and editorial database and trusted brand to enhance its
franchise.

Media's primary business is to communicate news, information,
and entertainment to consumers in a manner that is accessible, appeal-
ing, and relevant. In so doing, they create a credible and effective
mechanism whereby advertisers communicate with their customers and
prospects.

Today's consumers, the media audience, want to be part of the interactive dialog, and the advertisers want to target more efficiently and prove
the ROI of their advertising investment. Database marketing can help the
media address both of these challenges.

Let's look at our two goals:

* Building audience.
* Helping advertisers to target their customers.

In the past, traditional media efforts to build audience were pretty broad.
Media did a lot of advertising and ran a lot of contests and hoped enough
new customers would stick around to allow them to gain share. That didn't
always happen, and the more successful they became the harder it was for
them to keep growing incremental share.

Database marketing changes all that.

Now media can identify common attributes of their audience and
find prospects with similar characteristics. They can target small groups of
prospects and send a tailored message based on what they know about
them. If they know the prospect is a gourmet chef, they can talk about their
food or restaurant news. Because they will be speaking to their customers'
special interest, they can convince them to watch or listen or subscribe.
Newspapers can even target segments of the subscriber list, such as Sun-
day-only subscribers, and tailor special promotions to bring them aboard
as seven-day subscribers. Broadcasters can target special segments of the
audience for viewing or listening by appointment, promoting shows and
times based on known interests of audience segments.

Newspapers could even sell "tiered" subscriptions, like cable TV.

How many channels do you want? You can subscribe to the whole newspaper or just certain sections thereof like business or local sports, or pay extra for special crosswords or in-depth NFL news.

Media can profile their solid, core audience and go after look-alikes, thus focusing on prospects with the greatest likelihood of coming aboard.

Media will turn today's promotion investments to real relationship efforts to increase audience and *keep them.*

How important is it for media to keep readers, viewers, and listeners? It's not just that the rates they can charge the advertisers are based on circulation or viewer or listener rating points. It all comes down to a word media executives hate to hear—"churn." The churn rate is the rate at which audience is lost. Most people are aware of the constant ratings changes in the broadcast arena, where CBS is on top this month, then the leader becomes ABC. Few outside the industry know that churn is 30 to 70 percent in the newspaper industry. One media conglomerate told me their worst case is 208 percent turnover of subscribers. Their best case is 7 percent.

Subscribers who cancel are not likely to resubscribe. I am told that the average length of time between subscriptions is 170 weeks. That leaves newspapers with two strategic challenges: The continued erosion of newspaper dominance as the source for new information and entertainment, and the increasing difficulty to maintain and grow circulation base using traditional methods.

Thus, targeting consumers to build circulation and audience is what database marketing on the consumer side is all about for the newspaper industry. Database marketing can help the newspaper identify differentiated segments within the subscriber population. Then it becomes a matter of developing a long-range contact strategy and using the database knowledge to create targeted retention vehicles and communications appropriate to each segment.

Over time the newspaper marketer can develop benchmarks to track significant change warnings based on customer behavior and can learn to develop customized products and services to keep subscribers satisfied.

Beyond using the database for building audience, what are its possible applications for helping advertisers target their customers? Media can segment their audience and prospect database any number of ways, but what are advertisers looking for?

The advertiser wants to know a lot more about a medium's audience than most media now offer. More and more advertisers will want to focus on demographic and psychographic data and customer buying habits, rather than geographic data based on zip codes. More and more advertisers will be looking for ways to get a specific message to a specific portion of the media consumer base that is spread across the circulation or throughout the broadcast area.

With a solid database in place, broadcasters can know the different demographic or psychographic segments of their audience by age, income, or any of hundreds of variables, and they can know when each different segment watches or listens. It becomes a simple matter then to advise advertisers to make different cuts of their commercials to attract the different segments of the station's audience. More than that, they can match files with the advertiser to identify prospects who "look like" the advertiser's customers.

Some newspapers and broadcasters are already supplementing space or time buys with targeted direct mail pieces to those subscribers and nonsubscribers, or viewers and nonviewers, or listeners and nonlisteners who fit a particular profile. Because this is supplemental to the regular space or time buy, it often represents fresh, not recycled, advertising dollars. If the program is priced competitively, advertisers participate.

For years newspapers have sold "zoned" advertising, enabling the advertiser to buy only part of the circulation. Historically, these zones represented geographic quadrants of the circulation base, usually defined by compass headings. Now, most metropolitan papers allow the advertiser to buy selected zip codes, and some even offer "selects" down to the census tract level. It won't be long before some newspapers will allow advertisers to buy space only in the copies that go to doctors, or people over 65, or homeowners with pets.

There is really nothing new in this. It's called *selective binding*. *Farm Journal* has been doing selective binding for years. In *Farm Journal*, a dairy farmer and a pig farmer across the road from each other will be sent different ads. *Time* used sophisticated selective binding for Chevrolet. Newspapers will be the next selective binders. How long will it be before the broadcasters find a way?

The buzz-word for advertisers today is "interactive marketing." What the media will really be doing is helping their advertisers make the most efficient and effective interactive buy and they will be creating revenue from all of the parts.

Now all advertisers will demand results. They will demand a measurable return on their advertising investment. For years it has been said that the direct marketers, as we used to know them, had these measurable results, but mass media advertisers didn't have a clue. Now that we see that all marketers are direct marketers, we can expect all marketers to be looking for data-driven, provable results. Finally, the answer for Mr. Wanamaker and Lord Leverhulme!

Media will have to be able to prove that advertising works. The advertiser will be telling them each dollar spent on advertising must produce a visible return. Remember what we learned in Chapters 17 and 18. We can *measure* these things.

Here's the bottom line. We spent the last two decades developing *mass* marketing. We'll spend the 90s breaking that up to develop micro-marketing, relationship marketing, and database marketing. That means media must change to be competitive.

In the next chapter we'll look at consumer audience database building and use by media—things happening now and things about to happen.

CHAPTER **25**

Why Call the TV Station if Your House is on Fire?

What's happening with media right now.

We have already talked about magazines such as *Time* and *Farm Journal*. Others using subscriber database knowledge for selective binding have been well covered in the trade press.

The activities of television stations, radio stations, and newspapers have not been so well publicized. A look at current activities of a handful of each of these media will convince you that media database marketing is a force right now and can only get stronger.

Fisher Broadcasting's station in Portland is experimenting with on-line opportunities for viewers to call the station. They received 75,000 calls in the first four months. They're building a viewer database for their advertisers.

Looking for an easy means for viewers to access the station to create the "dialog with customers" we've talked about, 17 TV stations I know of have set up interactive phone systems—24 local lines plus an 800 number. Viewers can call for instant headlines, last night's winning lottery numbers, or the latest in fishing news. The station can ask 8 to 14 questions and offer advertiser specials, like Cadillac's recent Get-Away Weekend. All of these names go into a viewer database for these stations' advertisers.

I am reminded of the old story about the Lazarus department stores in Columbus, Ohio. They owned the market. Everyone shopped at Lazarus for every need. One day the store got a phone call from a customer saying her house was on fire. When asked why she called Lazarus instead of the fire company, the caller said, "I call Lazarus for everything I need." That's the kind of relationship these media marketers are trying to develop.

WCCO-TV Minneapolis-St. Paul is one of the best, with a state-of-the-art Web site. "Channel 4000" forsakes the usual talent profiles in favor of in-depth, sometimes real-time news, weather, and sports coverage. "Channel 4000" is a stand-alone profit center for WCCO and has proven to be a door-opener to TV advertisers.

WCCO Director of Sales, Bill Bradley, says: "Our position is to be the primary news and information supplier to our general region of the United States. That's our motivation, and the media we choose to do it is now broadcast and the Internet. That gives us a greater opportunity to be the primary supplier of news and information than our competitors, who may be operating in only one medium." WCCO looks to the day, coming soon, when the Web site will have the ability to create one-to-one relationships for the station with site visitors through personalized Web pages.[1]

KICU in San Jose, California put together a promotion for Warner Brothers to fill theaters for a movie opening night. They set up a small, unwired network. All stations sold the promo spots. A common in-bound telephone line took the calls. Since they mailed out the tickets, the stations have acquired the names and addresses of viewers who are moviegoers—exactly what we talked about in Chapter 24. I'm told this was so successful that Warners is coming back for more. And the best news is that these stations captured advertising dollars that had been going to radio. It was all new income.

NBC has started a viewer affinity club to get into database marketing by accumulating viewer names, addresses, and phone numbers. For a $24.95 annual fee, members will get discounts on NBC merchandise and savings on products and services from advertising partners. ABC is considering starting a similar club.[2]

In partnership with Sea Change Technology, Cable Advertising of Metro Atlanta has installed digital video systems that turn videotaped commercials into digital computer files. In addition to superior image quality, Sea Change's digital video systems enable Atlanta television advertisers to target segments of CAMA's 726,000 viewer households. CAMA has sliced the metro Atlanta television market into 17 separate coverage zones. Commercials can be displayed in any combination of zones, giving advertisers more control over what audiences their commercials reach.

The real database excitement is happening at the radio stations. In the research for this book, I found more than 50 radio stations building databases. They are helping their advertisers while increasing ratings and creating new revenue streams for the station.

One station executive told me, "The secret to our marketing is to program to the masses, but market to the 'diary keeper,'" showing he had an ever-watchful and marketing-efficient eye on Arbitron.

Ratings, plus new income, plus helping the advertiser. *Wow—the magic of database marketing!*

Stations building these database systems are calling them "loyalty marketing programs" to build a core of active, participating listener respondents. The most sophisticated stations are accomplishing this in almost every way imaginable: interactive telephone systems, direct mail, POS registrations, station remote registrations, telemarketing, and newspaper and magazine ads.

A number of very successful companies now specialize in database marketing for broadcasters. One of the most successful is Fairwest Direct. A loyalty marketing company for radio and TV specializing in interactive technologies, Reg Johns, President of Fairwest Direct, tells me most of his programs work as follows:

They sign up members using their Interactive Database Telephone System (Fairbase™). A profile is built on the listener. They assign the member a PIN number, then mail the new member a welcome letter and an interactive membership card, plus a welcome kit.

The ability to create a response and electronically track individual participation at advertiser locations begins with the interactive membership card and electronic card-readers. Interactive card readers are built into prize machine promotional displays like ATMs. Prize machine promotions are built around station events, remotes, advertiser locations, and manufacturer displays. Each day, members are encouraged, on-air, to visit participating displays/events where prize machines are located for a chance to win prizes, cash, and valuable, on-the-spot coupons. The prize machines provide instant awards based on random chance or matching membership numbers. Each day, members are invited to slide their cards through the prize machine for an opportunity to win. Winning numbers are changed daily, giving incentive for daily store traffic. As members slide their cards through the prize machine, they are asked yes/no survey questions, including demographic data and planned future purchases.

The station receives executive summary reports from Fairwest Direct, detailing demographic and zip code penetration definition of the member file, as well as daily transaction reports of member card usage. These reports are packed with valuable data for advertisers: male/female respondents, marital status, employment, household income, home ownership, length of residence and purchase data . . . all good stuff for the marketer. The winning numbers, survey questions, and coupon language are changed daily from the station each day, via a phone modem.

Stations are building enough demographic, psychographic, hobby, and sports interest data in members' files to create serious databases. This knowledge of customers gives the advertisers power. It also helps the station. They use this information to market back to their listeners, matching special interests with station events and advertisers' products. For ratings, they force members to listen during surge hours to win prizes and learn about members-only benefits at participating advertisers.

More than one station I talked to has found new ways to tap into retailers' *in-store* promotional vendor dollars. One station built a promotion to put its interactive prize machine in a supermarket's stores, with massive, freestanding product display build-ups from participating vendors. For an 18-week promotion, the station charged the supermarket $100,000. The promotion was so successful, the supermarket ended up raising $500,000 from vendor support. This supermarket was an advertiser that had spent only $8,000 in media in the prior year. They repeated this program three times.

Shoppers coming into the stores and swiping their cards at the product displays allow radio—for the first time—to provide verification of the amount of traffic the promotion brought into the stores. (And some of these efforts *are* bringing traffic.) Radio has found measurability and accountability.

Radio stations have also discovered interactive voice response (IVR) technology and are using it to register members, build databases, and generate revenue. IVR is the technical phrase used to describe automated phone systems—those awful systems most of us hate which instruct, "If you want X press 1, if you want Y press 2," and so on. Listeners not only call for information but also provide information about themselves. As much as many of us dislike these systems, they do help the stations build listener databases. And soon these machines will be able to respond to the natural way people talk. Ticker Talk, an interactive voice recognition response system is due sometime in 1997 from Nuance Communications, Menlo Park, California. Its vocabulary will exceed 2,000 words—roughly the equivalent of the average American's vocabulary.

One of Fairwest's clients, KABC Talk Radio in Los Angeles, has a

28-line IVR system with a current club membership at the 150,000 level. Its IVR Travel Program generates in excess of $1 million annually.[3]

Over 70 Fairwest radio station clients use the "pure" database of listeners in programming, marketing, sales, and research applications.

What about the newspapers? More than 200 of them now have reader loyalty programs which nurture relationships and reward loyalty.[4]

Two years after launching its Extra Card loyalty program, the *Houston Chronicle* has decreased its churn 6 percent, more than paying for the program. Of 360,000 subscribing households, more than 300,000 now pay in advance, reducing salesperson commissions and other costs. Similarly, *The Boston Globe* has achieved 92 percent retention among its GlobeCard members, although they make up only 8 percent of the subscriber base. With its loyalty program, the *Tucson Citizen* cut its subscriber turnover from 142 percent to roughly 70 percent, even though 35 percent of these readers are winter snowbirds who leave town when the season is over.[5]

In-house development of a consumer database was completed at the *Tampa Tribune* at the end of 1993. It includes names, addresses, demographics, and lifestyle information for all households in Hillsborough County—400,000 to 500,000 records. Demographic and lifestyle information is updated every six months. Subscriber information is updated monthly.

One of the *Tribune*'s first priorities was a detailed profile of subscribers and nonsubscribers. The difference between this profiling and media's usual research is that the database information adds the critical benefit of being able to target specific households for customized circulation campaigns and advertiser queries.

With all the money media are spending on research, most still don't know who their customers are. Survey data provides a description of the market but lacks the ability to apply tactics at the household level. A subscriber database changes all that. The database won't replace surveys, but it can substitute for some approaches and make vast improvements over surveys in others.

A key to the strength of a database is that it is not a sample or segment of subscribers, rather, it is much like a census of the full universe of subscribers and nonsubscribers. Research samples usually only represent a small portion of subscribers at a single point in time. This is where databases and surveys differ greatly.

The database offers a major advantage over surveys regarding noncoverage bias. There is none. The database is the full population. There is no margin of error to allow for noncoverage because full coverage is present in the database.

The *Tribune*'s database system was recently augmented by the purchase of Willowbend software for alternate delivery. This provides the ability to merge an advertiser's database or charge card files and other lists with the routing system for alternate delivery, thus eliminating a lot of labor-intensive hand sorting for projects involving alternate delivery.

The *Tribune* has used its database capability to sell a department store on a pilot project delivering catalogs to charge card customers through alternate delivery. At one point, the *Tribune* was delivering 20,000 store catalogs *every week* in 18 zip codes. The program is generating $100,000 in new annual revenue for the *Tribune*, and plans are in place to expand to more zip codes.

Think about this for a minute. Addressable home delivery just may help continue the newspaper's "monopoly" after everyone can distribute news. This can be a long-term business exclusive for the newspaper. AT&T, the Baby Bells, AOL, Microsoft, cable, and other TV stations are now, or soon will be, delivering news to the home, but the physical delivery of products or merchandise will not soon be done electronically. There is no need for more than two organizations, the US Postal Service (or the Canadian Post) and the newspaper, to pass every house once a day.

Much of the *Tribune*'s emphasis has been on testing applications for the circulation department. (Remember the importance of reducing churn.) For acquisition campaigns, the database is used to segment nonsubscribers into different groups for receipt of customized letters and offers. On the retention side, a "Keep in Touch" plan is showing improved retention rates. The *Tribune* also is experimenting with business-to-business files for advertiser prospecting and is building a database of classified customers to develop promotions for classified advertising.

One of the real newspaper leaders is the 160,000-circulation *Spokane Review,* which has created a strategic relationship with the Bon Marche department store. Admittedly, the leadership for this effort came from the store, not from the newspaper. Nonetheless, the early results are outstanding.

Bon Marche has appended complete newspaper subscriber data to its customer database, updating it quarterly. Both the store and the newspaper are learning a lot:

- 92.4 percent of the Bon Marche's credit card customers are *Spokane Review* subscribers.
- Of Bon Marche's sales, 91.7 percent are in key newspaper zip codes.
- Bon Marche's credit card customer subscribers have higher sales per customer than credit card customer nonsubscribers.

But the store only penetrates 30 percent of the newspaper file!

Michael Boze, Bon Marche's Sales Promotion Director, told me, "This database cross-analysis has allowed the newspaper to gain a greater share of the media dollars in our advertising budget." He also told me it wasn't easy to create this strategic relationship. They literally called in lawyers to draft this sharing agreement. They believe it was worth all the trouble. Both the store and the newspaper believe each side is bringing added value to the relationship.

The important thing about the Bon Marche/*Spokane Review* alliance is that sales management at the newspaper understands what most media executives don't. The advertiser must be able to target *individuals*—to find prospects who "look like" their best customers. If the store and the newspaper are overlaying geographic, demographic, and psychographic data on their files, they will be able to do just that.

Another leader in the newspaper field is the *Winston-Salem Journal*. The *Journal*'s database includes:

- Subscriber and nonsubscriber files.
- Household demographics and lifestyles.
- Voter registrations.
- County tax records.
- Names of parents of children attending public schools.

They use these files to support specific projects to generate new revenue. One is a niche publication called *Paws*. It is distributed to 18,000 households. Another 2,000 are distributed through selected racks. The database was built from appended lifestyle data plus tax records on dog licenses. *Paws* went from concept to launch in about 10 weeks. The first two issues of *Paws* produced $14,000 in revenue, with a contribution margin in excess of 50 percent .

Another project, *K-12,* is delivered to all households with children in the public schools. The *Journal* sells ROP (run of press display advertising) as well as ride-a-longs and sample delivery. No other local marketer has a more accurate list of households with children.

A recent project of theirs is the New Neighbor Program. The *Journal* serves as delivery agent for Bell South, making interim deliveries of telephone directories for new connects. Each directory is delivered to the door in a customized shopping bag that includes ride-a-long offers and an opportunity to sample the newspaper. Bell South provides the address list, and the *Journal* sells and delivers the ride-a-longs. Bell South saves delivery costs. The *Journal* earns new revenue, gets a free subscription shot at the new mover, and gains access to the most timely newcomers list available in the market.

The *Journal* is doing some of the best cross-pollination I have seen of database marketing and alternate delivery, and it's bringing in substantial new revenue.

Landmark Communications is using the *Greensboro News* and *Record* as its Beta site for database marketing; daily circulation 100,000, Sunday 127,000. They have chosen to build a preferred-member program involving discounts at local merchants. Here's how it works.

Shoppers who buy a 7-day subscription for 13 weeks or more receive a club card. Those who use the card at over 550 local merchants earn a 10 percent rebate on all purchases and receive a rebate statement listing all transactions to date. Every 90 days they receive rebate checks, in $10 increments. Nice perks for subscribers.

The newspaper captures all the live transaction information and extracts it for reporting and marketing analysis for its advertisers. Merchants are invoiced for rebate transactions at 15 percent. Merchants pay this to the paper to fund rebate accounts and pay for marketing and processing fees. Club members spend rebate checks only at participating merchants. Rebate checks are deposited into merchant checking accounts, just like other checks. Participating merchants get a 50 percent discount on space buys up to $5,000. Sixty percent of the participating merchants were not advertisers at the start. The paper developed $500,000 in new ad revenue from this group last year.

About half of all subscribers have signed up, and the paper tells me they no longer discount subscriptions, ever. Their database marketing manager says, "With detailed data on what our subscribers are purchasing, we can offer advertisers the ability to reach their best customers through targeted direct mail advertising." (A new revenue stream for the newspaper.) This is exactly what advertisers have been telling me they want from the media: "Know as much about your readers as I know about my customers. Then find ways to cross-feed this information to serve my objectives."

The *Denver Post* has a database that identifies families with children. Their business problem was low penetration in households with school age children. That was costing them some advertiser prospects. They needed a compelling sales proposition and a reason to communicate. They started a Colorado Kids page, then mounted a telemarketing campaign to parents of young children, identified from their database. They more than doubled response rates, decreased cost-per-order, and increased retention.

Denver seems to be a market of forward-thinking media marketers.

The *Rocky Mountain News* has found a way to give classified advertisers added value. A Web site allows car buyers to surf the Net for best car buys from the paper's classifieds. The consumer points and clicks to specify make, model, and year, and the home page shows details of all the qualifying cars advertised in the *Rocky Mountain News* classifieds.

An outstanding example of a "new rules" media company is Lee Enterprises, a 105-year-old company that owns 19 newspapers, 9 broadcast television stations, and more than 30 specialty publications in the midwest and west. Lee's Mark Roby stated the vision at a recent database marketing conference:[6]

> Our vision is to provide the best products and services to our advertisers, newspaper readers, and television viewers. Changing from a product-focus organization, to a customer-focus organization . . . what can we do for you, today?

Mark is the Marketing Director at Lee's *Quad City Times,* the *Muscatine Journal,* the *Kewanee Star-Courier,* and the five Lee-owned *Shoppers* in the Quad City region. He gave examples of how his papers are serving customers today. He listed targeted direct mail and database management products and services, targeted niche products that include special publications for senior citizens, pet owners, and youth sports, newspaper targeted marketing ROP products, and even production database tools for advertisers. They sponsor events to help build specialized customer data for advertisers. The *Quad City Times* BIX 7 road race attracts over 20,000 runners and adds to the database 20,000 prospects for athletic equipment. Advertiser services also include commercial printing, cable video pages to support classified ads, and of course, the Internet, with the *Times'* own home page.

Mark sums up the vision:

> Our goal is to have the best marketing database of our local community . . . know it better than anyone else . . . and then work with advertisers, helping them contact the correct customer or prospect for their product or service. In the process we don't want to forget our traditional newspaper product and the brand-building and image-building attributes that it offers.
>
> We feel we are not just a newspaper company anymore and are working hard to demonstrate that objective to our customers. We want to understand our local marketplace, household by household, better than anyone else . . . and that's what can make us a successful partner with our advertisers.

We could end this chapter right here. Mark Roby has delivered the sermon.

We can't end, though, because we still need to tell the story of Tony Coad's amazing Telegraph Group of newspapers. The group's flagship title is the *Daily Telegraph,* selling 1.1 million copies daily and claiming 2.6 million readers. Its associated title, the *Sunday Telegraph,* sells 750,000 copies. In November 1994, the group launched *Electronic Telegraph,* published on the World Wide Web, and it now has 400,000 registered readers worldwide.

The *Daily Telegraph* is a serious database marketer with a comprehensive range of databases. Their *transactional* database contains the records of over 5 million people and is updated with 8 million new pieces of data each year from 70 sources inside the newspaper. Their *lifestyle* database contains answers from 90-question surveys and grows by 80,000 new surveys each month. Their *editorial* database stores all the text and images from their papers, including advertising, and will eventually include video and sound. Here are some things they do with those databases.

- ◆ 24-hour advertisement access. Readers access *Electronic Telegraph* to get not just today's classified ads from the daily paper but also those that were previously published. Using powerful word-search facilities, readers quickly locate the ads that they want.

- ◆ Demographic append for the database *including* credit data. From this they provide advertisers with valuable market research, including predictive modeling.

- ◆ Big revenue stream from list rental of defined prospects. (The more you know about the customers in your database, the higher the list rental fee.) The *Telegraph* lists are some of the largest and most responsive in the United Kingdom and are a rapidly growing source of revenue.

- ◆ The *Telegraph* adds value to its advertising by generating new responsive leads for the advertiser's product. Advertisers put questions inviting a response into the *Telegraph* surveys and then telephone the respondents. Because of the trusted *Telegraph* brand and the fact that responders have asked for information, the calls are well received and generate high sales levels.

- ◆ They offer scoring techniques to advertisers enabling them to select names from the databases that are look-alikes to those who are the advertiser's best customers. Then the *Telegraph* writes to the selected readers introducing the advertiser.

- ◆ They have introduced a Telegraph Response Service, which enables readers who have telephoned an advertiser but have been unable to reach him to leave a message with the *Telegraph,* who will pass on the message. This service is being introduced by section; the first is for Financial Services advertisers.

- They send out "sponsored" direct mail offers under the *Telegraph* logo to niche segments of their database, using the brand to generate new revenue.
- They use their database capability to create "Bespoke" databases for others. Only a Brit could use the Savile Row "Bespoke," a word for custom tailoring, to describe custom databases.

Tony tells me the database allows real-time recognition of readers interacting with the paper. Because the database is linked to the call center reader information is provided instantly from the *Telegraph*'s database allowing each reader's pattern of interaction to be recognized and appreciated, and appropriate sales proposals to be made. He says that the mission at the *Telegraph* has changed from one providing superior advertising to one providing superior customer creation. That's a really important distinction. Finally, they build circulation by identifying responsive niches for different phases of the reader relationship, beginning with *trial* and culminating in *home delivery* and *loyalty reinforcement.* Their scoring techniques for this are particularly effective in determining the most appropriate amount of investment in calling each prospect.

You hear a lot today about newspapers going on-line. More than 1,100 U.S. newspapers use the World Wide Web to supplement their traditional outlets. The Boston Globe's boston.com is a leader. In addition to reporting the latest news, the site allows users to check radio and TV listings, preview current museum offerings, check real estate for sale, look for or post a job, check the weather, find a movie, and even check the menus of restaurants near a selected theater. The *Telegraph* gives a different view. We'll end this long discussion by hearing what Tony Coad told me when I asked about the newspaper's future: It's the quality of the relationship with the consumer that counts.

The increasingly electronic nature of media allows apparently more obvious opportunities for interaction. However, the issue is not whether newspapers will "go electronic" but whether media organizations sufficiently understand and possesses the necessary administration for interactivity. Newspapers may easily extend their old 'top-down' editorial and organizational paradigms into new electronic media, without understanding the *new concepts* that are needed to build reader/consumer relationships.

It's the *result* that matters. Newspapers can get excited about new electronic extensions of their products, but at the end of the day it is the result achieved for the advertiser that matters. Thus the *brand* and the *database* are more important than the medium the publisher uses to relay his message.

The culture of database marketing is not a natural bedfellow with that of newspapers dominated by the needs of the moment. Newspaper managers are not easily strategic in outlook or used to looking outside their particular and long-established disciplines. They will absorb *"new newspapers"* but will not readily respond to the *increasing consumer demands for interactivity and control.*

Thus, it is not new media that threatens newspapers but the reluctance of some managers to understand and respond to the implications of interactivity. What he was saying applies to more than just the newspaper industry.

Consumers don't express it in just this way, but they *are* looking for interactive relationships with retailers, with manufacturers, *and* with media. Tony Coad is telling us that the medium's brand and its database are more important than the medium.

This is what's happening, right now. It's exciting, and it can only get better. I can hardly wait.

CHAPTER **26**

Will You Tell Me, Please, Which Way I Ought to Walk from Here

Getting started: A step-by-step guide to building a working database marketing program.

We have made the case for the customer as a corporate asset and established the fact that technology now offers most of the tools needed to retrieve and use the base of customer information for more successful marketing. We have examined the process, the purpose, the tools, and the measurements. We have reviewed success stories. Our motion has been made and seconded. Now it is time to beg the question.

How do you get started? What are some of the basic considerations that will assure successful database marketing?

There are many answers. To be sure this effort covered all of the basics, I interviewed many of the experts: major businesses practicing database marketing, database marketing software providers, database marketing consultants, and agencies. Not all of the experts agree on every detail, but there was broad consensus on the ideas that follow.

Every single person interviewed agreed the most important basic for a successful start-up was having a good plan. That sounds a bit trite, until you consider the old insight from Christopher Robin, "A plan is something you do so it won't be all messed up."

When I quoted Christopher Robin to Bill Edgel, Credit Marketing Manager for Macy's West, he gave me an even better reference for advice on database marketing start ups . . . from Lewis Carroll's *Alice's Adventures in Wonderland:*

> Asked Alice, "Would you tell me, please, which way I ought to walk from here?"
>
> "That depends a good deal on where you want to get to," said the cat.

Before we talk about getting started, we must clarify the real meaning of database marketing. In fact, database marketing is a misnomer: What marketers are really doing is marketing using the database as a tool. Database marketing is a *competency*. The importance of this distinction is that the database tool can assist all of the marketing functions undertaken by a business.

Remember, a database is a marketing investment, often a very large one. It is an expensive tool with high fixed costs and low variable costs. The greater the usage, the less the cost per use and the greater the return-on-investment. Most marketers today underutilize their databases. Too many are data rich and information poor. It will pay great dividends to make the start-up process as inclusive as possible. Include all customer information that will have value for the most potential users. The more users within the company, the bigger the payback.

Before we look at the specifics of getting started, we have to ask, "How do you get the names and addresses?" This varies by industry. It is easiest for companies that can capture the data at point-of-sale. Of course, most large retailers already have the names and addresses of customers using the store's proprietary credit card, but how do they get the cash and bank card and check customers?

Some accomplish this by asking the customer directly. In this case, they are able to capture the data regardless of tender type. Having gotten the information from the customers, some have the capability to enter the data on the POS register; others ask the customer to fill out a form which is then processed back office. Many record the information from customers' checks and send bank card transactions to a vendor who provides names and addresses.

This latter process is called reverse-append. In these cases the retailer does not capture cash transactions, but they are usually the smallest share of the business. In the case of furniture or appliance stores, customer name and address are captured for warranties and deliveries. Auto dealers, banks, and others have the names and addresses of all customers. Packaged goods companies capture the data from 800 number calls, rebate offers, third-party sources, and surveys, and recently some are getting customer data from partnering retailers.

If you want to get maximum return on your database marketing investment, it is important to include as many potential users as possible right at the start. I asked a 20-year veteran about this. Bernice Grossman is President of Database Marketing Resource Services, Architects & Consultants in Database Marketing, a marketing consultancy that determines the complete scope of a customer's project, "architects" the solution, and integrates all of the systems. She told me, "Remember to involve everyone: MIS, customer service, telemarketing, promotion, advertising, sales, and nonpermanent members—list brokers, list managers, and direct marketing data processing service bureaus. Then use the Socratic design method, asking each of these future users of the database to prepare 25 questions they would like the data to answer."

Leo Rabinovitch, Vice President, New Product Development, STS Systems, echoes Grossman's comments, adding the admonition that before you even start, make certain to understand how customer knowledge will impact your whole business. Understand the real reasons for developing the customer information, then be sure everyone who can use this new knowledge understands its power.[1]

Karen Humphries Sallick, who heads the Marketing Planning and Analysis Group for Harte-Hanks Direct Marketing, goes a step farther and suggests the creation of a formalized database task force "because a strong foundation for success incorporates key issues and key people." Karen suggests it is helpful to involve any key players that show interest in the database creation, its evolution, and goal planning. But she stresses that the team should be a balance of interested, excited individuals and likely database marketing converts, and individuals who are slightly skeptical, as their captious perspective can often help refine a good plan into a great plan.[2]

Before Bill Edgel moved to Macy's West, he developed the customer database program for Merksamer Jewelers, a national chain of fine jewelry stores. He got the corporate database up and running in 60 days, so I consider him an expert on this question of how to get started. He says, "The key to a results-generating database marketing program lies in developing and executing a plan that supports the business objectives and marketing goals of the company." He lists five important steps:

1. Understand the corporate objectives.
2. Plan for database marketing results.
3. Develop a strategic partnership.
4. Achieve immediate success.
5. Communicate with management.

What does he mean by these?

1. Understanding corporate objectives:
   a. The mission statement
      (1) Defines the reasons your company exists.
      (2) Appropriate in scope, realistic to your capabilities.
   b. The corporate objectives
      (1) Must be reasonable, obtainable, and measurable.
   c. Corporate strategies
      (1) Determine the broad design for achieving objectives.
      (2) Must be linked to definite periods of time.
      (3) Must become objectives at the department level.
2. Planning for database marketing results:
   a. Base the plan on corporate strategy.
   b. Focus on database marketing the first year.
   c. Plan five years out for database marketing needs and ROI.
   d. Keep your plan on your desk.
   e. Review monthly progress with management.
   f. Anticipate changes.
3. Developing a strategic partnership:
   a. Determine your database marketing needs from the marketing plan.
   b. Prepare a formal Request for Proposal for prospect software vendors.
   c. Insist on scripted, relevant demonstrations.
   d. Review biographies of each of the vendor's support team members.
   e. Review your marketing plan with finalists for suggestions.
4. Achieving immediate success:
   a. Complete integration: all hardware and software packages and data appends completed and ready to use prior to training.
   b. Invest in training: enough off-site training for staff to expertly use the system before the executive management team starts looking for answers.

    c. Limit your start-up to three big-bang projects complete within three months of live date—three marketing programs that relate to established marketing strategies, have the potential to recoup first year costs, and whose success can be clearly communicated to management.

    d. Be sure to have clear reporting vehicles: develop a customer flash template that identifies lift and incremental sales for the total promotion, individual cells, and selected groupings of cells by product type, customer segments, markets, and geography, and reports that identify, by division and region, customer counts/growth trends, retention, LTV, and monthly marginal profit.

5. Communicating with management:

    a. Standardize expectations and reports.

    b. Educate management to database marketing opportunities.

    c. Share the customer flash reports.

Bill's five steps apply to any company in any kind of business.

The kind of study these experts are suggesting requires a multitude of questions:

- What will be the scope of the project?
- What type of data will you need to store?
- What kind of questions will you need to ask?
- What functions will you need?
  Analytical tools?
  Report generation?
  Campaign tracking?
  Statistical modeling?

At this point, another valuable question to ask is, "What do we need to know about our customers' needs?" This is the time to separate the "need to know"—highly relevant information—from the "nice to know"—items that do little to help understand the customer. Someone on the team must continue to ask, "What is the value of this information? How will it help us to market smarter and service the customer better?" Some of the customer information that is determined to be extremely relevant will be unavailable in existing files. Now is the time to explore sources beyond the legacy data to augment existing files. Always remember, the goal is not to build a database; the goal is to understand the customer better than anyone else.

Before more thoughts on getting started from another pro, more should be said about the "Request for Proposal" mentioned by Bill Edgel.

The first purpose of Karen's task force and Bernice's 25 user questions is to begin to analyze the company's needs in terms that will establish basic system requirements. This needs analysis should cover everything from file size to availability of data to anticipated marketing applications to query requirements and even the computer literacy of intended users. This is such a critical step toward the ultimate success of the database solution that it is important to have at least one member of the team with serious database marketing experience. If that experience is not present within the company, it will pay to add a database marketing consultant to the task force.

The basic requirements developed in the needs analysis provide enough detail for initial screening of software vendors and set the direction for the later writing of the formal Request for Proposal.

The Request for Proposal (RFP) is exactly what its name implies. It details system requirements, asks for information about a vendor and that vendor's system, gives the vendor all the facts required for developing the best solution, and requests a proposal defining and pricing a database software system that will meet the company's requirements.

But the RFP is not the next step after the needs analysis. There are a number of reasons not to rush into the writing of the RFP. A good RFP takes time (and some cost) to prepare. A better, more complete RFP can be drafted after several conversations with vendors. The vendor universe should be screened to manageable size before spreading proposal requests across the industry. No company will want to spend the time and go to the expense of fairly evaluating a dozen, or even a half dozen, proposals. It is also wise to respect the vendors. Proposals are costly to prepare. If vendors know your request is limited to a few qualified candidates, they will deliver more serious study and a better response. A good rule of thumb is not more than four vendors for demonstrations and probably not more than two for final proposals.

It is best to keep the initial process as simple as possible. Most marketers today know who the key players are or can easily find them through trade shows, conferences, trade press, or business associates. The challenge is to sort them down to the few most likely candidates.

Once the needs analysis is formalized as a checklist, brief phone interviews asking about vendors' system structure and performance, relative to the company's most important requirements, will eliminate some.

There is some discussion within the industry whether the formal RFP

comes before the official demo, or the demo before the RFP. I believe the
demo must come first. A good, two-hour software system demonstration
will create as many questions as it will answer, which leads to the final development of a more complete RFP. Also, the product demo will be
enough to screen the vendor list to the next level. It is important, in this
process, to be absolutely consistent in the requirements given to each vendor, and it is important to keep detailed, consistent notes throughout the
evaluation process. This not only assures the fairest possible evaluation,
but also provides the support that will be required to sell the final proposal
to management.

One of the best and most experienced pros in this database discipline
is David Raab. He has probably helped more companies through this process, studied it more, and written more about it than anyone in the field. He
lists eight "Big errors you should work hard to avoid":

1. Endless preparation: It is definitely possible to have too many
   meetings, too many memos, and in general, to simply drag the
   process out too long.
2. Lack of priorities which can be remedied with a more decisive
   management approach.
3. A current, rather than future, focus, which omits consideration
   of what the company could do with its system as it grows.
4. Letting your requirements be set by vendor offerings.
5. Holding vendor demonstrations prematurely, before you really
   know what you want.
6. Falling in love with a pretty interface. If you don't understand
   whether the system meets your other requirements, you may
   overlook critical deficiencies that lie beyond that nice surface.
7. Not finding all the candidates. It's never easy to find all the
   candidates, but be sure you give it a good try. You wouldn't want
   to find out later that you omitted the vendor who has the best
   solution for your needs.
8. Lack of a defined project path. If you don't have a clearly
   defined process, you may lose momentum and support along the
   way.[3]

Spencer Joyner, Senior Vice President, Harte-Hanks Data Technologies, sees seven challenges for starting up:

1. *Align database marketing objectives and functions with company goals.* Meet with senior management to confirm your com-

pany's short-term and long-term goals. Develop objectives for the database marketing team. Don't promise everything at once. Set priorities from this kind of list:

a. Financial
   (1) Increase incremental revenue.
   (2) Reduce operating costs.
   (3) Improve profitability.
   (4) Provide a process improvement.

b. Marketing
   (1) Increase marketing efficiency and effectiveness.
   (2) Increase average customer purchase dollars.
   (3) Increase customer purchases.
   (4) Increase number of items per purchase occasion.
   (5) Increase customer profitability.
   (6) Profile customers and develop customer segments.
   (7) Increase customer loyalty, retention, and customer LTV.
   (8) Gain and sustain a competitive advantage.

c. Merchandising
   (1) Decrease markdowns or discounts.
   (2) Increase up-sell to higher price point merchandise, products, or services.
   (3) Increase cross-sell to more profitable offerings.

2. *Set realistic goals and expectations.* Assess what the database marketing team can realistically do and what the budget can afford. The customer database will surface more new marketing opportunities than you ever expected, but unless you can act on the information, you won't be able to move the needle. Make sure objectives are measurable, and agree in advance what contribution thresholds will define success of each project.

3. *Establish transition plan from "old" system to "new" system.* Run parallel overlap in data audits, performance audits, and selection tests prior to going live. When detailed transaction data is first made available for detailed scrutiny, any errors in the legacy system come to light. Catalog and retail joint databases can be filled with errors relating to where sales and returns are credited, depending on how fulfillment is handled.

4. *Dedicate staff.* Assign and obtain responsibility for:
   a. Planning and organizing the database marketing function.
   b. System administration.
   c. Master user.
   d. Data integrity.

e. Database updates and refresh.
f. Prime user and secondary users.
g. Mail selection and execution.
h. Back-end event analysis.
i. Ad hoc management reporting.
j. Modeling/segmentation.
k. Customer performance audit.
l. Technical support.
5. *Commit to continuous improvement.*
  a. Always mail with control groups.
  b. Measure results.
  c. Identify responders/nonresponders.
  d. Learn from each experience.
  e. Model to improve next effort.
6. *Establish support channels: Internal - IS/IT.* You can't get around the IS people. Don't try. You need them.
  a. Timely data transmissions.
  b. Data integrity/audits.
  c. Communications networks, internal/external.
  d. Hardware/software maintenance and procedures.
  e. Preventive maintenance, backups, minor repairs (when the tape drive says "clean me," it means clean me!).
7. *Communicate successes and failures.* Share knowledge of what works and what doesn't. It is often surprising to management to find that marketing efforts that were perceived to have been successful end up not being successful at all, and vice versa.[4]

Bill Edgel talked about defining corporate objectives. He was kind enough to share an example.

GOAL: Increase the Lifetime Value of Our Customer Base 2.5 Percent over 5 Years

1. *Increase customer retention by 1.5 percent annually.*
  a. Identify customer segments with the highest likelihood of persistence, and test.
  b. Develop loyalty program: contact targeted customers four times annually.
  c. Reactivate 10 percent of recently paid off credit accounts annually.

2. *Increase sales among most profitable customer segments 10 percent annually.*
   a. Implement event trigger programs targeted to specific customer circumstances.
   b. Increase credit add-on sales among core customers by 15 percent annually.
   c. Contact core customer segments six times annually with targeted promotions and special events.
3. *Increase customer base (new customer purchasers) by 15 percent annually.*
   a. Insure maximum POS data capture rate through system modifications, training, and store data competitions.
   b. Use predictive modeling and zone analyses to reduce cost of prospect advertising 10 percent.
   c. Increase direct mail response 2.5 percent through segmentation, modeling, and testing.

One more real-life example, from Reece Small, Marketing Database Analyst for Pier 1 Imports. Pier 1 started their direct marketing, customer database marketing venture in mid-1995 with two major initiatives:

1. Marketing to prospects. Using the knowledge developed in the database to understand customer motivation, leading to finding prospects that match the profile of profitable customers, resulting in expanding the customer base in a cost-effective way.
2. Marketing to customers. Maintaining a close relationship with customers by providing them with special services and recognition, resulting in increased loyalty, reduced attrition, and increased sales.

From those initiatives, Pier 1 developed the important goals, objectives, and strategies to get the job done.

Goal 1: Develop and Manage a Marketing Database Using Harte-Hanks P/CIS System

Objective 1: Institute a database committee.
Strategies:

1. Involve key players.
2. Determine database goals.

3. Prioritize and schedule time for each goal.
4. Establish key measurement for goals.

Objective 2: Present and distribute written database plan.
Strategies:

1. Include project time frames.
2. Define success measurements and thresholds.
3. Condense to critical steps for each project.
4. Commit to objectives, timing, measurement, and continuous improvement.
5. Report on successes and failures.
6. Revise regularly.

Goal 2: Expand the Credit Card Base

Objective 1: Use targeted direct marketing to expand the customer base in a cost effective way.
Strategies:

1. Build "best customer" model.
   a. Load 12 months of transaction history into initial database.
   b. Capture future transaction detail for each customer. Keep detail activity for preceding 24 months and life-to-date totals.
   c. Identify predictive factors of "best customers" and create model for prospecting.
2. Use modeling to select mail lists.
   a. Test model on sample list to measure effectiveness.
   b. Apply working model to select lists for prospecting.

Goal 3: Augment Lifetime Value of Customers: Increase Retention Rate, Referral Rate, and Sales Volume; Decrease Direct Cost and Marketing Cost

Objective 1: Use customer-based marketing to build a relationship with credit card customers.
Strategies:

1. Implement platinum and gold credit card customer recognition program.

2. Supply "best customer list" and associated promotion tools to the stores.
3. Cross-sell existing customers.
   a. Send letter recognizing purchase and suggesting additional activity.
4. Utilize report analysis to plan future promotions.
   a. Report results of each strategy implementation using Lifetime Value calculations, recency, frequency, monetary analysis, response rates, etc.

Objective 2: Decrease Marketing Cost.

Strategies:

1. Segment customer base and target mailings to improve mail efficiency.
2. Use RFM analysis, testing, and modeling to optimize return on marketing dollar.

Reece tells us Pier 1 has added 400,000 names to the now 1.8 million name database since December 1995. By her use of RFM analysis, testing, and modeling, her database marketing is yielding double-digit response rates to targeted mailings.

I have included all of that detail from Merksamer Jewelers and Pier 1 to make the point that the start-up consists of little things that are mostly common sense—*a lot* of little things. The marketing champion will not be a programmer, a database administrator, or a techie. Many of the challenges of building customer information, both legacy and newly acquired, into a queriable database will be unfamiliar to her or his MIS team. The marketing database is not a stable system. Marketing dynamics call for all kinds of testing and retesting that will frustrate most MIS groups. Standard development methods will not always work.

The most important thing to establish at start-up is who is going to build the database, who will be responsible for updates and maintenance, and who will keep it up to the swiftly changing industry standards. Ongoing support of the marketing database will be a most important element of successful database marketing because marketing decisions from the database will only be as good as the marketing database support. Every expert suggests that support must be provided on the marketer's terms and conditions, not those of the MIS department or the vendor.

Our experience has shown that it is better to call in the proven software experts than to ask in-house MIS staff to try to re-invent the wheel.

Some years ago, I visited a small department store in Fort Worth, Texas. They proudly showed me their new escalator and explained how they had saved a lot of money. Otis and other major escalator companies, they said, wanted too much money, so the store operations staff built their own. After admiring their work, I asked why the man was sitting in the box-like enclosure at the foot of the escalator. "Oh," they replied, "every so often the mechanism will catch a customer. If our man is not there to shut it off the customer could get mangled." We have seen similar results from home-crafted database solutions.

The marketer starting into customer management must build a strong relationship with someone with the proven technical expertise to translate the company's objectives into routine, point-and-click, user-friendly functionality that the marketing team can use on their own without having to get into the queue at MIS for reports and queries and without having to station a man in a box at the base of the system to make it work.

The solution can be a proven, in-house desktop system or the use of an outside service bureau. To me, service bureaus are like training wheels. They can help at the start, but it's best to discard them once you learn to ride.

Why do some database marketing and customer management programs fail? Again, I asked many professionals, among them "Rocket" Ray Jutkins of Rockingham*Jutkins*Marketing,[5] who gave me seven reasons in about seven seconds. He called them "Seven things not to do when you build a marketing database":

Mistake #1—Thinking you can "test" before doing.

Mistake #2—Not getting a total commitment from management.

Mistake #3—Thinking you can stop the program at any time.

Mistake #4—Not making certain everyone understands.

Mistake #5—Expecting immediate results.

Mistake #6—Not planning to measure.

Mistake #7—Not using your database.

I would make Ray's number two my number one. Without a solid and total commitment from the most senior management, the project will fail. To make the customer database work, customer management must move to center stage and be central to the core strategy of the company. More than that, the program must have a dedicated senior executive champion with the strength to "sell" the program throughout the organization. This project will not run on auto-pilot. Without this champion, the project will fail. I have seen this happen. There are few things more frustrating than a database evangelist with systems in place but no corporate foundation, no cross-company task force, and no leadership authority. Trust and understanding of the database marketing program will never be developed throughout the organization.

I would move Ray's number five to my number two. A true customer management strategy requires a long-term investment, not just the up-front cost of software and hardware, but the manpower cost of time and attention. A customer database, established today, will not assure sales increases by tomorrow night. The old analogy of the fast nickel and the slow dime comes to mind. The brand manager, who will move on shortly to another assignment, wants a strategy to move more product in a shorter time and likes the fast nickel—a strategy in direct contrast with database/relationship marketing. The CEO must fight for the twice-as-profitable, slow dime. One expert has suggested the solution:

> If one can keep the focus on what is best for the brand—not in terms of what is best for the brand management people, the marketing people, or whatever political agendas may develop—then a DBM program has a chance of succeeding.
>
> If you have that "brand first" mentality and you can instill that throughout the entire team, in all the different functions of that team, then almost everyone will wind up being on the same page.[6]

Some database marketing projects fail for the simple lack of a marketing plan. The company falls in love with the concept of millions of customer names with no real plan for what they will do with the names once they have them. Others have what they call a marketing plan, but because it includes no numeric goal which will turn into profit and no detailed method to achieve that goal, the program loses support.

Many projects fail because of unreal payback expectations. Amy Hubbel, Strategic Information Manager, First Commerce Corp., cautions database marketers to start small. "That means segmenting an elite group of customers, making every action a test, evaluating results, and building bigger with experience," she says. "You have to invest time and money in testing so you can mine the response data and measure it against various customer models. Think about profits, returns, and high-end objectives, but go after the easiest projects to implement before you go to the more complex ones."[7]

In other words, for your first test efforts, go after the low-hanging fruit.

Not all projects that fail can be blamed on the marketing side. We have discussed the need for a strong marketing/MIS partnership. The road to this relationship can be bumpy. I have seen examples of well-built marketing databases that still leave marketing managers unable to answer fairly simple questions quickly and easily . . . or sometimes, at all.

The best explanation for this I have found came from Steve Leeds. He makes the point that while the marketing and MIS groups may appear to be in sync, in actuality they are following two completely different, hidden "tracks":[8]

Marketing track:

I'd like the ability to generate a lot of reports: demographic profiles, spending profiles, attrition by segment, lifetime value, model decile overlays. I'd like to look at mail history of customers and prospects, in addition to profiling customer acquisition history, and the sequence of mailings that they have received. Also, I'd like to track monthly performance before and after a particular event. For example, it would be a real plus to map certain areas and overlay model scores. Most importantly, there has to be quick turnaround of requests.

MIS track:

Where are all these files located? Who has the layouts? Who manages these ancillary files? Is there a data dictionary? Can these files be merged? Are any pieces of information seriously suspect? Why? I really need some "specs."

We all like to say that our MIS associates need to be more business savvy. One writer makes the fresh point that the overwhelming majority of businesspeople need to become more savvy about being an IS client. "Technical literacy—or even technical awareness—isn't the point," he says. "The reality—which absolutely stuns me—is that not one of a dozen Fortune 1000 firms I've talked with trains its general managers about how to be a good IS client. Not one!"[9]

Like Bernice Grossman, Steve Leeds proposes that the marketing group formulate a written list of specific questions to serve as a starting point from which both groups can work, while the MIS team compiles a nontechnical list of all available information that can be accessed. This combined exercise will surface the data that is unavailable and set the ground rules for what can be delivered and what will need more work. This short list will be expanded down the road. As marketing sophistication grows with the use of the data, requirements will quickly escalate. Remember, "The food begets the appetite." A limited list of immediate goals assures a strong start by creating manageable, short-term goals. Steve makes the point that, given these agreements, the company can develop short-term successes that will help project team members find ways to address new questions.

Looking at database marketing programs that failed to achieve success, I find one common thread. Those responsible failed to realize how complicated the follow-through must be. The process of database marketing customer management is the process of building profitable relationships with customers. Profitable customer management requires well planned, meaningful, friendly communications and recognition and caring that, together, become a web of connections between the marketer and the customer. It cannot be just another series of promotions, no matter how personally those promotions are addressed. Every consumer gets more promotional offerings than he or she wants or can handle. One more, or 10 more, are not going to impress. Customer management is not another add-on to the promotion schedule; it is the development of relationships that build customer loyalty. It takes a lot of work and serious investments.

Our final thought on getting started takes us back to the beginning. Database marketing is a misnomer. What marketers are really doing is marketing using the database as a tool to build the business. The information model, developed in the start-up, must be an integral part of the business model. The information must be committed to the business, and the business must be committed to the information technology. The database is a marketing investment, and an expensive one. The greater the ultimate usage, the less the cost per use and the greater the return on investment.

Make the start-up as inclusive as possible . . . and have a detailed plan. As Bill Edgel says, "If you want to get there, you had better know where *there* is, and have a good map before you go. Or you will certainly end up somewhere else entirely."

We have looked at the map to get started, but there is still a long road ahead as we use these new tools to build the web of connections between the marketer and the customer. In the next chapter we'll look at the three dimensions follow-through requires: the marketing side, the creative side, and a few of the details in between.

CHAPTER **27**

And Then What?

Following through: Lessons learned from the best.

Follow-through has more than one dimension: the marketing side that requires new and different strategies, the details that require careful attention and are vital to the science, and the creative side, where vision and inspiration can make customer management an art form.

With the customer database established, the marketer now moves from passive interactions with the customer to active interactions with the customer. There is a big difference.

Remember, the process of database marketing customer management is the process of building profitable relationships with customers—converting sales, market share, profits, and return-on-investment into customer targets. Profitable customer management is a *lot* of work. Building that web of connections between the marketer and the customer means listening to the customer, using the database to track the relationship, appreciating and acknowledging customers, and communicating with customers . . . relentlessly. In start-up, the marketer looks for the things he must learn right away. In the follow-through phase, he looks for the things he must learn to do better. There are some keys to following through to make the database marketing customer management program improve the bottom line.

THE MARKETING SIDE

Leaving the start-up phase, the marketer can now use the database to understand and manage the customer to maximize the business as it is today and to grow new strengths. For all of this, the marketer must build a new return on investment framework, establish the customer relationship, develop an ongoing dialog, maximize the value of the relationship, reward loyalty, and sustain the relationship—a tall order and a new challenge for most companies.

We keep talking about building relationships with customers. What are relationships based on? Communication, commitment, and common interest. All of this means *listening* to the customer. This has implications for employee training, customer satisfaction surveys, customer complaint management, redefining services, and product variety.

Concerning employee training and communicating the company's customer management strategy to front-line associates, recall Leo Rabinovitch's advice: "Make certain to understand how customer knowledge will impact your whole business." Remember, when we looked at the experts' reasons why some customer management projects fail, Ray Jutkins listed "Not making certain everyone understands." When a company changes its focus to the customer, management's past practices are affected. Much of the company culture will change. Not all things will be the way they were. This requires understanding at all levels within the company. The moment of truth arrives when the customer meets front-line employees.

Barbara Mowry was one of the people most responsible for the success of United Airlines Mileage Plus frequent flyer program when she served as President and CEO of MPI, a wholly owned subsidiary of UAL, Inc. She is now Senior Vice President of TCI, using database marketing as an underlying resource for TCI's service to its millions of cable television customers. She tells a story that makes the point for the urgent need for communicating any new customer strategy to front-line employees.

Since the whole purpose of the frequent flyer program at United and other airlines was to retain best customers, the frequent fliers, the programs were designed to give these customers special treatment to make them feel important. Back in 1981, this was all new and an immediate success. Customers willingly carried pads of mileage credit forms to be filled out for every flight and happily accumulated miles for their first ever free trip. All went well until the first frequent flyers began to show up for their free trips. When a young executive and his wife and their two small children arrived at the gate, free first-class tickets in hand, ready to be treated royally as they winged their way to Hawaii, they were asked to wait over at the side. Finally, after the long lines of tourists had boarded, after all of the overhead storage space was filled with other people's luggage, the not so happy frequent flyer and family were allowed to board.

What went wrong? The culture of the airline companies in 1981 was that free tickets were bad! Moreover, it was a given that first class was for business travel, and few families were seen in first class. United initially had failed to tell the front-line employees the rules had changed and how the economics of the program would benefit them.

Building the Framework

Our old method was to capture and retain customers by offering more coupons, more discounts, more promotions, and recently, more "frequent buyer" programs. There is more to life than 40 percent off. The traditional 40 percent off is history. We can't survive doing it, and the customer is looking for more individual attention. It is all too possible that frequent buyer programs are going to turn into just another version of 40 percent off, another way of raising customer expectations that we are discounting the brand.

The new rules of marketing involve all of the aspects of customer "bonding": awareness of the customer, identifying the customer by name and purchase patterns, building relationships, building a "community" of customers sharing experiences together, and, finally, developing that special customer relationship that makes the customer an advocate for the company. These will become the priorities for following through to maximize return on investment of the database.

As a company matures in its development of database marketing customer management, it moves closer to answering the question, "What is a lost customer worth to our company?" With the ability to measure the profitability of customer segments, and even individual customers, significant shares of the marketing budget begin to move from the conquest of new customers to the fight to retain best customers.

Establishing the Relationship

Most marketers think this relationship-building process begins by making the first sale and capturing the customer name for the database. I am indebted to Professor Katherine Lemon for a good many of my thoughts about customer management. She uses the analogy of a first date when talking about the customer relationship-building process. "Is the goal of a first date," she asks, "to get another name in your daytimer?" No. The goal of a first date is to begin to establish trust, to find a common interest, and to see if you want to have a second date.[1]

Most database marketers today focus on getting names. Instead, they should be learning more about the new customer, developing a mutually rewarding relationship, and deciding whether or not it is worth the time and expense to pursue a second date. Knowing what the customer is buying starts the process. The next step is to determine what needs the purchase is satisfying and what benefits of the product or service excites the customer. It may not be what we think.

One way to gain this knowledge is to learn who is the customer's customer. Who else is she concerned about when making the purchase decision? If a woman is buying apparel, she is concerned about the people she interacts with. If she is buying cereal, her concern is for her family. The marketer can get inside the customer's head by knowing the benefits that are being provided. It is not merely a matter of selling clothes or cereal: It is selling her the way she will present herself to her boss, her employees, and her staff as she goes to work each day, or selling her an assurance of good health for her family as she prepares the morning meal. The human dimension, the underlying motivation, is key to creating emotional connections with customers.

Developing an Ongoing Dialog

This starts with acknowledging the customer *as the customer wants to be acknowledged.* How do we get to know how customers want to be acknowledged? Ask them. A dialog is a two-way conversation. We need feedback from the customer. Customer surveys are one way of getting the customer to talk back. Even though there is an imperfect correlation between customer satisfaction and retention, customer satisfaction surveys are still one of the best tools available to understand exactly what customers are thinking and feeling and particularly how their evaluation is changing over time. This is as important as tracking purchase history over time. Tracking attitudinal history over time can predict when a customer is about to walk out the door.

Another way to create the dialog is to encourage feed back. Jordan's, a North Carolina furniture store, calls each and every customer who takes delivery of a piece of furniture that same day and just listens to what they have to say. The comments are all typed into a computerized database, word for word, and are saved for five years. They are reported the day of receipt to the company executives, in their entirety. The comments are not watered down. The executives read 18 to 20 pages of what customers had to say, every day. They know right away if a problem is brewing.

Maximizing the Value of the Relationship

The key to relationship management is maximizing the value of the relationship to the customer for the customer's benefit and the company's profit. What does the customer value about the relationship? What is the core service, product, or benefit? What does the customer really value about these? What is the value provided that differentiates your company from the competition? What product bundles will add value to the customer? Once the marketer knows what the customer values in the relationship, he can create custom product and service bundles to add additional value. The key is to maximize value to the customer by making each contact or communication positive from the customer's viewpoint.

We hear a lot about Saturn's excellent customer bonding efforts. I have a friend who owns a Saturn. She was offended by a Saturn communication that was intended to strengthen the bond. She is a loyal customer and loves her Saturn. She takes her car to the dealer every 3,000 miles. She missed one oil change because she was driving across country and was in Fort Collins where there was no Saturn dealership. On her return home she knew she was due for the oil change. She received a note from Saturn that said, "Good service depends on you, too. Make sure you don't forget to bring your car in, and bring this card with you when you come." It's not that she would get anything special if she brought the card. She told me she felt as though they were slapping her hand. It is important to remember that these customer contacts have the power to maximize or to diminish the value of the relationship.

Rewarding Loyalty

Whether the marketer rewards customer loyalty with a points program or with ego gratification or both, there are some key ingredients to any loyalty program. *Marketing Tools,* an excellent magazine published by American Demographics, is one of the very best at providing tools and techniques for customer management. Recently, in an article called "Lessons from the Experts," they reported the advice on loyalty programs from a number of hotels that have been in the frequent guest business for 10 years or more. Some of their points reinforce what we have been saying.

* Focus on what your customers want.
* Reward with benefits you can control, especially the cost.
* Reward for the behavior you want.
* The best rewards have greater perceived value than actual value. Customers perceive that they are really getting a benefit.
* Make use of the technologies that facilitate answering inquiries, but don't forget the personal touch. A computer doesn't have human ears or a human heart.
* Recognize that best customers will want exclusive privileges.
* Design a measure for evaluating the level and profitability of the incremental business developed from the loyalty program.[2]

Sustaining the Relationship

The secret of customer retention is that the customer develops a relationship with the company, over time. This relationship has value to the customer. To get that same relationship with another company, the customer has to reinvent the relationship, and that has a significant cost to it. This is the most important secret of success.

The follow-through phase of customer management is a matter of managing the customer relationship: building the framework, establishing the relationship, developing a dialog, maximizing the value of the relationship to the company and to the customer, rewarding loyalty in a way the customer feels appreciated, and working to sustain the relationship.

Professor Lemon has developed this checklist to help a company monitor its progress in relationship management:

1. Building the framework:
   a. Do we subscribe to the "old view" or the "new view"?
   b. Where are our customers on the loyalty ladder?
      (1) Awareness
      (2) Identity
      (3) Relationship
      (4) Community
      (5) Advocacy
   c. Do we know what a customer is worth to us? How much?

    d. Is everyone in our organization really on board and committed to relationship management?

2. Establishing the relationship:

    a. How are we now establishing trust with our customers?

    b. What new ways could we begin building trust?

    c. Do we know what benefits our customer is buying?

    d. Do we know what our products and services do for her?

    e. What are we doing, now, to create emotional connections with our customers? How could we do this more successfully?

3. Developing an ongoing dialog:

    a. How do we currently acknowledge our customers?

    b. How do our customers want to be acknowledged?

        (1) Satisfaction surveys

        (2) Formal and informal mechanisms for customer feedback

        (3) Personal communications programs

        (4) Other

4. Maximizing the value of the relationship:

    a. Maximizing value to our customer

        (1) What does our customer really value of the basic products and services we offer?

        (2) How is the value we provide our customer different from that of our competitors (as our customer sees our competitors)?

        (3) What product or service bundles could we create to add value to our customers?

        (4) Does every employee seek to maximize customer value in every customer contact?

    b. Maximizing value to our company

        (1) Have we isolated the drivers of profitability in our business? What are the drivers of:

           (a) Market share?

           (b) Customer retention?

           (c) Average profit per customer?

           (d) Customer satisfaction?

           (e) Customer delight?

        (2) What are the main drivers, and what are the key sub-processes for each of those main drivers?

        (3) Which quality/service improvements will provide the highest return on our investment?

5. Rewarding customer loyalty:

    a. Are we really focusing on what customers want? How do we know this?

    b. Are we able to control the cost of the benefits we project for our loyalty-building program?

    c. Are we sure we are rewarding customers for the behavior we want?

    d. Do our rewards have greater perceived value than actual value?

    e. Are we answering customer inquiries with a truly personal touch?

    f. What exclusive benefits are we providing best customers?

    g. How are we defining and measuring incremental business resulting from our loyalty program?

6. Sustaining the relationship:

    a. Do we use customer complaints as an opportunity to gain a customer for life?

    b. Do our customer contact people practice "customer retention" or "customer adjudication?"

    c. Do we use all three points of the customer retention triangle—customer service, quality management, and marketing—to our best advantage?[3]

THE PAYOFF TO THE MARKETING SIDE

For profitable follow-through on this business of customer management, it is important to have some kind of scorecard to measure the continuing payoff.

Different companies construct the scorecard in different ways, but all good database marketers measure progress, monthly, quarterly, and annually. Whatever form it takes, the scorecard gives the marketer a measurement of improvement in the size and quality of the customer base. It delivers a quantitative evaluation of the company's performance against targeted customer segments, allowing the company to track how well performance targets are being achieved, and it re-evaluates the new potential of each customer segment. The trends uncovered in the scorecard are like an x-ray of the business (as discussed in Chapter 23), alerting senior management to problems and/or opportunities for the future of the business. The bottom line is that, since loyal, quality customers are the ultimate measure of company success, the scorecard becomes a continuous track-

ing of customer quality and a measure of progress the company is making
against its goals.

THE DETAILS

If the information in the database is to deliver knowledge, the quality of
the information is paramount. The details of data maintenance are not very
glamorous, but they are critical to the success of this venture.

Wrong, incomplete, or outdated customer information can be costly.
Customers can err in their original input. It rarely occurs to them to make
their business affiliations their first priority for notification of change of
address. Double entry means duplication of customer addresses. Key-
punch operators can misread or mistype information in data entry. For a
frequent mailer, every bad address adds wasted printing and postage costs.
Worse than that, corrupt data makes questionable the valuable data analysis we have called the x-ray of the health of the business. Consumer data
degrade in usefulness approximately 20 to 30 percent annually. Business-
to-business data are estimated to degrade at a rate of 50 percent annually.

There are many solutions. The most common is National Change of
Address (NCOA) processing. NCOA is a database maintained by the U.S.
Postal Service from all of those change-of-address cards we fill in for the
post office when we move. A small number of vendors are licensed by the
Postal Service to perform this address correction service. Marketers send
tapes of customer records to these vendors for updating. The address for
every customer (or business) that has filed a change of address card is corrected and sent back to the mailer, updating the records to the new, correct
address.

We used to suggest that marketers clean their files through NCOA at
least once a year. The most recent postal reclassification changes that. To
qualify for best postal rates, mailers must now clean their files a minimum
of once a year for standard mail and twice a year for first class. The most
sophisticated marketers clean their lists each mailing. Since the NCOA database is updated every two weeks, this captures current updates for even
the most recent customers. The cost is very modest, and the return on investment is guaranteed.

At one time we worked with a marketer who had 7 million customers
and mailed more than 20 million pieces a year. For almost two years we
tried, without success, to persuade the marketing vice president to author-
ize the expense of NCOA. When we finally got him to clean the list, we

found 18 percent of the file undeliverable. That meant more than 3 million dollars a year in wasted postage, corrected for less than $15,000.

A lone California congressman has been fighting a six-year battle to outlaw NCOA and keep the USPS from providing marketers with address changes. He finally won a round in August 1996, when the General Accounting Office reported to Congress that the program violates privacy laws which prevent federal agencies from making available individuals' names and addresses. However, government and industry officials have said the GAO conclusion in itself will not lead to changes unless there is pressure from Congress or a lawsuit.[4]

Some think that a valid forwarding address will mean their advertising mail will forward to the customer's new address. First-class mail will. Standard class mail will not. Also, if the customer moved and left no forwarding address, expensive printing, and postage end up wherever dead letters go. Paying a bit extra to print a mailing with "Address Correction Requested" will, at least, clean up the dead mail and allow the marketer to save money by coding those undeliverable addresses as "do not mail." This process can get expensive. It should be used, but the frequency depends on the frequency of mailings and the firm's experience of address changes each time they do it.

The 20 percent of the marketer's customers who change addresses every year are not the only reason for undeliverable mail or wasted postal expense. Missing or incorrect zip codes can keep mail from reaching its destination, and missing carrier route codes mean a mailer will miss out on incentive discount rates. Here, again, the U.S. Postal Service has an official directory of all deliverable addresses in the United States called the Delivery Sequence File (DSF). Matching mailing lists against the DSF file catches all of the bad addresses, adds apartment numbers, applies correct zip codes, including zip+4, and adds the carrier route codes.

Duplications within the list can be another headache and money waster. A big-time cataloger, whose name I will withhold to save them embarrassment, has been sending me three catalogs in every mailing for several years: one to F.B. Newell, one to Frederick B. Newell, and one to Fred Newell. I have written these folks twice to ask them to clean up their list, pointing out the savings to them. I continue to get the three copies. I am happy to let them waste their money, but it is a small annoyance each time I lug in this mailer's waste from our box, enough that I toss all three copies without so much as a glance. So, duplicate mailings are not only a waste of the marketer's postage budget, they can also hurt potential sales.

There are solutions. Merge/purge/de-dupe software is based on match algorithms that can be adjusted to tighten or loosen the match limits. It becomes a matter of testing to get the right balance. Most mailers today "household" their customer files to combine individual family members living at the same address.

Even after NCOA, DSF, and de-dupe, there will be addresses in the file that are less than USPS valid—correct, but not in standard Postal Service address fields or zip code construction for automated letter-sorting equipment. They will likely get delivered but will probably be delayed and, under the new postal reclassification rules, will cost the mailer more money. Electronic address correction and standardization software solves this problem, and most NCOA/DSF vendors will include this as part of their processing, adding a confidence code to the file.

There is more to list hygiene than just the correction of postal irregularities. In any system, capturing customer transactions at point-of-sale, corrupt data can develop in the file. Incorrect customer ID numbers entered at POS will show up in the file as rejected transactions that cannot be assigned to any customer. Marketers using customer telephone numbers to identify customers will compile large numbers of transactions that cannot be tied to a mailing address even with reverse telephone look-up. Remember, we said 30 to 60 percent of telephone numbers will not produce a mailing address (and don't forget all those Californians with unlisted phone numbers). One marketer we have worked with insists he has 682,000 customers in his database. More than 250,000 of these customers cannot be identified by name or address. In other words, he cannot communicate with more than one-third of his "database." Although that makes it difficult to build relationships, this marketer insists on continuing the tracking (and back-office processing expense) of these "customers." We can't be sure whether he continues this wasteful expense as an ego trip so he can talk at marketing conferences about his large file, or whether he really believes the 682,000 file will someday impress a naive potential buyer of his business, or whether he lives with the hope that these folks will all march in one day and say, "Here we are. Here are our names and addresses." Profitable database marketing is not built on wishes.

Information integrity is vital to the success of any database marketing program. The smart database marketer will plan for the expense of constant checking for accuracy and understand the need to validate the database after each update. There is much more at stake than just wasted postage and undeliverable mail. The database will have little perceived value within the company if users discover information that is invalid. For the success of the program, a reputation for information integrity must be a first priority.

THE CREATIVE SIDE: VISION AND INSPIRATION

When I talked with Michelle Cerwin about her start-up and follow-through at Chanel, she told me, looking back, the two important things that helped her build a successful customer management program were to go slowly and be realistic throughout the start-up to make sure everyone came aboard with achievable expectations; then, in the follow-through phase, to "have a vision." She was reminding me that the start-up deals with technology, much of which is new to the company. Making the transition slowly with modest goals produces some "easy wins" (her words). But once the program is in place, it takes a lot more than technology to maximize results. The new knowledge about the company's customers opens opportunities that stretch so far the marketer must have a vision and must be able to develop creative ways to use the data to build real relationships that go far beyond promotion.

As David Harden of GE Capital once told me, learning database marketing is like learning to play a musical instrument: Learn the fundamentals (technique, chords, scales), be sure to get a teacher, practice, practice, practice, listen to others, then . . . incorporate your own creative ideas.

In our hundreds of interviews, we heard this in different words from all of the best and most successful database marketers. Exceptional customer management is more of an art than a science. Timothy Swigor said it best:

> Today, database marketing is a realistic proposition that will change communications and interactions with customers and prospects forever.
>
> However, it will only be the skillful and artistic implementation of the tools that will let marketers successfully manage individual relationships and differentiate customers.
>
> By creating and maintaining a dialog with each customer, information will come to light that will let marketers sell more products. Marketers can identify and solve customer needs from recorded information.
>
> These manifestations of database marketing principles are based on scientific analysis. But, because of the diverse environments marketers operate in, implementing all the tools, methodologies, principles, and discipline effectively takes this science into the realm of an art form.
>
> Like an artist who skillfully administers many different colours to create a masterpiece, marketers have many different tools from which to choose. Some artistic instinct is necessary to combine the appropriate tools to get the desired results. As artistic as it is to combine the correct amounts of blue and yellow to create the desired shade of green, it also takes "artistic" flare to combine and implement the correct database marketing tools

to create the perfect shade of meaning to a message that produces increased sales.

More important than what tools a marketing professional might use is how they use them. Database marketing is truly an art beyond science. The artistic implementation of the tools occurs only after constant evaluation of marketing programs.

Since database marketing produces measurable results, ongoing evaluation is a natural process. However, before creating their masterpieces, marketers must conduct a needs analysis, set realistic expectations, and artistically implement the tools that will yield desired results.[5]

The follow-through phase requires just as much leadership as the start-up, and it requires constant evaluation. The business of using the database to understand and manage the customer to maximize the business, grow new strengths, and improve return on investment will not run on auto-pilot.

The need for a champion persists.

CHAPTER **28**

CPU, MIS, UPS, LTV, TCP, MCI, EDS, IBM . . . BS

Just for the retailer: How to make customer information work for you on the selling floor.

The retailer has a special opportunity. Unlike the packaged goods marketer or some others who must rely on third-party sources for customer data, the retailer can capture all customer transactions and tie them directly to a name and address. Art Hutchinson, Senior Consultant, Northeast Consulting Resources, suggests it is not that simple, "It takes more than a technological breakthrough," he says. "The technology, by itself, is not going to have as revolutionary an impact in the retail environment as a lot of people like to think it will—especially without the proper incentives, a high level of training and making it a 'business priority' to capture data."[1]

We agree with that, so we went to another expert to find some answers. From the introduction of their earliest database software for retailers, STS Systems has always had a focus on the sales associates, their POS tools, and the importance of data capture on the sales floor. We talked with Leo Rabinovitch, Vice President New Product Development, about Mr. Hutchinson's challenge.

> Art Hutchinson is right; the technology, by itself, is not going to get the job done. Incentives and training are important and the sales associates have to know that name, address, and transaction capture is a "business priority,"

but the easiest way to capture data at the source—at point-of-sale—is with an in-store system. By its broadest definition, intelligent data capture is made possible by sophisticated software that facilitates customer data capture and customer matching and makes this as easy as possible for the sales associate and for the customer. Then the sales benefits and the data look-up capabilities in the system can provide the incentive for both sales associates and store management.

In the past, companies could only capture house-card purchases—that was their definition of capturing transactions. Today's intelligent systems enable companies to capture customer data regardless of means of payment. The sales associate simply scans a credit card or enters a name at the point-of-sale terminal and the system determines whether that customer is already on file. If not, a hot key enables the sales associate to create a new customer account on the spot. All of which contributes to a higher capture rate. And a higher capture rate means that the head office can more accurately measure the effectiveness of promotions.

Of course, there are companies that manage to capture customer information without using sophisticated data capture systems. In this scenario, every time a customer buys something, the sales associate must ask for name and other particulars and enter this information in the register [or, worse yet, on paper for later back-office entry], even if the customer is already on file. Since dumb name capture (as this method is called) increases a busy sales associate's workload tremendously, Mr. Hutchinson is right; it inevitably decreases the capture rate. And since it also puts the burden of matching customers to transactions on the host end, twice the work is needed to get the same result. The end result is a less meaningful customer/transaction record, so its potential use for tracking customer buying patterns, targeting promotions, and creating better sales and service opportunities is diminished.

Richard Penn of Puritan Clothing of Cape Cod, a regional specialty store chain, says it differently:

Data capture is not a software issue.

Sales associates don't go to marketing conferences or read marketing books. We have to teach them that acquiring, developing, and retaining customers is mission-critical for their jobs. Anything else is nonmission work and it is our job as management to get rid of it. That's why, in our store, we have changed delivery times so floors can be restocked pre-opening. We have limited interstore transfers, and we are doing everything possible to allow sales associates more time for their mission-critical work.

Having done that, we make sure sales associates know data capture is a business priority. We review every individual's capture rate every week. Twenty-five percent of a store manager's bonus is based on customer retention. We make this part of our corporate culture. We won't fail because of software. Data capture is a minimum requirement to work for our company.

Having established the data capture, what can sales associates do with all of this enriched customer information? Back to Leo Rabinovitch, who works with more than 100 companies on database marketing:

> First of all, they can easily identify their best, or highest-spending, customers and keep them loyal. They can access reports detailing any customers who may not have shopped in the last few months, so they can call them up and invite them in for a special promotion. They can keep electronic customer "black books" on-line, recording their customers' specific events so they can contact them for birthdays, anniversaries, or holidays. (As an added corporate safeguard, this priceless information will stay with the company should a sales associate leave.) Because they have their customers' purchase history on-line, sales associates can easily suggest cross-shopping opportunities—say, the designer name blouse that goes with the pants they just bought. And marketing as well as management can measure which sales associates are creating cross-shopping scenarios and which ones are dropping the ball.

How does this work in the real world? We asked Kaye Hutchins, Advertising Director for Stanley Korshak, a fine specialty store in Dallas. She is one of the best I know when it comes to using the customer database in-store. By working closely with her 50-member sales staff, she accomplished the store's goal of capturing customer data on 90 percent of all transactions within two months of installing the database software. By developing a strong relationship between the sales staff and the marketing department, she successfully empowers her sales associates with valuable customer information. She agrees that the computer is not the thing to concentrate on. She says:

> Forget the computer! To make customer information work for you on the selling floor the first thing you are going to need is a cheerleader, someone who will be able to respond to the sales associates and talk their language. If you present your database as a bunch of cables and silicon chips, you're not going to empower anybody with anything. The sales associates simply will not use it. They won't get it. I don't talk mips and bits and bites and chips and CPU, MIS, UPS, LTV, TCP, MCI, EDS, IBM. They're just going to say, "BS."
> You must be willing to invest the time required to make sure your sales associates know what they're doing—they get it, they understand why they're doing this and how it can be of value to them. You must authorize

them to get involved with the system. You can't buy the best, most expensive system, then sit back all calm and comfortable and go, "Oh, OK now we'll be successful." Training, training, training. The sales people must know what they're doing. During this training, remember salespeople are very competitive. Give them something to compete about. For our first week, the associates who captured the most data received lunches and dinners. At the end of the month, the associate who had put in the most data received a sports car . . . for the weekend. We post a top-10 list, daily, in the common employee area. Most important, listen to your sales associates. They are on the selling floor. They are your contact between your customer and you. They are your business lifeblood. If they don't understand the system, they won't use it.

Lauren Goldberg, who spent four and a half years involved with the in-store workings of the customer database at Bergdorf Goodman and is now Database Marketing Manager at Escada (USA), is another pro we talked to. She agrees with both Leo and Richard. She uses the STS Marketworks software, so things are easy for her sales associates, but she doesn't believe the software is the key:

It isn't the system. You [the database manager] are in charge of the information. You need the system, but you can't get caught up in the box of what the system can or can't do. You need to be able to manipulate the system any way you want and know what to do with it. It's not a matter of saying I can get this report and I can get that report then trying to figure out what to do with them. You must come up with the program that's right for your organization.

We all talk a lot about relationship marketing, but after you have established your database marketing program, you have to do relationship marketing in-house. This is a really important issue. You have to be the one to educate your market, in-house. You have to be the one to define and penetrate your market, as you start out, and your market includes everyone from sales associates to upper management.

To accomplish this, Lauren has set up a database "point person" in each store. This person is the vision-keeper, the enthusiasm builder, Lauren's eyes and ears in the store. She has also put together a cross-functional task force of the director of stores, store managers, database point persons, buyers, merchandisers, and MIS.

Lauren stresses the importance of setting up a procedure manual for in-store personnel to be certain all sales associates know how to access the information. She has strong beliefs about how that should be done:

I've been to all my stores. I've done training on top of training, but I still had to go back to my office and re-do the manual, not in terms of the way

I think or the way we think, but in terms of the way a sales associate would think and in terms of the way that they sell. Most of them would rather that I stood behind them as they were on the register and told them which keys to press, instead of really thinking about: OK this is how I access my information. What do I want to know? What do I want to get from my system, and how to I apply it to make more sales?

Lauren's final advice for all retailers was to think carefully about how to define their database marketing strategy in terms of the way the company looks at its business. She says:

Every company looks at their business differently. We're all looking at the same things, but what are the most important things to analyze in your business? At Bergdorf's it's department, it's division, it's floor, it's store, it's men's store versus women's store. That's the way they look at their business. At Escada, it's more division, line, product line, and penetration in terms of lines. It takes a while before you can really figure out, within a company, which way is best to look at the business. It's not just a matter of asking, because "they" don't understand the way you're thinking. "They" are not used to thinking in terms of database marketing and don't understand it, at first.

Both Lauren and Kaye gave me great examples of what all this in-store, sales associate effort can mean for sales payoff. Lauren told me about taking 50 customers in each of her stores, who had average purchases of $5,000, and moving them up to the $7,500 to $10,000 level. When she converts just 10 percent of these customers, she has added $500,000 in business. And she says:

I didn't even do anything. I didn't send out any direct mail. I didn't do anything. All I did was, I alerted my sales associates and my store managers as to who these customers were, and asked them to just focus on them, to give them a little more attention. Tracking these kinds of results makes it easy for me to show upper management what our database has been able to do for our business.

Kaye's story was remarkable. The Korshak men's department was overstocked in some sizes. They had 12 size 36-short sport jackets at $700 each. Stanley Korchak is not a sale store. They sold all 12 jackets by calling the customers who wore size 36-short. Only seven people bought all of this—$8,400 worth—but once they were in the store that day, the seven people spent $35,000 more. Kaye says, "Show that report to management."

What can we look forward to for the development of in-store database marketing? Personal information managers (PIMs) are available today to enable sales associates and store managers to book appointments, track alterations, even find gifts on the fly without having to tie up the register or leave the selling floor. Hand-held devices, which can be carried by sales associates while they are serving the client, are appearing in stores. Kiosks and customer workstations will ride the popular interactive wave, but they may not spread as widely as first predicted because of the growing presence of the Internet and electronic shopping. The emergence of holography and imaging will enable a virtual customer to "try on" clothes for look and fit before buying. Finally we may see the model store concept where merchandise display is minimal and the customer is served with merchandise from back room stock.

Whatever the retail format, we can count on the fact that it will continue to grow more and more important to empower the front-line forces— the folks who meet the customers—with customer information from the database.

To recap, the retailer has a special opportunity, but the technology by itself will not make the revolutionary impact. Richard Penn gave us the challenge. We have to teach everyone on the front line that acquiring, developing, and retaining customers is mission-critical. Anything else is non-mission work. To make the customer database work in-store, we must have in-house relationship marketing. We need a cheerleader.

And we need to listen to the sales associates who are the lifeblood of our business.

CHAPTER **29**

Why "Big Brother" was Mentioned 542 Times

What every marketer must do about privacy and why it is important for every company.

As marketers (and, not so incidentally, governments) develop more and more information about the lives and lifestyles and habits of customers (and citizens), The Privacy Issue heats up around the world. The explosion of cyberspace capabilities will bring completely new issues that will be unique to the new technologies. Privacy issues will have to be examined from fresh perspectives if we are to continue the delicate balance between the marketer's need for information and the consumer's desire to control that information. The marketing community, so anxious for a continuing flow of customer information, must work to keep the balance by sharing more positive stories of customer benefits, to balance the media focus on Big-Brotherism, and the legislators' zeal to "protect us" from ourselves.

That's why, at our Database Marketing Conferences, we always include an important session on The Privacy Issue. At the most recent Seklemian/Newell Database Marketing Conference, the featured speaker was Jennifer Barrett.

As Senior Vice President, Interactive Services Group at Acxiom Corporation, Jennifer is responsible for evaluating and shaping Acxiom's presence and participation on the Information Superhighway, and provides oversight for Acxiom's corporate-wide privacy initiatives and its internal privacy measurement activities. She is a pro's pro on privacy.

Her research highlighted the focus of our national press with some startling facts:

> In articles on the Eye-Q database between January 1, 1995 and January 2, 1996:
>> The word privacy was found 31,374 times.
>> Under 'privacy and technology' were 4,720 articles.
>> Under 'privacy and the internet' were 2,552 articles.
>> Under 'privacy and database' were 983 articles.
>> Under 'privacy and medical records' were 550 articles.
>> Under 'privacy and public records' were 236 articles.
>> The term 'big brother' was used in 542 articles.
>> Compilation of any list for any reason was portrayed as a threat or potential threat to personal privacy.
> Privacy advocates are concerned about both commercial and governmental use of databases.
> There was little or no information on the merits of Database direct marketing. All such articles were found in trade publications, not publications the average consumer will ever read.

Then, she shared some untold stories of consumer benefits:

> American Student List helped locate 15 missing children by matching names of missing kids to its own database.
> The Ritz-Carlton has established the highest standards of service by discretely fulfilling the *unexpressed* wishes of their guests, supporting their highest mission to provide genuine care and comfort.
> Product guarantee registration information from NDL's consumer database has been used as proof of ownership of items that were stolen or lost in a fire or disaster.
> Motor vehicle records are used to contact owners for recall service.
> Direct mail users of customer databases have raised over $50 billion in charitable contributions to such causes as The National Wildlife Federation, The American Heart Association, Father Flanagan's Boys Home, and more and more and more.
> The Advertising Mail industry (those folks who need customer information) employs over 3,500,000 individuals (approximately one in every 30 jobs).
> Direct Mail (to consumer lists) has generated over $150 billion in sales for the last five years.

There is an important opportunity here for all marketers to share more positive stories developed from customer data.

Based on some of the negative reporting Jennifer capsuled, polls tell us about 50% of American consumers are deeply concerned about privacy and 80% are concerned. The last poll I saw said 25% of consumers would like to prohibit secondary use of their name without approval, 55% want privacy and choice, and 20% don't care. There are some who say people don't care about privacy unless prompted by a pollster's question.

The 50% deeply concerned may best be represented by this actual letter received by a direct marketer:

Sir:

I would like to inform you that I am no longer interested in receiving any catalogs from you. I would like you to stop issuing them to me at my current address. Please don't hesitate to remove me from your mailing list which includes my name and address.

Also I would like you to stop sending me magazines associated with your company advertising your products. I cannot afford to take the time to look over them and to make any future purchases.

To assure you my current request for complete privacy, my name and address is not included in this letter.

After you have completed my request to be cleared from your mailing list, please discard this letter.

Thank you.

Anne

For whatever reason, the legislation mounts.

In the last ten years there has been a 100% increase in the number of privacy bills that would restrict or eliminate our access to certain types of information. Politicians consider privacy a "can't lose" issue. In 1996, Rep. Robert Franks (R-NJ) and Sen. Dianne Feinstein (D-CA) sponsored a bill to make it a crime to "knowingly sell information about children without the express written consent of the parents." Their interest came from the tragic stalking death of little Polly Klaus in California, but that twelve year old's death had absolutely nothing to do with the techniques of database marketing. This bill, as proposed, would end the livelihood of any number of fine companies that market excellent quality products that enhance children's lives.

Even more colorful was Rep. Edward Markey (D-MA) who introduced into Congress the "Privacy Bill of Rights for the Information Age." His bill would instruct the Federal Trade Commission to closely examine whether the rights of consumers are being threatened. No matter that this bill is meaningless, since it proposes the FTC do something it is already doing, listen to his rhetoric.

He talked about business' present ability "to sneak corporate hands into the personal information cookie jar." With all of Congress' priorities focused on election issues, Rep. Markey's bill didn't get far, but privacy legislation does and will continue.[1]

We will hear more noise whenever some irresponsible person treats the privacy issue in casual fashion. The Ohio based data firm Lexis-Nexis was overwhelmed with angry faxes, phone calls, and e-mails recently after someone posted notices on the Internet warning that the firm was selling social security numbers and other personal financial information to anyone willing to pay for it. Actually, Lexis-Nexis sells only names, current address, up to two previous addresses, month and year of birth, telephone number, and in some cases, a person's maiden name.

Surprisingly, there has been little uproar about the enactment of the new federal health-care bill that gives the federal government the power to create a national computer database with the medical records of every patient, without any option for individuals to request that their files be excluded.

Some folks are beginning to express concern about "smart cards" which will soon be issued by banks and other financial institutions. These cards will be embedded with computer chips capable of keeping a record of every transaction. Because consumers are expected to use them for small transactions, there are those who believe they could make cash obsolete. One columnist had this to say about "smart cards."

> Even if people have absolutely nothing to hide, they really don't want any-
> one—not the government, not their employer, maybe not even their family
> or friends—tracking their daily activities. But if the information on "smart-
> cards" is made as readily available as the personal information that Lexis-
> Nexis offers, then no "smart-card" user can be confident of his or her
> privacy.[2]

Telemarketing is under the gun, as well. The telemarketing and Consumer Fraud and Abuse Protection Act of 1994 allows consumers to choose whether or not they want to receive telemarketing calls. Nothing wrong with that. I always answer my phone during the cocktail hour by saying, "OK, what are you selling tonight." But in-house name-suppression has always been a part of DMA's ethical guidelines.

Another good part of the balance was the Driver's Privacy Protection Act that provides Federal guidelines for states to allow responsible use of drivers' license information, while giving consumers the choice to opt-out.

States have enacted opt-out legislation for everything from credit bureau and health data to video rental. Eleven state bills were passed in 1994 to create "do not call" lists for telemarketers.

We can expect to see increased legislative activity as lobby groups build pressure on legislators. The leader is the American Civil Liberties Union. Because of the ACLU's many independent affiliates, their cohesive action is hard to predict, but they consider privacy a priority initiative.

There are others: The Electronic Privacy Information Clearinghouse, a group continually railing against the sale of consumer data, The Center for Democracy and Technology who are fighting for a Federal medical privacy bill, and Privacy International, London, a watchdog on surveillance by governments and marketers. The Privacy Rights Clearinghouse at The Center For Public Interest Law at the University of San Diego is a bit less of a lobbyist group. It's goal is to educate consumers to empower them to control their own information. They focus, primarily, on California state issues.

The good news is that the Direct Marketing Association and the direct marketing industry have been doing great work for years to help keep the balance. In 1989, DMA and concerned industry leaders formed the Privacy Task Force. It's mission: to assure consumers and policy makers that their privacy concerns would be addressed and their options increased by marketers' responsible use of databases. The Task Force developed the DMA Mail and Telephone Preference Service, allowing consumers to opt-out. They also formulated the Privacy Action Plan which provides marketers with a course of action to address the privacy issue.

Recently the DMA launched "Project Positive" a broad based industry education initiative to underscore the importance of consumer privacy protection practices. Hundreds of industry leaders have signed the declaration. Then DMA President, Jonah Gitlitz said those industry leaders are "expressing their belief that the continued success and growth of direct marketing depend largely on our ability to meet consumer expectations for the protection of personal information in the direct marketing process."[3]

In June 1996, after eight months work, the DMA issued its cyber-space principles for self regulation. These guidelines continue DMA's efforts to keep the balance between the protection of consumer privacy and the commercial interests of business. DMA's guidelines are a near match to the set of principles issued by the International Chamber of Commerce which call for companies that market on the Internet, World-Wide-Web, and On-line services to reflect the highest standards of ethical conduct, conform to on-line sponsors' policies, always disclose their identity, and offer users of interactive services the option not to receive unsolicited commercial messages.

At the 79th Direct Marketing Association conference October '96 in New Orleans, the DMA announced a major communications effort for members and consumers. The new campaign is called "Privacy Action Now!" and offers a kit giving tips for marketers dealing with consumers, lawmakers, and the media. The kit includes messages that can be used to address three major concerns: data collection and use, on-line and children. It outlines the major privacy and direct marketing issues, covers the various audiences to whom marketers may be speaking and provides the messages that the DMA is using on each subject.

We'll hope self regulation will work so the government won't feel it has to turn the Internet into a playpen to protect adults from things that might harm infants.

Now, a company called Junkbusters Corp is offering consumers a free opt-in/opt-out preference service accessible on the Internet (www. junkbusters.com). Consumers are asked to fill out a form specifying what kind of information they deem acceptable and what they don't from direct marketers using distribution such as direct mail, telemarketing, or e-mail.[4]

For cyberspace in the next century or "snail mail" today, privacy is the most important customer service issue that marketers face. I recently asked Jennifer Barrett, "Who needs a consumer privacy initiative?" Her reply:

Any business involved in:
- Maintaining transaction information on consumers
- Collecting household or individual information on consumers
- Using database marketing
- Direct marketing
- Internet activities

Here are Jennifer's recommendations for corporate privacy initiatives:

Follow laws and other legal restrictions.

Establish a privacy "Champion" and Oversight Committee.

Develop a question and issue resolution process.

Publish a corporate information practice or privacy policy.

Perform the DMA privacy audit.

Develop an opt-out or opt-in practice.

Use the DMA Mail and Telephone Preference Service.

Include language in contracts with suppliers.

Protect your data internally with secure facilities and systems.

Seed data and lists you rent or sell.

Develop employee education and awareness programs.

Establish a public relations process.

Use a privacy employee acknowledgment form.

Support and participate in trade association initiatives.

Publicize consumer benefits.

I urge all marketers using a customer database to get a copy of DMA's Fair Information Practices Manual and the Privacy Action Now! Kit. The manual was developed to provide marketers with answers to the most commonly asked questions about implementing corporate fair information policies and complying with DMA's self regulatory programs.

The manual also includes information on the Fair Information Practices Checklist. The checklist gives companies the opportunity to evaluate their compliance with the fair information principles detailed in DMA' s Guidelines for Personal Information Protection. It is an important first step in determining a company's strengths and potential areas for improvement.

The bottom line of the privacy issue is that consumers fear what they cannot understand. The application of advanced technology to information management has created a feeling of discomfort among American consumers.

This was best explained by Watts Wacker, Resident Futurist at SRI International:

> Individuals stand planted with one foot in a comfort world (the past) and the other in an anxiety-ridden world (the future). Their attitudes and behavior are becoming increasingly inconsistent and difficult to read. Consumers want more privacy, yet they realize that there are benefits to providing companies with additional data. They want more knowledge, yet they don't want to process more information. They want to know more about

others as they tune in to Hard Copy and Geraldo, yet they want their own privacy respected.

How each marketer responds to the privacy issue will play a major role in helping to strengthen customer satisfaction and preserve our right to market without overly burdensome regulations. Developing pro-active policies like those outlined in the Fair Information Practices Manual is the first step in showing that a company can be responsive to consumer privacy expectations—and to prove to our critics that self-regulation is effective.

Another step—perhaps really the first—is the establishment of controls to ensure the internal security of the company's database. After all, the information in the database is a complete profile of the company and its customers. There must be no way for outsiders to ever get their hands on this information. In the retail industry, this becomes especially important as salespeople who change jobs will want to take the data on their best customers with them.

A first copy of the Fair Information Practices Manual is free to DMA member companies. There is a $25 charge for each additional copy. Nonmembers are charged $50 for each copy ordered. To order, write to the Direct Marketing Association, Fair Information Practices Manual, 1111 19th Street NW, Suite 1100, Washington, DC 20036, or Fax James Crow in the DMA's Washington office, 202 955 0085.

Acxiom Corporation was kind enough to let us share their Corporate Privacy Policy as an example.

ACXIOM'S CORPORATE PRIVACY POLICY

Axciom Corporation supports the protection of consumers' privacy rights as a fundamental element of our business. Both from the company and the associates level, we support industry initiatives and have developed internal policies that protect the privacy of consumer information. Acxiom and its associates pledge to conduct their business according to the following principles:

* To recognize the consumers have the right to control the dissemination of information about themselves.
* To conduct our relationships with you and information providers in an ethical and professional manner.
* To respond immediately to questions about the accuracy of information we process for you.
* To provide products and services to you so that you can improve the accuracy of the information you maintain about consumers.
* To monitor privacy issues on an ongoing basis to assure that any changes in legislation or industry standards regarding privacy issues are reflected in our privacy policy and understood by our associates.
* To maintain strict data security systems that ensure specific individual information will not be made available to any unauthorized person.
* To educate our associates about the issues and laws surrounding individual rights to privacy.
* To work with recognized trade associations and organizations that support consumer privacy.
* To provide services that benefit both consumers and marketers.

Courtesy: Acxiom Corporation

CHAPTER **30**

5 Percent of the World's Population = 25 Percent of the World's Purchasing Power

The global future is now.

The United States is only 5 percent of the world population and only 25 percent of the world's purchasing power. That means that 75 to 95 percent of the total world market exists outside America's borders. We are told that Asia is a $3 trillion market, growing at the rate of $3 billion a week. There are 400 million customers in Eastern Europe and Russia, supposedly aching to buy western products. By the year 2000 there will be 11 million net new customers in Europe. In the Pacific's wealthiest countries there will be another 13 million. Add another 68 million in Thailand, Malaysia, Indonesia, and the Philippines, and 100 million more with disposable income in China. It is predicted that the Asia Pacific region will overtake the United States as the top credit card market in the "medium term."

In a recent issue, *Advertising Age* proclaims:

MULTICOUNTRY MARKETING APPROACHES: Although cultural interests continue to be defined largely by national borders, there is a clear trend towards media globalization. Helping to spread global messages/images/icons are such world news services as CNN and the BBC, as well as the Internet. This is all part of a deepening sense that the "global consumer" is becoming more of a reality and that marketing messages can—and should be—transmitted across borders.[1]

One brand expert has said, "It was more difficult to carry our brand name across the river to New Jersey than around the world."[2]

That certainly is enough of a challenge to force marketers to take the global view. Of course companies like Coca-Cola, IBM, Unilever, and the big automakers have been doing worldwide business for years. Nestlé does more of its business out of its home country than any of the multinationals. In 1993, the latest figures I could find, 98 percent of sales came from outside Switzerland. It is still a new opportunity for the distribution industry and the database marketing process in particular. The real business of global database marketing and customer management is underway and will be in full force in the new century.

In October 1996, a new International Federation of Direct Marketing Associations was organized to tighten cooperation among the many global organizations. To date, most of the retail expansion outside the United States has been provided by the catalog retailers, and some has been significant. Just a few examples make the point.

The $800 million Viking Office Products Company catalog is now in Ireland, the United Kingdom, France, Germany, Netherlands, the Benelux countries, and Australia. Next they will reach into Scandinavia, Austria, and the Czech Republic. New markets contemplated include Asia, with Japan being the most important target. In 1995, the company gained almost 44 percent in revenues and net income, with less than half the revenue coming from U.S. operations.

Viking knows about learning to understand customers. Their catalogs are produced in local languages, and local products are included where it is appropriate. In Germany, where the standard sheet of paper is larger than in the United States, Viking has paper sourced in Germany. We're told this applies to almost 98 percent of the offerings in Viking's international division.[3]

National Pen sells low-cost, disposable pens in every country in the European Union. Dell Computer reaches out to its worldwide customers from Dublin, Ireland. Quarterdeck Software sells in England, Germany, Spain, Italy, Russia, Sweden, and the Czech Republic. Both companies are building huge global databases.

After the completion of successful, year-long Japanese tests of its Horchow and Trifles catalogs, Neiman Marcus will test a 140-page version of its famous Christmas catalog sent to 100,000 Japanese buyers in

1996. Neiman's built the prospect list to start their database with Japanese language ads in upscale magazines, large circulation newspapers, mail order publications, and promotional inserts in credit card mailings. It's easy to see why Neiman's is targeting Japan: DMA reports the U.S. catalog business in Japan has grown to $750 million in sales.[4]

Lands' End has taken its catalog to Hong Kong and Singapore[5], and *Sports Illustrated* will have a stand-alone edition of its swimsuit issue in 30 countries, in February 1997.[6] The famous swimsuit edition is not a catalog, but this new global distribution is a sure sign that global marketing has arrived.

Japan seems to be welcoming American catalogers. Under a program called International Mail Order Support Services (IMOSS), qualifying catalogers get to have their books displayed at 1,300 Japanese post offices across the country. For Japanese consumers, a post office display is the mark of instant quality. Consumers feel safe about things they see there. So far the Japanese have approved only a very few catalogs. Last year it was one British and one American firm. So far, in 1996, three other American companies have made it.[7]

China is becoming a lucrative market for U.S. mail order goods, with consumers willing to pay a premium price to get them. The Chinese know American brands, and they are not interested in goods made in China. This could be a big market for upscale American brands and stores. When author Martin Baier, founder of the University of Missouri's Professionals in Direct Marketing course, lectured in Singapore, Manila, New Delhi, Hong Kong, and Bombay in 1996, CEOs and marketing executives of banks, insurance companies, utilities, real estate developers, and manufacturers turned out to learn about database marketing.[8]

There are good reasons marketers are interested in these new markets. Emerging markets' lower postal rates can reduce marketers' expenses by as much as $100 per thousand and response rates are averaging double the average response generated from developed countries in Western Europe.

It's not just U.S. companies in the direct marketing business. In Russia, high-fashion boutiques now use direct marketing for customer feedback. Luxury automobile dealers stay in touch with customers through after-sale services, offering spare parts by mail and pushing sales of second cars for family members.

Newly democratized South Africans are counteracting high crime rates by shopping by mail. While the currently affluent are fueling this growth, it is predicted that the rising purchasing power among South Africa's black consumers should offer marketers lucrative opportunities. In 1995, blacks and individuals of mixed-race represented nearly one-third of the country's affluent households, up from 16.4 percent in 1994.[9]

Direct mail programs are not the exclusive domain of catalogers. Mariott has launched a Europe-wide direct marketing campaign to sell time shares in its 288-apartment vacation complex in the United States to 14,700 potential one-week owners for an eventual gross of $190 million. They began dropping mailings in the United Kingdom in March '96 and have sent out 150,000 pieces to prospects in the United Kingdom, Germany, Spain, and France, as well as to Saudi Arabia, Kuwait, and Egypt. The worldwide Mariott chain has a million name database including 200,000 European names.[10]

Heinz has been building a consumer database in the United Kingdom for two years and now has 4.6 million households on file, one of the largest consumer databases in the United Kingdom. It has been reported that their baked bean brand has increased its UK market share from 49.1 to 53.1 percent since the company began exploiting its database. A spokesman was quoted as saying brand shares in all Heinz categories—about 360 products—"are steaming ahead—the highest shares we've ever had."

In March 1996, Heinz sent a carefully segmented mailing with versions based on consumer type, cluster groups, prior purchases, and category of purchases. The most loyal Heinz customers received the big "At Home" mailing. A different mailing targeted the "healthy eating" segment featuring the Heinz Weight Watcher line. A "Winter Warmer" piece featuring seasonal soup and pasta recipes went to heavy purchasers of particular food categories.[11]

In November 1996, Unilever mailed out seven custom magazines to its million-household database in the United Kingdom, each targeted to specific households. Data from consumer questionnaires enabled Unilever to target the magazines containing product coupons to different groups of consumers depending on whether they rated health, convenience, or value most important.

It goes in the other direction, too. City Index, a UK betting establishment, has launched a direct response print campaign in the United States to attract and build a database of American bettors. City Index Sports is taking bets on the NFL, the Dow Jones Index, and U.S. unemployment figures.[12]

List rental for consumer database marketing is still a problem in Europe and many other countries. Though the Japan Direct Marketing Association recently began to publicize more than 2,000 Japanese mailing lists, I am told many Japanese lists are not very reliable. Lists are not as clean as U.S. marketers demand, and merge/purge is costly and inefficient because Japanese characters can have seven different meanings.[13]

In some of the smallest countries, the only option is to rent all of the addresses in the country without any way of evaluating best prospects. In Sweden there are evaluation opportunities because every citizen is registered in a database—where he lives, members of his family, income, if he has a house or apartment or a country house.

The CCN Marketing Group is out to make things better. CCN serves the retail and consumer credit industry with MOSAIC, its geodemographic classification system that, like PRISM in the United States, groups consumers into clusters of identifiable categories, allowing marketers to analyze and profile their customer addresses. They are now expanding the MOSAIC service to Belgium, Italy, and South Africa, raising the number of countries where it can be used to 14. The system now classifies more than 700 million consumers worldwide. CCN's 240 clients with MOSAIC installed include banks, major media companies, retailers, cable companies, and packaged goods marketers.[14]

Catalina Marketing Corp. has taken its coupon and marketing programs to Japan, where 99 percent of large chain stores are equipped with point-of-sale scanners.

Another service provider making things easier for international clients is ICLP, the folks who help companies like Motorola, Holiday Inn Worldwide, American Express, Citibank, Virgin Atlantic, and Saudi Arabian Airlines manage their international loyalty programs. ICLP has added to its Dallas, Singapore, and Hong Kong offices an office in Dubai to service the Arab countries. Mary Carse, Marketing VP, told *DM News,* "As markets develop and become more sophisticated, the concept of customer retention becomes more important and our services are more in demand."[15]

Still another service provider, Master Card International, is making things easier for global marketers and global shoppers in Latin America. In a joint venture with Ocasa, the largest transportation company in Argentina, they have set up a "Master World" office in downtown Buenos Aires that displays a wide selection of American catalogs. Locals can receive the U.S. mail order goods through a mail box in Miami and have them delivered direct to their homes in Buenos Aires.[16]

We could go on and on with examples. The point is that the U.S. population represents only 5 percent of the world's population and 25 percent of the world's purchasing power. International mail order sales are proving the success of the pioneers. In 1995, per capita mail order sales in Germany reached $345 (compared to $328 in the U.S.), Canada $237, Switzerland $231, Japan $212, Austria $194 (latest figures 1993), and the United Kingdom $169. For the total European population of 372.7 million, per capita sales averaged $156.[17]

It's not all good news around the world. Many European economies are uneasy, and the Maastricht Treaty is under the strain of its commitment that the EC nations adopt a common currency by the year 2000, with no agreement in sight. Uncertainty is never good for business growth.

As more direct marketers reach out to world markets, the competition heats up. In countries like Germany, France, and the United Kingdom, households are now receiving 50 to 60 direct mail offerings a month. In Switzerland, it's up to 150 pieces a month, the top position in Europe, even more than the United States. Even in the hot Japanese market with 126 million affluent customers, high credit card ownership, and a favorable foreign exchange rate, too many catalogers mailing to too few lists are beginning to show diminished response. Two-thirds of the top 3,000 advertisers in the United Kingdom now have an individual responsible for direct mail. One in five report direct mail expenditures in excess of 75 percent of total advertising spending.[18]

As attractive as these markets appear, they are not easy. I have been told Germany has the highest labor costs in Europe, the highest postage cost, the most stringent recycling laws, the most restrictive privacy laws, and the tightest marketing restrictions (sales are limited to specific weeks each year). Telemarketers can call consumers only if they have been given prior permission. Cold calls are against the law. The same is true in Denmark, where a telemarketer cannot contact a customer at home or business to sell goods or services.

The New Zealand Privacy Act requires that personal information be collected directly from the individual, with the individual's authorization to collect it. The New Zealand Complaints Review Tribunal has the authority to award damages up to NZ $50,000 for interfering in the privacy of an individual.

In July 1995, the European Parliament adopted a directive to protect the rights and freedoms of individuals, including rights of privacy with respect to the processing of personal data. Some experts are predicting that China will set some tough rules, but others are quoting the old Chinese saying, "The mountains are high and the Emperor is far away." That's their way of saying, "Don't worry about the rules, China is a very big country." There are numerous regulations from Beijing, but to what extent they are policed will vary from market to market. It is certain that we will see more of these restrictions develop as database marketing continues to explode around the world.

In two years the new European Union's data protection directive will take effect. Article 25 of the directive prohibits data transfer to a country outside of Europe unless the country ensures an adequate level of protection. They may not accept ours.

Direct marketing around the world is not all direct mail. Just about every country has some form of infomercial programming. Mark Hershhorn, CEO of infomercial giant National Media, says, "We want to build a pre-eminent global marketing transactional TV programming company that can deliver a box anywhere in the world efficiently from selling direct to the customer." He envisions a future where people in Jakarta, Perth, or Helsinki can tune in their local cable station, discover the merits of Touchless Car Wax, order it locally, and have it shipped to their door. Through its Quantum International division, National Media has gone in early to Asia, Indonesia, Eastern Europe, South America, and Africa, locking up partnerships in media time, telemarketing, and fulfillment. On the European channel alone, National Media owns six and a half hours per night.[19]

Direct response TV is moving just as swiftly. The global direct response TV giant Interwood Marketing Group has recently added Latin America and Japan to its around the world distributor network, bringing them into 94 countries.[20]

In 1995, QVC's U.S. sales reached $1.6 billion, and its UK sales were 37.2 million British pounds from just 4 million British viewers. At year-end 1995, Home Order Television beat the competition into Germany. Against the wishes of German media regulators, Bavarian regulators gave H.O.T. permission to broadcast their 24-hour a day home shopping channel. The channel now reaches viewers in Germany, Switzerland, Austria, and Eastern Europe. When the EC's Frontiers Without Borders legislation opens home shopping across Europe, QVC, TV Shop Europe, and broadcast group CLT are expected to jump into the market.[21] QVC hopes to have all the legal obstacles resolved before going on the air in Germany, but they plan to begin broadcasting whether they are or not.[22]

In Switzerland, DRTV is relatively underdeveloped, as it is in Australia and New Zealand, but DRTV surged ahead 26 percent in Canada in 1995 with the lifting of government restrictions.[23] Some are saying the global window of opportunity for DRTV is closing fast, it is now time to get in or miss out.

The point of all this in a book about database marketing and customer management is that the new rules of marketing, coming at us so fast, will move these direct response TV marketers deeper and deeper into the name game. Many are collecting customer data now, but few have begun to explore serious target marketing. We can count on that to happen quickly, adding yet another group of marketers learning to create the dialog with their customers.

Our quick trip around the world would not be complete without a few thoughts about what the Web will mean to international marketers and where it will fit into the new rules of marketing. Bob Runge, Vice President, Marketing, Broad Vision, Inc., a California software company with offices in Paris, Singapore, Tokyo, and Zurich, has strong words for the global marketer:

> The future for U.S. direct marketers looking to embrace the globe lies in their ability to reach their customers over the World Wide Web. Working on the Web can be the most powerful direct marketing system. Companies can now target individuals by their e-mail address, just like aiming at their home address and mailbox. But the Web is much more efficient. Over the next couple of years, the Web will be an extremely important tool for direct marketers all over the world. In fact, within the next two decades, online will be the major selling channel in the world. This is a juggernaut in the evolution of the direct marketing industry.[24]

One could argue that those words are a little strong and that Mr. Runge may have just a bit of a biased opinion, since his company specializes in software and services specifically designed for conducting international, interactive commerce over the Web. The counterargument must be, who is in a better position to see and evaluate these opportunities? There is certainly no question—instant global communications will mean buyers and sellers will be able to build relationships in the global marketplace. We see the only force holding back the kind of growth Mr. Runge predicts to be the high telecom pricing in many parts of the world. In the United States, Internet access is virtually free. In Europe, most telecoms charge by the minute, and the charge can be steep, as much as the equivalent of more than three U.S. dollars per hour in Germany. As AT&T expands in Europe, and other telecoms tighten the competition, it is a safe bet that access prices will drop by at least half and the global playing field will level out.

The expansion of on-line services will add to the growth. In the first six months of 1996, America Online opened services in Germany, France, and the United Kingdom. AOL plans to be in Japan before the end of 1996.

This now puts AOL head-to-head with Compuserve with a strong European presence, and power-players like T-Online, the dominant, government-owned German service. This combination of global service providers is already having its effect. Thirty-five percent of Yahoo! accesses are now coming from outside the United States. In the first three months of The Limited's Express on-line store, 20 percent of the sales came from abroad.[25] Ten percent of its daily one million hits are coming from outside the United States. Since opening up access in August 1996, traffic is growing at an average of 10 percent per day.[26]

NBC has expanded is NBC.com web site to Europe and Asia, offering program schedules and show descriptions for the network's Asian and European channels. With its e-mail capability, people worldwide are talking back to NBC, creating the dialog we keep talking about. NBC Asia viewers are talking back to CNBC.[27] Down the road direct marketers and advertisers could use the website to reinforce the message the viewer has seen on Superchannel or CNBC Asia in English, with a message in the viewers' local language.[28] The planet gets smaller and smaller. The one-on-one target gets closer and closer.

It is now predicted we will see the development of web-specific direct marketing tools. These will be satellite sites; small, focused web sites whose only goal is to build customer and prospect databases. The existing home pages that are evolving into giant, corporate, on-line brochures are not working for the direct marketer who needs clear data, like cost per customer, to measure success. Dedicated satellite sites will help justify direct marketing advertising expense.[29]

Direct, in its conclusion of a discussion of applying traditional direct response strategy with new web-specific tools, sums up with these words:

> There are no experts, only leaders. There is very little history, only ongoing experimentation. There are no proven models, only evolving prototypes. But by applying strong direct response strategy with new website-specific tools, anyone can participate in shaping the future of [global] marketing.[30]

A fitting conclusion for this quick trip around the world. Regardless of the medium, there are no experts, only leaders. There is very little history, only experimentation. There are no proven models, only evolving prototypes.

It's not too late for you to participate in shaping the future of global marketing!

PART THREE

You have learned the basics of direct marketing that will help you use customer knowledge to assure your position as a successful growth company.

You have seen examples of the many ways some smart marketers are making customer management work for them, and we hope you have discovered some new ideas you can borrow to make this happen for you.

How will today's challenges and opportunities present themselves in the near future—from the year 2000 on?

Let's take a look.

CHAPTER **31**

Changing Channels of Distribution

A look ahead.

Looking ahead makes us think, again, of Tim. Where will he be in the year 2000? Will there be tools not yet imagined that will help him to know the perfect gift Jenny wants most? One visionary suggests just such a possibility.

As keynoter speaker for the opening gala dinner of the Montreux International Direct Marketing Symposium, June 1996, Nicholas Negroponte, professor, founder, and director, MIT Media Lab, got the delegates' attention by suggesting, "The human body is a valid and viable conductor of electronic data. In the future, by simply shaking hands with a new acquaintance, the data about that person, their company, and other pertinent information will be downloaded into a micro PC in the heel of your shoe."[1]

Others suggest Tim will not have to search the ponds or the marshes or the meadows, or even a retail store, to find his special gift. One estimate suggests that by the year 2010, 55 percent of American shopping will be done non-store: a combination of the Internet or on-line services, catalogs, shopping channels, interactive TV, CD-ROM, and so on.

Survey after survey reports respondents saying they plan to shop at malls less often. Some are even saying it is conceivable that, during the next five years, as many as 350 of the 1,800 regional and super regional malls in America will be shut down or converted into warehouse-style discount centers.[2]

Some of that will happen, of course. Some already is happening as market demographics have changed. We have already seen some regional malls give up their department-store heritage and convert, with great success, to off-price centers, bringing many of the big-box, power-price retailers together. That's all part of the changing channels of distribution we reviewed earlier, but that hardly suggests the end of the mall. We don't see that happening.

Seklemian/Newell works with some savvy mall clients. We can safely report the regional and super-regional malls don't have their collective heads in the sand. Some have already built strong web sites. Some have become adept database marketers, building relationships with customers that will last beyond technology. All are becoming more than just a place to shop and grab a quick meal.

It's getting harder to tell what's the biggest draw of a big, regional shopping mall—the stores or the entertainment. When mall developers began adding 20-screen movie theaters and giant food courts, they started to change what malls were all about. You no longer went there just to shop; you went to have a good time. Now, some regional centers are extending their hours to accommodate moviegoers who start coming in midmorning and keep coming until midnight. Entertainment has gone beyond music and fashion shows. Disney Stores and Warner Brothers' Stores have brought giant-screen entertainment into the store. At many mall book stores, customers can relax on comfortable couches or enjoy a cappuccino. Mall developers are open to almost anything that makes shopping fun, that gets customers into the stores and keeps them there, encouraging them to buy. The malls will remain, but they will no longer be the apparel centers of old.

We are already seeing such new, nonapparel "stores" as fitness clubs, Internet access centers, airline offices, even a service called The Great American Back Rub. Cynthia Cohen Turk, President of Marketplace 2000, a Miami consulting firm says, "Retailers now have to keep up with an entertainment standard that keeps being raised. There is no turning back now that we are producing consumers from the MTV generation and sensual stimulation is throughout our everyday lives more than it's ever been before."

Barbara Ashley, Senior Vice President, Retail Services, for leading mall developer The Taubman Company, says there's much more involved than "entertainment retailing." She calls it a process of "creating an enjoyable experience." She makes the point that doing new, exciting things that make people feel good—that make people want to come into the store—is not always just entertainment. She cites the fantasy of merchandise presentation at Ralph Lauren's Polo X2 store in Manhattan, the tasting bar at Williams-Sonoma, Biltmore Fashion Park, Phoenix, the Hollywood Freeezway ice cream store on Universal City Walk in Burbank, and the Nike Town stores that are among the top tourist attractions in every city where they are located.

Pier I Imports understands this. Part of their mission statement is to make the store fun. Marvin Girouard, President and CEO, goes even further, saying, "If Pier I is to be a fun place to shop, it must be a fun place to work." At Pier I, they back that up by making everything from memos to sales training fun.

Of course there will be shopping "malls" on-line. Time Warner has completely redesigned its entry and is expected to unveil, before this book will publish, Dreamshop, Internet—an interactive TV shopping service with 18 merchants including Spiegel, Eddie Bauer, and Williams-Sonoma. IBM has announced World Avenue, an Internet shopping mall to feature more than 30 retailers, said to include The Limited's Express, Omaha Steaks, Eyemate, and Canadian department store Hudson's Bay Company. Even Microsoft will join the fray with its acquisition of eShop, whose clients include 1-800 FLOWERS and Spiegel.[3]

In the Spring of 1996, 160 CEOs and corporate presidents gathered for IQ 1996, a national retailing/manufacturing conference devoted to exploring the benefits of new technologies. Panelists included Bill Fields, President of the Wal-Mart Stores division, Bob Rockey, President of Levi Strauss North America, and Microsoft's Bill Gates. Fields expressed confidence that people will still go into stores, noting that traditional merchants already compete with $65 billion in annual sales direct to the home. "All consumers really want is to get what they want when they want it in the most cost-effective, convenient way," he said, "That's all that's important to them."[4]

"That's one of the reasons Wal-Mart is exploring the Internet as a way to reach customers," Fields said. Then he joked about the possible effects of the Internet on traditional, in-store retailing. "We are very interested in the Internet because one day consumers may turn around and find they don't need to come to our stores anymore, and we don't want to be sitting around on our hands with nothing to do."[5]

Most panelists agreed that the Internet would not replace personal shopping. They concluded that that it will complement traditional shopping for most consumers and perhaps replace some shopping trips for younger, highly computer literate shoppers short of time.

Bill Gates made the point that even if those potential customers didn't end up buying on-line, they will use the information they found on the Net to make a more savvy buying decision. "Consumers can find a wealth of information on the Net to help them make more educated purchases," Gates said. "A customer who is comfortable using a computer can tap into almost anything. The amount of information they will have to choose from will soon be overwhelming."[6]

Bob Rockey agreed that closing the sale on-line may not be the wisest use of the Internet for retailers and apparel makers. "One of the missed opportunities with the Internet," he said, "is the opportunity to dialog with customers. That dialog may be more important than the actual sale."[7] In other words, many of those selling on the Internet today are as ignorant of retail as most retailers are ignorant of the Internet. They have no conception of the importance of the sales person.

While it has yet to reach critical mass, new media will grow to be more and more important; however it will not spell the end of retail stores or catalogs or plain old television. The man who signs the checks for the number one advertiser on network TV, the number one advertiser in syndicated TV, and the number one advertiser in cable TV should know. Robert Wehling, Senior Vice President responsible for Procter & Gamble Company's $2.69 billion in U.S. marketing expenditures, says, "I cannot imagine a time when more than two-thirds of the population—I have trouble seeing even half—won't be interested in collectively watching regular quality TV programming like today's 'ER' . . . something that people can talk about around the coffee machine the next morning."[8]

Research supports Mr. Wehling's belief. Americans each spent an average of 1,575 hours watching TV last year, about 4 1/3 hours a day, according to the investment bank Veronis, Suhler & Associates, Inc. TV watching is expected to grow to 4 1/2 hours a day by the year 2000.[9]

Spiegel rolled out its Spring/Summer '96 catalog on CD-ROM, but said at the time, that they are not totally convinced the technology is the wave of the future. Just 18 percent of their customers have multimedia home computers, compared with a national average of 12 percent. More than 100 million U.S. households do not have home computers.[10]

So we can look for a lot of excitement on the Web and with interactive television. By the time this book is published, the software will be in place to assure secure credit card transactions on the information superhighway. The "Big Box" retailers will build more stores, and new, "Big Box" concepts will emerge. Improved technology will continue to open more global markets to American marketers. As trade barriers come down and new markets open, many U.S. marketers are already enjoying faster growth in foreign markets than they are earning at home.

But retail stores will change to add more and more of the excitement that will stimulate customers' senses or emotions. As long as retailers like Recreational Equipment Inc. build stores like REI's newest 98,683 square-foot flagship in Seattle—with the 65-foot REI Pinnacle, billed as the world's tallest freestanding indoor climbing structure, a 470-foot outdoor mountain bike trail to test mountain bikes, a campsite and stream to test camp stoves and water filters, and a rain room to test Gore-Tex rain gear—there will still be stores.

We don't believe many consumers will find they don't need to go to their local Wal-Mart anymore. We don't think Bill Fields needs to worry about having to sit on his hands with nothing to do.

Included in the changes of distribution channels will be changes for catalog marketers, the original direct marketers. As Harris Gordon said, they will need to understand the dynamics of engaging customers in interactive dialog. That's the big message of the new century. To put this in perspective it is worthwhile to go back to 1990 when the publication "A Special Report on the Impact of Technology on Direct Marketing in the 1990's" was prepared by Deloitte & Touche, as commissioned by the Direct Marketing Association, Inc. The introduction rings true today:

> Forecasting the future, particularly where technology is involved, is a difficult task. While technology has always had a great impact on the direct marketing field, its impact has never been greater, nor the rate of technology-driven change ever faster, than it is today. One does not need a crystal ball to see that the **future of the direct marketing field and the survival** of many of its current players, will be dictated by the use, or the ignorance, of technology.
>
> Change is coming in many ways. The field of direct marketing itself will become fundamentally different as new, powerful entrants, bolstered by the innovative application of technology, change the nature and scope of direct marketing. Large consumer products companies are gathering customer information and targeting their marketing efforts directly to their customers. In addition, these companies are likely to form partnerships with retailers, their main channel of distribution, to improve the effectiveness of retail promotions. This changing relationship between retailers and their suppliers will likely have considerable impact on direct marketing by bringing new players to the field—players large enough to **change some of the rules of the game.**

The innovative use of technology has changed the rules. The Deloitte & Touche study made the point that the manner in which direct marketers approach and implement the array of available technologies will determine who will be tomorrow's direct marketers. No question, the report was right on target for 1990. Now the picture has changed a bit.

The 1990 report said the key *finding* of the study was that "the direct marketing industry has not widely absorbed important technologies." One of the primary factors then holding some direct marketers back from full-scale adoption of new technologies was the apparent lack of trained technology professionals, particularly in data management, with the requisite understanding of the direct marketing business (they could have included marketers in every business). The report also saw a perception among many direct marketing managers that there was insufficient payback on many of the technologies available then. All of this has changed.

The report's second significant finding was that if there is a common thread tying together the important technologies, it is the concept of a database. To quote the 1990 report, "The database plays a vital role in direct marketing, from customer acquisition through the creative process, then the customer transaction and fulfillment, and finally analysis. Smart marketers will take note of how databases are applied in each of the crucial technologies discussed, and prepare themselves to exploit their own databases in the future." As we have seen, many marketers heard the call.

The third finding of the study has proven just as true. The study foresaw technology bringing many large, powerful, new entrants to the direct marketing field, suggesting that the nature of direct marketing itself would change radically as consumer products companies and retailers gained expertise in direct marketing methods. "Both of these players," the report suggested, "will bring significant marketing experience and well developed technology infrastructures to the field. They will change the way in which both consumers and direct marketers do their business."

All of this fits with what we have seen in the changing channels of distribution and the blurring of the lines between the original direct marketers and others in the distribution industry.

Such blurring of the lines is occurring even within the direct-to-consumer marketer group. By-mail marketers now accept the TV infomercial buyer as a live prospect. In the early 90s, when high postage and paper costs caused some catalogers to close down, and the pool of catalog-buyer name lists shrank, the by-mail folks began to test TV-buyer names. Now, TV shoppers have gradually been integrated with by-mail buyers. With the cross-renting of names, there are now few distinguishing characteristics. Some infomercial companies are now producing mailers, and some catalogers are using the phrase, "As Seen on TV."

And now the Internet is said to be the most prolific driver of new name lists for high tech catalogers. These new lists include Internet specific names, Internet-sold buyers, and e-mail-sold buyers. Mailers can even rent 500,000 names of computer owners who buy by mail from Victoria's Secret. The list owners expect catalogers to use it to reach mail-order-responsive women who might not show up on male-dominated high tech lists.

At the Montreux Symposium, Professor Philip Kotler observed: "Electronic media is just another part of the integrated marketing mix, blurring the lines between direct marketing, integrated direct marketing, database marketing, and now, Internet marketing." Here are his predictions on the Internet and its effects:

1. Start-up companies now have a greater chance of finding a critical mass of customers faster because of the worldwide reach.
2. There will be a reduction in the number of retailers, leading to fewer jobs for the unskilled.
3. The Web will reinforce the spread of the English language.
4. Companies will find it faster and easier to test new products.
5. New product diffusion will take place more rapidly.[11]

These changes extend beyond the blurring of the lines between by-mail shoppers and TV shoppers and the Internet. TV infomercials have become powerful ads, driving consumers into retail stores. When Marvin Traub was CEO of Bloomingdales, he saw surges in the sales of electric juicers in his housewares department and discovered that these surges—as much as 10 times normal sales—were tied to juicer infomercials appearing at the time on television. The experience impressed Mr. Traub so much he went on to found a company to produce a Thai cooking set and wok with its own infomercial.

The point is that even the simple infomercial has caused further blurring of the lines between retail and direct response, to the point that it is now common to see special "As Seen on TV" displays in retail stores. Perhaps Don Libey was right—we may yet see "Directail."

So these changes in channels of distribution continue. Many of yesterday's differences are nothing but history. Moving with these changes, in many cases forcing the changes, we see customers now empowered by technology and information controlling the buying interaction. Retail stores and retail catalogs will remain, but increasingly the marketer will need to understand the dynamics of how to engage the customer in interactive dialog. The bar has been raised. Today's customer expects more: more service, more customized products, a more interesting and entertaining shopping experience, and above all, more understanding, care, and respect. The new customer will demand to be involved, to be seen, and to be heard.

CHAPTER **32**

Changing Perceptions of Value

A look ahead.

The changing perception of value we discussed in Chapter 3 will continue and in fact will become an even more significant element for marketers learning to sell to the new customer.

Don't count on your next handshake to download enough customer history into the heel of your shoe to build a relationship. It will still be the value each company adds to customer services that will make the difference, and that will have to be value as perceived by the customer.

The important change is not the technology. It is the fact that customers will be empowered by the technology. As Bill Gates said, customers have more access to information than ever before. They will soon learn how to use this information to begin to control the buying-selling experience. They will use this power to secure value as they perceive it.

This was verified by a study on electronic marketing done by A.T. Kearney, Boston, for the Direct Marketing Association. Presenting highlights of the study at the Direct Marketing Association's 31st Spring Conference, Harris Gordon, Vice President of A.T. Kearney, said, "The rules have changed. Marketers no longer drive the communication with customers. The customer now has the power. Marketers need to understand the dynamics of how to engage customers in interactive dialog."[1]

Or, as Martha Rogers explains it, "We've put the rifle in the hands of the deer."

The rules indeed have changed. This is the message of *The New Rules of Marketing*. It is more than technology. It is a whole new paradigm of understanding the customer and the customer's perception of value. The business of creating a dialog with customers cannot be overstated.

"Companies will have to change key aspects of customer service," Gordon said. The study showed 23.5 percent of on-line customers expect a same-day response from businesses that they e-mail. Gordon used that fact to make the point that the on-line culture promotes instant gratification, and that raises the service bar not only for those on-line but for all marketers.

Companies will have to know what their customers want and will have to understand *the customer's* perception of value. They will now have to zero in on the customers who want what they can best provide. Then they will have to keep up with changing customer interests and changing perceptions of value to continue to offer the wanted goods. This is using one-to-one relationship marketing to become the leader in your industry. We have been married to the concept that advertising produced awareness that led to interest that became desire and finally action to buy the product. The new rules tell us that companies with a true customer focus must start with the knowledge of what the customer considers to be "value" and show the customer that they understand.

This will lead to smaller "shares of market" and much larger "shares of customer." Remember the dictum: It is much more profitable to have 100% of 10% of the market than to have 10% of 100% of the market. The numbers are the same, but the costs are far different.

In Chapter 3 we talked about the customer's changing perception of value, the reemergence of the good old American value system, and people coming to grips with what's really important in their lives. Authors Al Reis and Jack Trout have chronicled some of the basic reasons why marketing programs have succeeded or failed in the competitive 90s.[2] One of their 22 laws is *The Law of Perception*. Briefly stated, the law declares that marketing is not a battle of products and services; it is a battle of perceptions. In the long term the best products do not always win. In fact, the law says, there are no best products. The only reality is the perception in the minds of potential customers. Marketing programs, the authors tell us, must focus on these perceptions, which may be totally opposite to the logical way to market a product. Minds of customers are very difficult to change— their own perceptions are always right.

The bar has been raised for customers' perceptions of quality and service, but more than that, the new customer wants to be involved, to belong, to be heard, and that means developing comfortable relationships. There is a longing for high-touch to balance the anxiety of all the new high-tech.

I read recently that Hugh McColl, Chairman of Nation's Bank, admitted to *The Wall Street Journal* that he is scared of what technology might do to his business.[3] I would suggest that bank executives worry less about technology and more about customers and customer relationships.

Last month when I came to that check reorder form in the middle of my check book, I took it on my next trip to the bank and handed it to a teller with my deposit. I was told the local branch couldn't process the reorder; I would have to mail it in to the head office. After the head office sent the new checks to my branch . . . and after the branch lost them . . . and after I raised a big enough fuss to get my branch to reorder them . . . and after that reorder came through as my wife's checks instead of mine . . . I went in to insist that *someone* at my local branch get this thing right. The branch manager told me no one there could help me: I would have to use the phone on the wall and go through the digital response procedure to correct the error. I went to the phone on the wall. I used the digital response procedure. And I closed the account I have had at that bank for 25 years.

Did technology cause this service problem? One could make the case that technology was the culprit because it changed the *official procedure* for reordering checks. The fact is that the real problem develops from the fact that customer focus is not a core element of this bank's business plan.

> The globalization of commercial communications does not mean reaching customers a billion at a time. It may seem like a paradox, but a global communication gives us the chance to speak individually to each and every customer.

What's the point of quoting Mr. Esrey again?

The customer now demands to be treated as an individual. The consumer has lost faith in institutions. The faith Americans once had in their corporations to provide good jobs and good products has been ripped apart by the downsizing revolution. Fear of urban disorder, school systems that continue to decline, and the breakup of the family increase social insecurity. People have turned away from the nonstop consumption and ego gratification of the 80s and shifted their focus to the security provided by emotional and financial stability, a conscious, considered effort to make everyday life more manageable and secure. If that means less lavish lifestyles, most consumers are saying "So be it." Good, simple food, easy-fit clothes, and family, family, family, all affect the customer's perception of value.

Americans moving out of the big cities is a sign of these new value perceptions. The U.S. Census Bureau reports a startling reversal in trends. Between 1990 and 1994, 74 percent of America's nonmetropolitan areas grew, reversing what had seemed an irreversible trend in the 80s when 55 percent of them lost population.

In the past four years, employment grew faster in rural areas than in urban ones, and unemployment dropped more steeply. One factor for this resurgence of smaller towns is "urban refugees." Significant numbers of people are finding their way to these towns from cities and suburbs, reflecting social insecurity. The U.S. Agriculture Department estimates that 56 percent of nonmetro growth in this decade is attributable to newcomers moving in. A recent newspaper article summed this up:

> All the urban fears of the 1990s are coinciding with a renewed nostalgia for the face-to-face-communications of small-town life. Asked by pollsters whether they would prefer to live in a small town, suburb or city, Americans of all backgrounds rather consistently chose the small town over the city by roughly 2 to 1.[4]

In the future, consumers will demand value not only in products and services but in quality of life. Whether it is corporate commitment, environmental responsibility, elimination of stress, or the quality of the dialog and relationship, the customer will be choosing business partners by new standards.

Elimination of stress will be one of the most important standards. *The Yankelovich Monitor®* Hour makes the point that stress is no longer confined to bad circumstances or negative events. The list of "positive" stress triggers grows every day.

> Stress is everywhere consumers look, live, work, and breathe. Playing with your kids, going to the mall, meeting friends for dinner . . . these are all good things. Add them all up in one day or several hours, however, and they translate to stress.[5]

The advice to marketers from Yankelovich: "Don't just make it 'faster' or 'easier' when consumers have to detour out of their lifestyles to use your products—don't make them detour at all!"

This goes a long way in explaining why speaking individually to each and every customer and understanding the dynamics of how to engage customers in interactive dialog will be such important elements of the new rules of marketing.

CHAPTER **33**

Changing Generations
A look ahead.

What will changing generations mean by the year 2000? We will still be marketing to people, and their differences will continue to be important. As we have said many times, it will no longer work to market to the "averages." We will have to learn to market to the "differences." Age, income, expectations, perceptions, and peer groups will still affect how people spend their money.

The GI Generation, average age 83, will not get much attention from product marketers. The Silent Generation, whose youngest members will turn 58 as the century starts, will still have spending power and for many, good health. The travel and entertainment industries will still love them. One in four seniors still works, and many more have part-time jobs. Though we think of senior consumers as brand loyal, research has shown they are as likely if not more so to try or switch to a competitive product or service if given the proper motivation. One challenge these two groups face is mastering new technologies that go far beyond the skills they learned years ago.

By 2010, the Boomers will have the clout to elect a 72-year-old president from their group, but, having invented youth, they probably won't want to. The Boomers will continue to look for a more forgiving fit in their blue jeans, while they become the ultimate prize for Detroit, Stuttgart, and Tokyo. As *Advertising Age* notes:

> As boomers age gracefully, car makers are offering vehicles with high-intensity headlights, larger digits on speedometers, and easier car entrances. But don't call buyers hitting 50 old fogies quite yet. As one Toyota executive put it, "The boomers will reinvent what we call middle age. They were always young. They invented youth. Fun is part of this generation's psyche—even as they hit 50 they're snapping up advance offers for the Plymouth Prowler and BMW Z3 as their children leave the roost for college or new jobs."[1]

The Boomer group may just prove to be a large enough audience for the NBA, the NFL, and the National and American Leagues to start Senior Leagues for basketball, football, and baseball. Look for the PGA to develop an Alumni Tour for pros too old for the current Seniors. Perhaps each pro will have to shoot his age to qualify.

Marketers will continue to sharpen their message and their products for the tech-babies of the 13th Generation. But this will require a balancing act. Studies show that members of this generation are the most enthusiastic about technology and also the most skeptical of technology. Traditional media may or may not win them back.

They will be the Web buyers, and as long as they continue to fill the lines at movie theaters and restaurants and gather up the latest in clothing and TVs and stereos and computers, marketers will be in the chase.

The Millennial generation, the even more realistic group we called harder to sell, the group that tells us they don't think advertising is generally truthful, will be a strong force making the new-century marketer learn the dynamics of engaging customers in interactive dialog.

More than a third of teenagers say they never read a newspaper.[2] In the first month of the new Fall '96 television season, ratings for the children's shows dropped precipitously from 7 percent at ABC to a frightening 61 percent at CBS. That set media pundits to question whether CBS, like NBC before it, will abandon children's programming altogether.[3]

Here's the way one trade paper describes these young generations:

> Kids today play video games and park in front of computers to noodle with CD ROMs or explore the Internet. The on-line market, in particular, is emerging as a serious contender for kids' leisure time. Jupiter Communications, a New York research and consulting firm specializing in on-line advertising, estimates there will be 4 million on-line users under age 18 by year's end and 15 million by the year 2000.[4]

The new media, particularly the Internet, are at the heart of a new youth culture and a new generation who, in profound and fundamental ways, learn, work, play, communicate, shop, and create communities very differently from their parents. There is no issue more important to marketers than understanding this new generation.

The oldest members of this generation are 29 and pioneering the new media. The youngest are 3 and taking the mouse out of their parent's hands to manipulate it through colorful CD ROM programs. They don't view the new technology as new technology at all. Unlike their baby boomer parents, they have no fear.

There are more than 7 million North American children under the age of 18 on the Internet. Internationally this is doubling every six months.

Over 90 percent of students at public universities and community colleges have the potential to access the Internet. Unlike the baby boomers who witnessed the technological revolution, this generation has no awe of the new technology.

They have no fear. They have grown up with computers and treat them like any other household appliance. To this generation it takes no more expertise to go on-line or install software than it does to open a box of crayons or write in a notebook.[5]

The great opportunity lies in understanding all these new consumers as individuals, to create honest, open relationships with them, and to manage customers, not just products. It may just be we *will* be able to communicate with them if we use their media wisely.

CHAPTER 34

Still Looking for Meaningful Relationships

A look ahead.

Everything we have seen so far leads to the meaningful relationships predicted in Chapter 5. Everything we saw happening in the late 90s magnifies as we look ahead.

In 1996, a *Target Marketing* cover story stated that "Consumers are moving from passive status to involved participants." The A.T. Kearney study for the Direct Marketing Association confirmed that when they said, "The rules have changed. Marketers no longer drive the communication with customers. The customers now have the power. Marketers need to understand the dynamics of how to engage customers in interactive dialog."

That means customers, in the new century, will all be sending the message, "I'm looking for a meaningful relationship." This requires far more than good, or even great, quality products and services. Even the famous Nordstrom reputation for service will not be enough. What was yesterday's great competitive weapon quickly becomes state-of-the-art and all too commonplace. Products and services and retail stores must fill the needs of *individual* customers. Don Peppers and Martha Rogers have suggested that we will see a new marketing executive called the "customer manager," each one being responsible for a specific segment of the customer file.

Lester Wunderman, founder and Chairman of Wunderman Cato Johnson, speaking at the Direct Marketing Association's fall '96 conference, made the same point:

> Corporations will manage customers and how they behave rather than products and what they represent. The brand manager will be replaced by the customer manager, who will be responsible for satisfying consumers' needs. A "share of loyal customers" and a consumer-centered strategy will build profits better than old-fashioned concepts such as "share of voice," "share of mind," and "share of market."[1]

I agree. I suspect we will see something like what used to happen 20 years ago in the big department stores, when fashion buyers would go into market looking for special outfits for individual customers. The big difference will be that the merchandise fulfillment to satisfy the customer relationship will, in many cases, be performed electronically. One aspect of satisfying customers' needs is to never be out of stock of a wanted item. Wal-Mart Stores, Inc. and Warner-Lambert Company have developed an electronic partnership exchanging information formerly guarded closely by both groups. The pilot project, known as the Collaborative Forecasting and Replenishment Initiative, allows the two firms to jointly develop sales forecasts that shorten product cycles, slash inventory costs, and assure customers in-stock availability of most wanted goods. Wal-Mart plans to expand this partnership program to many of its vendors.[2]

Advances in communication capabilities will make it even easier for marketers to sustain "personal" relationships. On-demand technology now allows mass mail customization by using computers, flexible printing techniques, and sophisticated design to narrowly target mailings to a market of one.

What makes that possible are computerized printers that can merge a database of images, graphics, and text with a customer database of names, addresses, and profile information. The printers can then be given a set of very specific instructions. For example, send person A from geographic area B who bought item C this type of brochure and ship person D from geographic area E who bought item F this one. The possibilities are limited only by one's imagination, according to Jeff Hayes, Director of Cap Ventures, which specializes in print-on-demand. "For example," he said, "a 1,000-piece mailing could have as many as 1,000 variations in image, text, and color."[3]

And now, for $49.95, a marketer can buy NetMailer software from Alpha Software, Burlington, Massachusetts, and apply individual mail-merge capabilities from his or her database to the Internet. The program can customize e-mail with multiple custom elements including name, address, salutation, offer, contacts, and other information particular to the recipient and can handle mailings of a few dozen up to 500,000 or more.

The significance of this, of course, is that personalization further enhances the one-to-one communication that is the key to relationship building. With 25 million businesspeople and more than 15 million consumers with e-mail addresses, the marketer can keep up a dialog with many customers in a very cost-efficient way. To understand the potential, realize that 776 billion e-mail messages crisscrossed the globe in 1995, and that number is expected to hit 1 trillion in 1996.[4]

And it's not all business. I read recently that people are now e-mailing Mother for advice, such as what they should serve on a first date.

In tests performed by Alpha Software, NetMailer was able to send 2,000 personalized messages per hour on a PC linked to an ISDN line. A more advanced Windows NT server-based edition will handle e-mailings of 1 million or more and will be capable of sending 50,000 to 100,000 personalized messages per hour via T1 line.[5]

Meanwhile, the U.S. Postal Service is developing a series of services to mirror those of first-class mail. The first calls for a time and date stamp to represent the electronic postmark. Other services will include return receipt, certified, registered, verification of sender, and recipient archiving services. They are also designing a certificate of authority for individuals to use to prove who they are when sending e-mail or other electronic documents through the Internet and other networks.[6]

The critical thing is not the available tools of communication. They are, after all, only tools. They will make it easier to maintain the relationship, but the marketer must, first, learn enough about each customer to understand the customized products and services that will provide individual solutions. That will add convenience for the customer. One of the new rules of marketing is to sell solutions, not just products. It will be up to the successful marketer to take all of the available information and intelligence and use it to identify specific needs that can be addressed, remembering that customers will be buying the experience as well as the product. Remember the advise of Don Peppers and Martha Rogers—"establishing relationship quality" will build "a barrier of inconvenience"—a reason for a customer never to want to deal with your competitor again.

One last, entertaining word about maintaining relationships through customer experience. We used to say that a customer having a bad experience with a product or a store will tell 17 people. That number escalates exponentially with the Internet. I received this in my e-mail from Jean-Claude Larreche, Alfred H. Heineken Professor of Marketing, Instead, France, who said, "The enclosed message I am forwarding from Charles Kossman is a great real-life example of customer relationship breakdown and concept of 'justice' in action."

From: Charles Kossman,
Date: 7/8/96 05:09 PM
RE: Cookie Recipe

This message is sent to you with the hope you will forward it to EVERYONE you have ever seen the e-mail address of. In the spirit of the originator, please feel free to post it anywhere and everywhere.

My daughter and I had just finished a salad at a café of a well-known department store and decided to have a small dessert. Because our family are such cookie lovers, we decided to try the "special Chocolate Chip Cookie." It was so excellent, that I asked our waitress if she would give me the recipe and she said, with a small frown, "I'm afraid not." "Well," I said, "will you let me buy the recipe?" With a cute smile, she said, "Yes." I asked how much, and she responded, "Two-fifty." I said, with approval, "Just add it to my tab."

Thirty days later, I received my VISA statement from the cafe, and it was $285.00. I looked again and I remembered I had only spent $9.95 for two salads and about $20.00 for a scarf. As I glanced at the bottom of the statement it said, "Cookie Recipe—$250.00." Boy was I upset !!

I called the store's accounting department and told them the waitress said it was "two-fifty," and I did not realize she meant $250.00 for a cookie recipe. I asked them to take back the recipe and reduce my bill, and they said they were sorry, but because all the recipes were this expensive so not just everyone could duplicate any of our bakery recipes . . . the bill would have to stand. I waited, thinking of how I could get even or even try to get any of my money back. I just said, "Okay, you folks got my $250.00 and now I'm going to have $250.00 worth of fun." I told her that I was going to see to it that every cookie lover will have a $250.00 cookie recipe for nothing. She replied, "I wish you wouldn't do this." I said, "I'm sorry, but this is the only way I feel I could get even, and I will." So, here it is, and please pass it to someone else or run a few copies . . . I paid for it; now you can have it for free. (The recipe can be halved.)

2 cups butter
4 cups flour
2 tsp. baking soda

2 cups sugar
5 cups oatmeal (blended)
24 oz. chocolate chips
2 cups brown sugar
1 tsp. salt
1 8oz. Hershey Bar (grated)
4 eggs
2 tsp. baking powder
3 cups chopped nuts (your choice)
2 tsp. vanilla

Measure oatmeal and blend in a blender to a fine powder. Cream the butter and both sugars. Add eggs and vanilla; mix together with flour, oatmeal, salt, baking powder, and soda. Add chocolate chips, Hershey Bar, and nuts. Roll into balls and place two inches apart on a cookie sheet. Bake for 10 minutes at 375 degrees. Makes 112 cookies.

Have fun!! This is not a joke—it is a true story. Please pass it along to everyone you know.

Mr. Kossman, I hope this reaches millions.

Customers do indeed now have the power. In spite of the fact that I have heard the store maintain that this correspondence never occurred, won't it be great if some customer, some day, is so pleased by the relationship a company has established that she or he will spread the word at the rate of 1 million or more e-mail notices per hour from a PC?

CHAPTER 35

Will the Three Magic Words Still Have Magic?

A look ahead.

In Chapter 10 we said that recency, frequency, and monetary were the three magic words for the database marketer because the real power of segmentation starts with customers' purchase behavior. The recency, frequency, and monetary value of customers are the simplest measures of customer value and the easiest to use for list selection. They are the most used today, but they are still only the most basic of tools. They don't allow for consideration of customers' age, sex, or other demographics, and they fail to take into account product interests.

The next step in sophistication is modeling, where the marketer adds to the purchase behavior history geographic, demographic, and psychographic customer data to create a statistics-based model to predict propensity to buy. There are those who are already suggesting that RFM should be relegated to history's dustbin because regression models, neural networks, genetic algorithms, and the various tree analysis processes are far superior.

Without going into the kind of detail that would surpass this writer's understanding of these processes, the regression model scores customers on a combination of variables and ranks them in deciles. It is an excellent technique for determining whom to promote, but because each decile contains customers with multiple characteristics, regression does not give the marketer the important clues on how to personalize the promotional message to the interests of each individual customer. To develop the meaningful customer relationships required for the new rules of marketing, communications must relate to personal interests.

Tree analysis, like CHAID and CART, create homogeneous groups with each scored decile producing customers with identical characteristics. This specific knowledge of age or hobby interests or marital or parental status or product interest allows the creative team to target the selling message to known personal interests.

Neural networks build predictive models by testing and "learning" cause and effect. They give the marketer answers but do not show the modeler how or why the model developed its predictions.

Moving beyond RFM to predictive modeling is no longer a question of when. It is happening now, but it is still in the mini-mass marketing stage of segmenting large groups of customers. The future will require even more accurate models that define the most important message for each person in the database and the timing of that message, not just for response, but for maximum customer satisfaction.

This means more than statistics-based models. It will require an intense focus on the customer, supreme respect for the customer, and a great deal of listening to the customer.

The Milliken Company started listening to customers in 1985, asking if it was doing the right things and asking how it was doing. The replies were surprising and could be misunderstood based on just a snapshot of one year's performance. Milliken now reports it has enough historical data to discern six clear trends:

1. The things that matter to the customer are not always what the company expected.
2. Customers are becoming more demanding over the years.
3. The competition is not standing still, and that means extra effort is needed to maintain the performance gap.
4. It does not matter how good you are; it is how good your customer thinks you are that matters.
5. If you improve something be sure to communicate this to your customer, otherwise he will think you are still doing things as you used to.
6. Price is never the most important factor for customers.[1]

Perhaps the best suggestion came from Kay Partney Lautman, a 34-year veteran in the nonprofit fundraising industry who was recently honored with the 1996 Fundraising Achievement Award from the Direct Marketing Association. In an interview with Cathy Asato, associate editor of *DM News,* she was asked to name the biggest challenge today. Her reply gets to the heart of the matter and should be included in the new rules of marketing.

> In some ways we need to go back to the old way of treating people when they were on 3-by-5 cards—they became real people and you had a certain respect for them. Now that everything is computerized and on printouts, I don't think they are thought of as people, but as segments. I think that's a major challenge—to accept all the good things that computers and technology bring us but remember to treat people as people. That means mailing a little less to them.[2]

There will still be some easy magic to recency, frequency, and monetary. Marketers who use their databases for promotion will still have success with the RFM formula. The marketer who really buys into the concept of building relationships with customers will treat them as real people and show them respect. RFM, regression modeling, neural networks, genetic algorithms, and even CHAID and CART are only tools. They will make it easier to maintain the relationship, but the marketer must first learn enough about each customer to understand the customized products and services that will deliver individual solutions and bring individual satisfaction. A new rule of marketing is to sell solutions, not just products.

CHAPTER 36

From Frequency and Reach to Relevance

A look ahead.

Marketing communication is locked in the teeth of a hurricane. Change is blowing hard and fast all around. New media are sprouting like flowers in a desert seeing its first rain for a decade. All of this has major implications for brands and their agencies as they face ever increasing competition for the attention of the consumer.[1]

With change occurring everywhere, the new consumer will force media to be more accountable. When we discussed this earlier, we said all advertisers will be demanding results. They will demand a measurable return on their advertising investment. For years the direct marketers have been able to measure results, but mass media advertisers have not. In the new century, all marketers will be looking for data-driven, provable results. This was stated even more forcefully recently by Mike Becker, Chief Creative Officer at Wunderman Cato Johnson:

In five short years, or 1,328 days, I predict that 90 percent of print and 75 percent of all broadcast will be measurable and accountable. The tide will change. Clients will change.

Agencies will change and, therefore, the advertising people in these agencies will have to change. It won't be how loud and how often is your message, but rather how personal and how relevant is your message. The new, wired world is coming at a great velocity. There's a core convergence of computers, kiosks, on-line services and videos. The need for personalization in advertising and the new electronic capabilities will require a new generation of advertising people. Ad people will have to emerge from caterpillars to soaring, accurate, responsive butterflies. The question for tomorrow is how personal can we be without intruding? With more information-driven advertising, there will be less time for selling. The new advertising superstars will require the ability to walk the bridge to the consumer.[2]

When I talk to advertising agency executives about this new challenge, they tell me it will be especially difficult because so few of their creatives have been trained in direct response database marketing. To the creatives, database marketing advertising is less than exciting. Letters and postcards don't enhance their portfolios. Up to now, there has been a real question whether or not there is any place for traditional "creative" in this one-to-one marketing. Some have wondered if traditional advertising agencies should even get involved. As Mike Becker suggests, the new rules of marketing will change all of that thinking.

As I have tried to get advertising agency folks to change their thinking, I have often quoted Gary Wolson, Executive Vice President and Chief Creative Officer, Ross Roy Communications. He encouraged advertising agencies not to fear these changes, but to see them as opportunities:

> In the early days of TV, commercial producers thought that there was no room for creativity, that a commercial should just be someone from the program praising the virtues of a refrigerator.
>
> You can have all the technical knowledge in the world, but without a creative idea behind it, you don't have a chance of moving the client's product.
>
> Consumers must be rewarded for spending their time reviewing our messages.
>
> We, as professionals, need to realize that the textbook definition of advertising is being redefined and, therefore, we must accept the ways in which new technologies will fit into the new descriptions of advertising and marketing.
>
> Creative (interactive) communications build relationships between customers and advertisers by facilitating *dialogs* between them. The information customers provide in the dialogs can be used to create databases that enable advertisers to follow up with more personalized communications. It is all about getting closer to the customer. By embracing this media, agencies can learn more about what to say and how to say it to individual customers.

> It all comes back to creativity—to the big idea. Agencies should not
> lose sight of the fact that creativity will continue to be paramount, just as it
> has been in more traditional forms of media.
> Be innovative or be gone . . . be creative or be gone.

That last proclamation is, indeed, one of the new rules of marketing. You can have all the technology in the world, but without a creative idea behind it, you don't have a chance of moving product.

The second new rule of marketing comes from Gary Wolson's reminder that creative communications can build relationships by facilitating dialogs. Only by creating dialogs can advertisers gain the knowledge to be able to follow up with the kind of personalized communications that will be required.

It is all about getting closer to the customer. While a big piece of that responsibility starts with the agencies and other creatives, it will be up to the media to develop their relationships with listeners, viewers and readers to make these personalized messages welcome.

As media build customer databases, they will have to learn to handle them with care for their own benefit and the benefit of their advertisers.

Shelley Wagner, Marketing Director, KABC Talk Radio, Los Angeles, knows this. He says, "Our listener database is extremely pure. These are people who listen to *this* radio station. *We only want our members to hear from us when we have something of great value, and only with their pre-qualified approval.* We take care of these people—they're offering information about their lives and lifestyles that generally we want to keep private. Names aren't sold. *We also pick and choose the clients we do mailings for.*"[3]

That kind of protection of the customer is another new rule of marketing, and one media must learn to heed.

We can't look ahead at advertising media without a word about e-mail and the Internet. Direct marketers have built their business by renting names of direct mail buyers for new customer acquisition. That suggests that the first question is whether or not marketers will now have the opportunity to rent names and electronic addresses of e-mail users, on-line subscribers, and Web surfers. In October 1995, a list brokerage firm offered the first list of e-mail addresses and caused so much controversy in the industry they pulled back. Now, again, there are a few companies offering files of e-mail addresses by category of known interest, such as travel or investing. We don't know how this question will ultimately be resolved, but some things are certain.

Already, advertisers who have sent mass e-mail offerings (a process referred to as "spamming") have been "flamed" by return mail bombs that tie up their mail service and eat up disk space. As one writer said recently, everyone in the world has a megaphone via the Internet. People need to think about what they do before they do it. The important thing for marketers to remember is that e-mail is a service consumers pay for. Therefore many consumers view unsolicited advertising as an invasion of their privacy. It will be up to marketers in the new century to protect their rights as advertisers by preserving the rights of consumers to maintain their privacy.

One company has an answer. Aristotle, a San Francisco software and database publisher, is conducting a test to allow California voters to receive their November 1996 ballot pamphlets by e-mail, with Aristotle paying them for doing so. If the test proves successful, this could save the state millions of dollars and open up exciting new opportunities for marketers.

By October, 130 million registered voters across the country will have an Aristotle mail box in their name on the Internet-based universal e-mail system. The company is offering the free e-mail address to every registered voter who prefers to receive commercial and government mail electronically. Aristotle is compensating voters to pick up e-mail, and charging the e-mail senders.

Aristotle will make money by charging the direct marketer $1.35 to deliver a catalog electronically that might otherwise cost $1.50 to print and mail. Mailers only pay Aristotle for mail that's opened. Aristotle pays the consumer $1 to open e-mail from a direct marketer, with or without a catalog, 25 cents to open the first piece of e-mail, 25 cents to open e-mail sent from a government office, and 25 cents to open personal e-mail.[4]

This is a completely voluntary solution. Consumers will get the mailbox free, but won't get any ads they don't want. Aristotle's program may be the start of the capability for consumers to manage the use of their own name. Some industry pundits think so well of the idea they are predicting the end of spamming.

The strongest winds of Tom Brannan's "hurricane" are coming from the Internet, and like real tropical storms they are hard to predict with precision. The Internet by itself is a boring network. Just a few years ago it was used only by academics and researchers. The advent of the object-oriented Mosaic browser suddenly allowed the most casual user to make searches without a technological knowledge of the net. One of the things we can count on is the fact that the Internet will be as familiar to the next generation as television, VCRs, and cellular phones are now.

In a recent technology audit, 48 percent of those surveyed agreed with the statement, "I could not live without a modem—it's vital to keep me in touch." In comparison, only 24 percent indicated they could not live without a telephone.

It is a fast growing medium. As of January 1995, only 4 percent of the population had been on-line. By November of that year, 19 percent of the population had been on-line—a 400 percent increase in less than a year.

Never before has a new advertising medium sprung up so quickly. With the Web now just two years old, the penetration of PCs in American households is now 38.5 percent. Thirty-six million households are on-line. It is predicted there will be 180 million households worldwide with Internet access in 2000. By the year 2000 the viewing of PC screens will be almost double the viewing of TV screens, and worldwide Internet commerce will reach $7 billion.[5]

In Northern California in 1995, 16 percent of local calls could not connect due mainly to high Internet usage. The number of public pages on the World Wide Web is 66 million and will grow to 1.1 billion by the end of 2000.[6]

And folks are shopping. Twenty-seven percent of heavy Web users are already buying on the Net, and 84 percent say they will be buying more in 1996. Thirty-one percent of existing on-line shopping is done by women. A recent study by Jupiter Communications projects the number of women on-line will more than triple between now and 2000. Twenty-seven percent of users aged 40 to 49 buy on the Net. Almost 25 percent of users over 50 are making purchases.[7] These customers are valuable. Although Internet households shop less often than non-Internet households, Internet households spend 18 percent more per shopping occasion. In one category, Internet households spent 68 percent more per year than non-Internet households.[8]

But where are the big advertisers? The best answer I have heard for this came from Katie Muldoon, President of Muldoon & Baer, Inc., a direct marketing catalog consulting firm: "It is said that the Internet is like high school sex: everyone thinks everyone else is doing it, everyone wishes they were doing it, only a few are actually doing it, and the few doing it aren't doing it well."

Companies spent $66.7 million to advertise on the World Wide Web in the first half of 1996, with second-quarter spending up 83 percent from the first quarter. But two-thirds of that spending came from Internet search engines, telecommunications, and computer companies, all with a vested interest in the success of the Web.[9] The big consumer goods advertisers were noticeably absent: Toyota, in 13th place, spending roughly $900,000, and Procter & Gamble at 24th, with less than $500,000.[10] It should be noted that this was a measure of pure advertising dollars. Many of the big consumer goods marketers are building Web sites. Looking ahead, we can assume they will be advertising those sites to add value. Jupiter Communications forecasts that ad spending on the World Wide Web will reach $5 billion by the turn of the century.[11]

Traditional direct marketers appear to be ahead of the consumer goods companies. A study commissioned by the Direct Marketing Association, Grey Direct, and Litlenet, and conducted by A.T. Kearney, reported that 54 percent of the direct marketers polled said they are already using the Internet for sales and marketing, while 48 percent are using on-line services. Of the companies not active, 47 percent said they were looking into media investments. Nine out of ten predicted increases in new media investments over the next three years. Three out of four expect increases of 100 percent or more. Their reasons for using the Web were the real clue to the future. More than 50 percent see the Internet as a new distribution channel, 47.2 percent see it as a way to increase revenues, and 30.2 percent see it as a way to reduce costs.[12]

Others see more benefits. American Entertainment, with The Marvel Comics On-line Store and two other sites, reports that about half of its on-line orders came from new customers.[13] James Pisz, National Direct Response Manager of 13th-ranked Toyota says, "We want to build a sense of community with our customers and our prospects." Since 80 percent of luxury car owners use a PC, Toyota is betting that useful and interesting features on the Internet will generate repeat traffic that over time will build Toyota's image and sell more cars.[14]

One of the big changes, as more folks actually learn how to use the Internet, will be a new ease of capturing consumer and transaction data. The interaction between buyer and seller, between advertiser and consumer, will generate this information in new ways. For perhaps the first time, marketers will be able to learn specifics about prospects, not just customers. More than that, this new interaction will open the door for packaged goods marketers to obtain direct data from consumers instead of having to rely just on third-party studies. A current browser feature called the "cookie" allows Web site owners to capture visitors' actions—which sites were visited, which products ordered, and so on. Since not all consumers really want that much information stored about them, the next versions of Netscape Navigator and Microsoft Internet Explorer will allow users to disarm the cookie file. Marketers will still be able to gather user data, but increasingly that will require user permission. The Internet will open the door for serious database marketing, customer management, and two-way communication with customers for every kind of business.

Firefly Online (www.firefly.com) allows a user to rate products such as music, albums, or books; the user's intelligent agent then suggests additional albums or books rated highly by other Firefly users with similar tastes.

Now other Web sites are using the intelligent agent software from Firefly Network to deliver personalized ads. They will be able to recognize users with passports and offer them customized information and personalized ads.

When signing on to Broad Vision's The Angle (www.theangle.com), users are asked to fill out a lengthy questionnaire which enables the agent to make recommendations unique to each user. This is the kind of customer empowerment we have been talking about.

And Amazon.com knows enough about its customers to e-mail notices of new books on specific topics they know will interest the customer.

More benefits coming from the Internet that will change the rules of marketing came out of the DMA/Grey Direct/Litlenet study. The study showed that new media speeds up the pace of marketing activities. Processes that took weeks or months can be reduced to days and hours. The study proved that the marketers who were planning to use the Internet to lower costs were on target. As opposed to paper, printing, and mailing for traditional direct marketing, the new media lowers the cost of an accessible address. Also, since these new channels don't require extensive advertising support, many smaller companies can now have the same technological presence as large advertisers. Finally, the new media enable companies to communicate and sell directly to customers without the need for wholesalers, brokers, or retailers. The study suggests that businesses will need to overhaul their sales, marketing, and service organizations to serve the needs of interactive markets.[15]

And now we are seeing what some are calling the community-based Internet newspaper. KOZ has developed software to help newspapers use the Internet to save costs. To report Little League scores and standings most local newspapers rely on Little League parents to fill out a form on paper, maybe getting the information to the paper on time but more often not. The community-based Internet newspaper uses an electronic form. The Little League representative is given a password and enters the data on the electronic form; the stats go right into prepress at the paper with no labor involved. The representative is rewarded by having access to the newspaper's file on line-ups and schedules. Others can access the more detailed stats file for a cost. Newspapers are using the same electronic reporting by community groups to report town meetings, social functions, and club news.

And it looks like there will be another new kind of publication—the digital electronic magazine. Michael Ovitz, former President of Walt Disney Company, spoke to the American Magazine Conference in Bermuda, October 1996, and offered publishers the Disney view of the magazine of the future.

Mr. Ovitz showed attendees a video and a model of a handheld, digital electronic magazine with a liquid-crystal display screen. The video demonstrated digital newsstands where consumers would download all or parts of their favorite titles from CD ROMs and access updated information and archival material.

Mr. Ovitz said Disney's Imagineering Unit has been studying the idea of an electronic magazine for five years and all the technology for such a product currently exists.[16]

The new rule of marketing on the Internet is that it will grow to be different from the Internet of today. Bill Rolinson, Vice President Marketing, Internet Shopping Network, explains it this way:

Today, the Internet is one-way broadcast; the future will be two-way interactive. Today, anonymous users; the future, registered viewers. Today, no well-known preferences; the future, well-known preferences. Today, standard content; the future, customized content. Today, standard advertising; the future, targeted advertising. Today, standard promotions; the future, custom promotions.[17]

One thing is certain: People will be looking for a personal experience. The Internet sites that use engagement and interactivity will be the ones to attract users and keep them coming back. But marketers must learn to create dialog with customers better than they are doing now. Many companies are inviting the dialog, but few are really prepared to keep up their end of the conversation. One recent survey randomly checked Web sites of 100 of the 500 largest U.S. companies, and only 17 of them sent back replies. *The Wall Street Journal* sent e-mail inquiries to 24 corporate Web sites. Nine never responded. Two took three weeks to reply. Others sent canned responses that failed to address the questions asked. Only three adequately answered within a day. Seventy percent of larger companies can receive e-mail but only about half accept requests for information. We can now predict that e-mail traffic to Web sites will parallel the swift growth of telephone inquiries more than 20 years ago.

That just about sums up the new rules of marketing for the Internet, but perhaps Don Libey summed it up best.

> The Internet will usher in an intensely challenging new business climate.
>
> It will be infinitely more difficult, infinitely more complex, infinitely more analytical and infinitely more costly, but you can't afford to ignore it. If you do you will be irrelevant within five years. You can come back from bankruptcy, but you can never come back from irrelevance.
>
> Mind the customer and embrace the technology and you will experience growth on a scale you cannot have conceived of.[18]

CHAPTER **37**

Privacy is History?
A look ahead.

As stated previously, from January 1995 to January 1996 the national press used the word "privacy" 31,374 times. The term "big brother" was used in 542 articles. The February 1996 issue of *Wired* carried the prophecy, "Privacy Is History—Get Over It." We don't believe that. We looked at all of the current legislative attacks on commercial speech, but it is important to remember the constitutional argument for free commercial speech is on the side of the marketer. The Supreme Court upheld that with these words in 1976:.

> Advertising, however tasteless and excessive it sometimes may seem, is nonetheless dissemination of information as to who is producing and selling what product, for what reason, and at what price. So long as we preserve a predominately free enterprise economy, the allocation of our resources in large measure will be made through numerous private economic decisions. It is a matter of public interest that those decisions, in the aggregate, be intelligent and well informed. To this end, the free flow of commercial information is indispensable to the proper allocation of resources in a free enterprise system, it is also indispensable to the formation of intelligent opinions as to how that system ought to be regulated or altered.[1]

The Direct Marketing Association has been fighting this battle for marketers for 22 years. Looking ahead to when the Internet and other new media will make it possible for all marketers to address consumers, individually and personally, the stakes grow larger. It is time for all marketers to join the efforts of traditional direct marketers—to join the DMA's efforts, to sign the declaration of "Project Positive," to sign on to the cyberspace principles of self-regulation.

How each marketer responds to the privacy issue in the new century will be the key factor in helping to strengthen customer satisfaction and preserve our right to market without overly burdensome regulations. Developing pro-active policies like those suggested by Jennifer Barrett and those outlined in DMA's *Fair Information Practices Manual* will be the best way for companies to show that they are being responsive to consumer privacy needs, and to prove to our critics that self-regulation is effective.

CHAPTER **38**

Finally, the Customer
A look ahead.

Even when there is great risk inherent in change, it is the responsibility of leaders to shake things up. To be truly successful we have to learn how to deal, react, adjust, survive, and be comfortable with change. Change before you have to.

At the very outset we said that changing world trends have left many marketers as confused as Dorothy in Oz. Everything has changed. Few have been able to find the Yellow Brick Road.

Finding our way will not be as simple as clicking the heels of our ruby slippers and saying, "There's no place like home. There's no place like home."

We cannot, like Dorothy, go "home" again—to the 70s or 80s or 90s. The new consumer trends are changing everything we ever thought we knew about consumer marketing. The changes involve virtually every link in the marketing chain, from manufacturer, through the retailer, to the consumer. The changes are tearing apart the efficient and delicate marketing process that has worked for the past 60 years.

In 1993, Lester Wunderman, the Grand Master of direct marketers, told a DMA conference audience:

Direct marketing as I have described, practiced, and predicted it for the last 30 years, is over. It must be replaced by a marketing force so effective that it will become not just an alternative form of marketing, but the predominant practice of the future.

Building brands by creating and managing profitable consumer customer relations.

Owning the customer is the new priority.

Lester Wunderman was right, as always. The challenge is to find the ways to *understand* the new customer in order to create and manage those profitable consumer customer relations—to learn how to use one-to-one relationship marketing to be the leader in your industry. This calls for new rules of marketing.

We must have the ability to accept change.

Having said that, at the beginning, it is important to remember the quote from Brett Shevack, who said it is the responsibility of leaders to change before they have to. The real leaders will accept change and use it to their advantage.

We have talked about many of the changes marketers will face—the limits of growth, the changing channels of distribution, the changing perception of value, increased time poverty, the growing importance of changing generations, the changing definition of service, the changed consumer, the need to build relationships, and the need to concentrate on the individual. That adds up to an enormous groundswell of change for marketers to accept. It will require real leadership.

In October 1996, I went to Dallas for the 14th Annual symposium sponsored by the Center for Retailing Studies, a privately funded center housed in the Department of Marketing at Texas A&M University. Each year, Dr. Len Berry, Director of the Center, puts together what I have come to consider the premier conference on retail strategy. This year, the Conference theme was "Hyper-Competition in Retailing—Leadership Lessons." I went to hear the wisest marketer I know, and the Conference keynoter, Stanley Marcus, Chairman Emeritus of Neiman Marcus. As promised, he talked about leadership.

Mr. Stanley, as I will always call him, listed the characteristics of great leaders. The number one characteristic on his list was: "The ability to accept change." He went on to say, "Great leaders must be visible, articulate, gutsy, considerate, and willing to take a reasonable chance." Then he concluded, "Great leaders in business must have the vision to accept the new, even before it is commercially proven."

That was a perfect keynote for a day and a half that featured an impressive platform of great business leaders, including the presidents of Pier I Imports, Saturn Corporation, and LensCrafters, and the powerful, dynamic Herman Cain, Chairman and CEO of Godfather's Pizza, Inc.

I like to think it is an even better introduction for this summary chapter, where we look ahead and try to understand what the new rules of marketing will mean for all marketers.

The new marketing leaders will have to shake things up, to learn how to deal, react, adjust, survive, and be comfortable with change. Change before they have to. And, as Mr. Stanley said, they will have to have the vision to accept the new, even before it is commercially proven.

It all starts with the customer. The 90s and the pace of technological developments have changed the customer.

> Science empties its discoveries on you so fast you stagger beneath them in hopeless bewilderment.

That quote could have come from yesterday's *New York Times.* It didn't. It came from the *Atlantic Journal,* June 16, 1883. Nonetheless it can be used to make a point about the staggering load of information—particularly commercial information—and technological change the new-century customer must bear. Marketers must learn to understand this new consumer.

Wendy Lieberman, President of WSL Strategic Retail, describes some of the changes in a recent article in the RAMA Bulletin:

> The 1995 Christmas selling season will be remembered by those in the American retailing [marketing] community as a defining moment—when they could no longer ignore the fact that consumers had changed so dramatically that low prices, sale signs and the perennial deals were no longer sufficient to encourage them to shop.[1]

Quoting from her firm's recent study, "How America Shops," she says:

> Consumers said that price was no longer the singular reason why they chose a specific retail outlet. Forty-four percent said convenience, defined as location and ease of shopping was more important than price. This is the first time since 1992 that price has slipped from first place.
>
> They told us that they will shop anywhere—department stores, mass merchandisers, catalogs—regardless of their income levels, education, or family size.
>
> Consumers have changed . . . and changed dramatically since the beginning of this decade. And only those who recognize this fact will make the successful transition into the new millennium.

That takes us back to the start of this book. One of the new rules of marketing will be that price has lost much of its appeal. The marketer must change from price to more personal appeals.

In the same issue of the RAMA Bulletin Elliott Ettenberg, Chairman/CEO Prism Communications, looks at the changing, new-century "Boomers" we talked about in Chapter 4:

> The "Nasty 90s" reflect an aging boomer who is growing concerned about life, death, and retaining wealth. So value now has a price and opportunity cost as its components.
>
> What comes next in the decade of 2000–2009 will be what we at Prism call the "Converse Naughts," a "Decade of Solitude." It will be a time marked by retreat, withdrawal, and remorse. (The converse of the boomers earlier behavior patterns, hence the name.) Driven by their past experiences and facing frightening prospects of their own mortality, boomers are changing their purchasing behavior once again. And, once again, you will have to align your marketing strategy in order to succeed by offering up "value" to the boomers.
>
> In the coming "Decade of Solitude," value will consist of price, craftsmanship, and simplification. Price is the traditional cost component. Craftsmanship is the degree to which the product or service is durable, unique and elegant. Simplification is the degree to which the product or service enhances life by making day-to-day maintenance easier or reduces the stress and anxiety that accompanies the "Converse Naughts."
>
> Classifying people by income, age, education, color, religion, or any other common demographic will be ineffective. These are one-way communication tools. To be invited into the household means you must be relevant or even important to their lives. To do this successfully you must understand how to present your selling argument in words, icons, and symbols that appeal to the values of the cells you are targeting.
>
> What you communicate had better be a shared value.
> Information is not power. Information is confusing. Information is frustrating.
> Knowledge is power. Knowledge is knowing how to use information.
> Help them understand how to buy what you want to sell and they will come to associate your company with the category.

The customer will teach us what she/he wants if we will only listen. Marvin Girouard, President of Pier I, calls this "Integrity Selling." He tells his people to "listen to the customer so we can know how to serve her needs." The more the customer teaches the company, the better the company becomes at providing just what the customer wants. The customer will not give up this relationship easily, which means it will be more difficult for the competition to take the customer away.

That brings us back to relationship building (relationship marketing). A purchase is simply one brief event in a customer's life. The first step to begin to use one-to-one relationship marketing is to focus on the relationship *process,* not just the transaction. I have heard the famous relationship folks at Hallmark say, "While a series of transactions that are not embedded in a thoughtful relationship process will inevitably fail, a series of mediocre transactions that are well integrated into the total relationship process will succeed."

Relationship marketing is a process that attempts to modify people's behavior over time. Its goal is to strengthen the bond between the customer and the company or brand. Remember the difference between Pavlov's classical conditioning—teaching the customers to salivate at the mention of price—and B.F. Skinner's instrumental conditioning that depends on reinforcement.

Vernon Tirey makes this distinction between database marketing and relationship marketing:

> For many people database marketing and being customer focused are in principle the same thing but in practice very different. Typically, database marketing is reduced to the application of technology, which makes sales-driven companies faster, better and cheaper. It is not the agent of change required to help companies become market driven.
>
> Relationship marketing enables a company to observe its relationship with a customer from the customer's point of view. Terms such as acquisition, growth, and retention are inherently flawed because they do not present a customer view of the relationship, only the seller's view. Customers do not think about being acquired, being grown, or being retained. By adopting a life-cycle framework—knowing the customers, where they are in the relationship with the company, how effectively they are being moved through the process, where they are falling out of the relationship—a company learns to think like a customer. All of this enables a company to identify the product, process, and communications requirements to maximize shareholder value, market share, and customer satisfaction.[2]

Looking ahead, successful companies will cultivate intense, reciprocal, interactive, one-to-one relationships with their customers. This will require a redefinition of understanding customers. Some companies have already recognized the need. One example comes from a marketing discipline you would least expect—telemarketing.

Many telecommunications companies have mastered the numbers game, pushing their dialers to the max, charting their decreases in talk time, perfecting scripts, capturing psychographics, and continually improving processes. And yet these same telecommunications companies are scrambling to hold on to all of those customers they have worked so efficiently to bring to the door.

Telemarketers who only meet customers' expressed needs are ignoring potential opportunities to secure long-term customer brand loyalty . . . Telemarketing results should be required to extend beyond simply satisfying customers, to delighting them.

Companies like Sprint are taking an innovative approach to salesforce training which seeks to teach employees how to *interact* with the customers in order to improve the quality of transactions. The training moves away from the more standard approach in which representatives are supplied with a script and required to meet pre-established goals at almost any cost.

Instead, Sprint's telemarketing approach seeks to focus on each individual customer interaction as a unique exchange of needs and solutions.[3]

One writer calls this, "Adaptive Marketing—using advanced technology to better the interaction process with the customer by understanding his or her real-time needs, and then managing and leveraging the selling and service opportunity."[4]

Satisfying the new customer will require more than managing and leveraging the selling opportunity, however. Sprint's focus on a unique exchange of needs and solutions suggests that the marketer will have to know enough about his customers to customize his offerings. We will be hearing more and more of the new term, "Mass Customization."

Here is more from the report of Alvin Toffler's presentation to the Strategic Leadership Conference:

> Typical of the industrial revolution was the move toward mass production and mass consumption, or massification, as Toffler calls it. This concept will increasingly be turned on its head as the move is on toward diversity and differentiation. The application of knowledge-based technologies is leading to a reduction in the cost of diversity, so that there is an enormous profusion of new products, models, sizes, etc. Eventually, customers will be able to order exactly what they want, to their own specifications and have it delivered to them at no extra cost than if the same item were mass produced. Remember, we're handing the rifle to the deer. Ultimately this will lead to production lines of one, or mass customization.[5]

The apparel industry has already developed high-speed, single-ply cutters that will help to mass customize made-to-measure clothing.

Lutron Electronics, the leading manufacturer of lighting controls in the United States, is a leader. To compete, Lutron has not lowered prices to match competitors. They are offering their customers the ability to customize the products they need. In using mass customization they have not only been successful in keeping customers from switching to competitors, but they also have developed many new product designs. Lutron's engineers hold a majority of the patents in their industry.[6]

The makers of the Saturn car plan to invite customers soon to "Come to Spring Hill to design and help build your own car."

We can count on the Internet to help us move from simply satisfying the customer to adding a true sense of delight. Web transactions will enable us to decrease the customer's time investment, increase value, add convenience, lower cost—to be there at the customer's exact moment of need—and quite possibly entertain.

Michael Rollens, the former President and CEO of *NBC Direct,* is in the process of launching an interactive entertainment, information, and retail network on the Internet. In a recent article in the *Arthur Anderson Retailing Issues Letter,* he forecasts the look of virtual shopping:

> Shopping in tomorrow's virtual world will be like shopping in today's physical world. How can this be? It is because a major paradigm shift in the way we experience reality is now possible. Technology allows us to immerse ourselves in this new electronically created world. In the future, we will experience in the virtual world everything that today we see, hear, and touch in the physical world. This overwhelming fact will change everything. We will enter this virtual world to be entertained and to be informed.
>
> People will enter these new virtual stores not only to shop but also to be entertained. Interactive storytelling will involve us in the use of goods and services, and we will be able to immediately purchase items that appear as part of a fictional experience. For example, a retailer might create an interactive drama with highly interesting and likable characters. Shoppers who identify with these characters might want to buy the clothes they wear. The consumer, by using his or her electronically generated body image, may try on the clothes.
>
> In this and other ways lifestyle correlations with individual users will be designed to attract buyers to specific products. Once that happens the migration of economic activity will accelerate, and virtual shopping will exponentially grow.[7]

I smiled when I first read Mr. Rollens' description of tomorrow's virtual store. In 1982 I worked with a man named Chris Keith, who had formed a company called "Interact" to try to develop an electronic retail chain to be called Telestore. Michael Rollens' 1996 thoughts are a perfect description of Chris Keith's 1982 idea.

The Telestore chain was to be developed around a theme similar to a soap opera. The individual retail outlets within each Telestore were to be located in "Jake's Landing," a quaint community filled with highly interesting and likable characters. Our plan called for two kinds of stores: Theme stores which were to be an integral part of the Jake's Landing story line—designed to optimize the medium and exist only in Jake's Landing— and real stores, which existed in the everyday world and would not be part of the story. Each theme store featured a special character to create the emotional involvement of the customer with the store and its proprietor.

The Gift Box was to be owned by a kindly, avuncular figure—patient, knowledgeable, the Mr. Whipple of gift shops. Fiona's Foolishness was to feature Fiona, a lovable flake, sort of like the Toad of Toad Hall in *The Wind in the Willows*. Thorndyke's home store was to be a bigger company, complete with office politics, a harassed delivery manager, and ambitious young men and women in a corporate environment. The Tomorrow Store was to be managed by a young heartthrob bachelor who had received an advanced degree somewhere and decided not to continue working at Mega Industries on war machines—a man who believes the turning points of western culture were the invention of Aspirin, flush toilets, and the double boiler.

Jake's Landing was to have a members' bulletin board for customer participation—even a Clubhouse Grill where new shoppers could be filled in on the story line by a loquacious bartender.

Some of this is already happening. Ragu has a Web site where Mama encourages visitors to return to see a new episode every 48 hours.

Ah well, we were just a bit ahead of our time.

Where does all this leave us as we take our last look at the customer? In any transaction between a buyer and a seller there is always some kind of an emotional response. Satisfaction makes the buyer feel good and a satisfied customer, at the extreme, will become an advocate. But customer satisfaction is not a surrogate for customer retention. We must move beyond mere satisfaction to great experiences of delight.

We must accept the fact that not all customers are created equal, remembering that if a marketer treats best customers like everybody else, he can expect them to treat his brand or his store like any other.

The marketer *must* learn how to create a dialog with customers. Dialog is what relationship marketing is all about. If the only time your customer hears from you is when you are trying to sell something, and the only time you hear from her is when she has a complaint, that's not dialog.

I hope every reader will remember Simon Anholt's term, "Friendship Marketing"—the kind of dialog that enriches the relationship and shows you can give without expecting to receive . . . and his suggestion that socializing with customers is almost more important than pitching to them

. . . nonselling customer communications are the mass-market equivalent of the after work drink.

Customer management, customer development, and responding to the needs of *individual* customers is now the only formula for success.

To accomplish retention and loyalty, the relationship marketing program must shift the marketer's emphasis from inducement to rewards. With price as the only inducement we are rewarding promiscuity. Relationship marketing rewards loyalty. This represents a profound change in the way we market.

Building relationships from the customer point of view will be the only way we will be invited into the household. If we can make every customer contact more meaningful and mutually profitable than the last, we will be building brand equity from the customer up. Every point of contact with the customer will help to create brand value.

Those who accomplish this will finally have learned the new rules and how to use one-to-one relationship marketing. They will be the leaders in their industry.

End Notes

CHAPTER 2

1. Murray Raphel quoting Jane Perin NCH Promotion Services, Association of Coupon Processors, September 1995, "Happy Birthday, Dear Coupons . . . ," *Direct Marketing,* November 1995, p. 42.

2. Frankel & Company.

3. Pat Sloan "P&G tops rivals in no-coupon push," *Advertising Age,* January 15, 1996 p. 3.

4. *Ibid.*

5. Brett Shevack "Staying ahead means changing the rules," *Advertising Age,* October 16, 1995.

CHAPTER 3

1. "Not change, but revolution," *Strategic Direction,* published by MCB Business Strategy Publications, Bradford, England, pp. 16–17.

2. *Ibid.*

3. *Ibid.*

4. *Direct Marketing,* July 1996, p. 59.

5. "Procter & Gamble out to simplify its product lines," *Advertising Age,* September 30, 1996, p. 21.

6. "Co-branding," *Advertising Age,* October 14, 1996, p. 20.

7. Arnold Fishman "Mail Order Report," *Direct Marketing,* August 1996, p. 50.

8. *Ibid.*

9. WEFA Economic Impact Study for the Direct Marketing Association, *Direct Marketing,* November 1995.

10. *Ibid.*

11. *Ibid.*

12. *Ibid.*

13. Jane Hodges and Mark Gleason, "McCann hires Rapp for DM prowess," *Advertising Age,* October 7, 1996, p. 1.

14. *The Friday Report,* Hoke Communications, August 23, 1996, p. 1.

15. Bruce W. Frankel in an interview in *Outlet Retailer,* a supplement to *Shopping Center World,* November 1996, p. OR6.

16. *Ibid.,* Jeffrey Kerr, October 1996, p. OR4.

17. Mary Kuntz, Lon Bongiorno, Keith Naughton, Gail DeGeorge, and Stephanie Anderson, "Cover Story," *Business Week,* November 27, 1995, p. 92.

18. Tony Priori, Vice President Marketing, Pea Pod, DMA's 3rd Annual Retail Senior Executive's Forum, New York City, September 17, 1996.

19. "Pea Pod signs on with largest grocery retailer in U.S.," *The Friday Report,* Hoke Communications, September 6, 1996, p. 2.

20. "The Competitive Advantage of Virtual Retailing," Fred Schneider, Executive Director SMART STORE, Center for Retailing Studies Texas A&M symposium, Hyper Competition in Retailing - Leadership Lessons, Dallas, TX, October 18–19, 1996.

21. *Ibid.*

22. Cathy Asato, "Visitor Survey Drives Wine Site Content," *DM News,* August 26, 1996, p. 20.

23. Jean Holliday, "AutoNation and CarMax gear up for used car clash," *Advertising Age,* October 28, 1996, p. 3.

24. *Ibid.*

25. "Cover Story," *Business Week,* November 27, 1995, p. 88.

26. Miguel E. Tersy, "Used-Car Chain Seeks Loyalty Through Database," *DM News,* November 4, 1996, p. 4.

27. Cathy Asato, "Auto Site Lets You Buy, Lease and Insure," *DM News,* September 9, 1996, p. 21.

28. Ridd McGinty, "Deal Brings Auto Loan Approvals On-line," *DM News,* October 21, 1996, p. 18.

29. Keith Naughton, Kathleen Kerwin, Bill Vlassic, Lori Bongiorno, and David Leonhardt, "Revolution in the Showroom," *Business Week,* February 19, 1996, pp. 70–76.

30. *Ibid.*

31. Cathy Asato, "Catalog Biz Is Good and Getting Better," *DM News,* June 24, 1996, p. 14.

CHAPTER 4

1. Karen Ritchie, *Marketing to Generation X,* Lexington Books, The Free Press, 1995.

2. "During the Boom," *The San Diego Union Tribune* quoting from the January issue of *Modern Maturity* magazine, January 21, 1996, p. D-2.

3. *American Demographics,* December 1995.

4. "During the Boom," *The San Diego Union Tribune* quoting from the January issue of *Modern Maturity* magazine, January 21, 1996, p. D-2.

5. Michael Goldberg and Jaikumar Vijayan, "Data 'wearhose' gains—Victoria's Secret to weave profits from store data," *Computerworld,* April 8, 1996, p. 1.

6. "Engendering Loyalty in Your Customers," *Retail Ad Week* quoting Don Peppers, President Marketing 1:1, Media/Options '95 Show, July 31–August 7, 1995, p. 7.

7. Coopers & Lybrand LLP, Consumer Enhancement and Development, *Chain Store Age,* January 1996.

CHAPTER 5

1. Judann Pollack and Pat Sloan, "ANA Told: Remember Consumers," *Advertising Age,* October 14, 1996, p. 17.

2. Kate Fitzgerald, "In Credit Card Business, Relationships Count," *Advertising Age,* October 7, 1996, p. s18.

3. "The Experts Predict," *Target Marketing,* quoting Ralph Stevens, President, Stevens-Knox referring to observations about the 1990s as the "Decade of Rude Awakening" made by Stan Rapp and Tom Collins in their book *Beyond Maxi-Marketing,* January 1996, p. 14.

CHAPTER 7

1. *DM News,* November 6, 1995.

2. *Ibid.*

3. Carolyn Gould speaking at the Seklemian/Newell Retail Database Marketing Working Weekend II, Durham, North Carolina, May 2–4, 1996.

CHAPTER 8

1. Ramon Barquin, Steve Crofts, Alan Parker, and The Data Warehousing Institute, "Data Warehousing: The Road to Knowledge Production," *Fortune,* October 1996, p. S-2.

CHAPTER 9

1. "Database Marketing: Pre-1950 Mass Marketing Through the Mail," *Journal of Direct Marketing,* Vol 7, Number 3. Summer 1993, p. 28.

2. Doug Henschen, "Club Med Moves to Segmentation From Global Model, Mailing 1st Prospect Test to 60,000," Database Marketing, *DM News,* October 14, 1996, p. 25.

3. Michael Wilke "Subaru Adds Lesbians to Niche Marketing Drive," *Advertising Age,* March 4, 1996, p. 8.

4. David Schmittlein, Professor of Marketing, The Wharton School, University of Pennsylvania, *The Attrition of Inclination in Customer Histories: Where "When" Matters More Than "How."*

CHAPTER 10

1. David Schmittlein, Professor of Marketing, The Wharton School, University of Pennsylvania, *The Attrition of Inclination in Customer Histories: Where "When" Matters More Than "How."*

2. Brian P. Woolf, "Measured Marketing, A Tool to Shape Food Store Strategy," The Coca-Cola Retailing Research Council, 1994.

CHAPTER 11

1. Suzanne E. Gallagher, "First Union Relies on DB Mktg, to Retain Best Customers," quoting Mark Schultz, Marketing Representative, Okra, *DM News,* May 13, 1996, p. 23.

2. American Banker/Tower Group 1995 Survey of Technology in Banking.

3. Alice Z. Cuneo, "Great Western Bank Toughens Ad Strategy," *Advertising Age,* June 24, 1996, p. 12.

4. *DIRECT,* September 1, 1996.

CHAPTER 12

1. "Catalogers Reveal Dearth of Planning for the Future," *Adveristing Age* reporting on The Dean Report, presented by Bill Dean, President W.A. Dean & Associates at the Catalog Conference & Exhibition, June/ July 1996, p. 12.

2. "Measured Marketing A Tool to Shape Food Store Strategy," a study conducted for the Coca-Cola Retailing Research Council by Brian P. Woolf.

3. Paul Wang, Ph.D., Associate Professor, Integrated Marketing Communications Program, Medill School of Journalism, Northwestern University, *Response,* an STS Systems Publication, Issue 2, Spring, 1996, p. 1.

CHAPTER 13

1. Mark Horey, Manager Service Marketing, Nissan Motor Company, USA; National Center for Database Marketing, Orlando, Florida, December 1995.

2. *The Cowles Report on Database Marketing,* June 1996, Vol. 5, No. 4, p. 1.

3. Marketing Services Department, *San Diego Union Tribune.*

4. Leah Haran "With 4M+ Cards VonsClub Helps Target Shoppers," *Advertising Age,* October 16, 1995, p. 24.

5. Jim Emerson, "Supermarket Throws Vast DB Weight Behind Coupon Program," *DM NEWS,* February 26, 1996, p. 1.

CHAPTER 14

1. John Cummings & Partners.

2. *The Cowles Report on Database Marketing,* June 1996, p. 8.

3. Beth Negus, "Life's a Niche," *Direct,* October 15, 1996, p. 43.

4. Interview with Victor A. Grund, former Manager Database Marketing Corporate Marketing Services, Kraft, July 1996.

5. *Case in Point* is a publication of Acxiom Corporation, Conway, AR.

6. Peter Cobb, Marketing Director Samsonite, SRI Conference, New York City, February 1995.

7. "Reinventing the Bicycle," *Strategic Direction,* April, 1996, p. 30.

CHAPTER 15

1. Suzanne E. Gallagher, "Hyatt Moves DB Marketing to the Fore," *DM News,* November 20, 1995, p. 25.

2. *DIRECT,* December 1995 and *DM News,* November 20, 1995.

CHAPTER 19

1. Donald R. Libey, President, Libey Incorporated, "Keep One More Customer," *Target Marketing,* September, 1995, p. 30.

2. Brian Woolf, "Measured Marketing, A Tool to Shape Food Store Strategy," The Coca-Cola Retailing Research Council, 1994.

3. Simon Anholt, Managing Director, World Writers, London, "Of Friendship Marketing and Customer Magazines," *DM News International,* January 22, 1996, p. 22.

4. *Ibid.*

5. Frederick F. Reichheld, Bain & Company, *Harvard Business Review,* March-April 1993.

6. RAM Research, as quoted in *The Cowles Report on Database Marketing,* June 1996.

7. Kate Fitzgerald, "Credit Cards Toughen Their Rewards Efforts," *Advertising Age,* May 13, 1996, p. 20.

8. Brian Woolf, "Measured Marketing," 1994.

9. Garth Hallberg, *All Customers Are Not Created Equal* (New York: John Wiley & Sons, 1995), p. 40.

10. *Ibid.*

11. American Society for Quality Control.

12. F. Reichheld, D.W. Kenny, "The Hidden Advantages of Customer Retention," *Journal of Retail Banking,* Vol. 12, No. 4, Winter 1990–91.

13. Frederick Reichheld and W. Earle Sasse, "Customer Retention: A New Star to Steer By," Working Paper, Bain & Company, November 1987.

14. R. Buchman & M. Plantevin, "Customer Retention—The Key to Profitability, Marketing Management," *EFTA's Newsletter* (European Financial Marketing Association), July 1991.

15. F. Reichheld, "Loyalty Based Management," *Harvard Business Review,* March-April 1993, p. 70–71.

16. Al Malony, Best Customer, Inc, Seklemian/Newell Retail Database Working Weekend, Fuqua School of Business, Duke University, August 1995.

17. Brian Woolf, "Measured Marketing," 1994.

18. Kate Cullum, "Customer Loyalty—A Quick Look at the UK Today," *DM News International,* October 21, 1996, p. 14.

19. Don Peppers, Martha Rogers, *Enterprise One-to-One,* A Currency Book, Doubleday, 1997, pp. 177–179.

CHAPTER 20

1. Jennifer MacLean; "Putting the Service in Service Merchandise," *Retail Ad Week,* February 5–12, 1996.

2. *Direct Marketing,* April 1994.

3. Brian P. Woolf, "Measured Marketing," 1994.

CHAPTER 21

1. Cathy Asato, "Philip Morris, Hachette Team for New Mag," *DM News,* October 7, 1996, p. 4.

2. Raymond Serafin, "VW gets into gear with catalog for 'Drivers wanted'," *Advertising Age,* February 5, 1996, p. 9.

3. "Pepsi Catalog Promotion Earns Spot in History Books," *The Friday Report,* Hoke Communications, October 4, 1996, p. 2.

4. Lynn Dougherty, "McDonald's to Serve 500,000 via DM," *Direct,* September 15, 1996.

CHAPTER 22

1. Bradley Johnson, "Camry may ride new ads to No. 1," *Advertising Age,* September 23, 1996, p. 59.

CHAPTER 23

1. Nicholas G. Poulos, Hunter Business Direct, "Customer Loyalty and the Marketing Database," *Direct Marketing,* July 1996, p. 33.

2. *Ibid.,* p. 32.

3. Garth Hallberg, *All Consumers Are Not Created Equal* (New York: John Wiley & Sons, Inc., 1995).

4. Brian Woolf, Retail Strategy Center Inc, "Frequent Shopping Cards: The Aisle to Success," at Food Market Institute, May 1996.

5. Al Malony, Best Customer, Inc, Seklemian/Newell Retail Database Working Weekend, Fuqua School of Business, Duke University, August 1995.

6. Frederick F. Reichheld, "Loyalty-Based Management."

7. Terry G. Vavra, *Aftermarketing* (Burr Ridge, IL: Irwin Professional Publishing, 1992, 1995).

8. Garth Hallberg, *All Consumers Are Not Created Equal.*

9. Brian P. Woolf, "Measured Marketing," 1994.

10. *Ibid.*

11. *Case-in-Point,* a publication of Acxiom Corporation, Conway, AR, p. 3.

12. Viewpoint, "Better Days for Brands," *Advertising Age,* October 14, 1996, p. 30.

13. Richard A. Dunn, Vice President Carlson Marketing Group, "Loyalty Programs Beyond Typical Industries," at National Center for Database Marketing Conference, December 10–12, 1995, Orlando, Florida.

CHAPTER 24

1. *New York Market Radio Update,* May/June 1996, p. 1.

2. Arbitron Ratings, Fall 1995.

3. Cathy Asato, "Free calls from cell phones give DR radio a big boost," *DM News,* August 26, 1996, p. 1.

4. Robert McFarlane, CFO, Clearnet Communications, Inc., Pickering, Ontario, "PCS proponents hail wireless phone as the next wave," *The Globe and Mail,* September 12, 1996, p. C-2.

5. "Time, Inc.: Time Captivates Advertisers," *Case in Point Case Study,* Axciom Corporation, Fall 1995.

6. *Ibid.*

7. "How do you create a newspaper brand?" *Editor & Publisher,* October 14, 1995, p. 17.

8. *Ibid.,* p. 16.

9. Peter Levitan, "Never fear, oh newspapers," *Advertising Age,* September 23, 1996, p. 31.

CHAPTER 25

1. *Inter Media,* July 1996, p. 1. A loyalty marketing publication of Wolfe Communications.

2. Chuck Ross, "NBC wields new viewer club," *Advertising Age,* July 29, 1996, p. 1.

3. *Inter Media,* May 1996, p. 1.

4. *Cowles Business Media Direct,* December 1994, Vol. 6, No. 12.

5. *Ibid.*

6. Mark Roby, "Newspapers and Retailers: Maximizing Converging Database Marketing Opportunities for Both," at National Center for Database Marketing, Orlando, Florida, December 1995.

CHAPTER 26

1. STS Systems, Montreal, was among the pioneers in the early development of marketing database software with the Customer Profile System. In 1996 they introduced the newest generation of marketing software, MarketWorks.™

2. Karen Humphries Sallick, *Journal of Database Marketing,* Vol. 1, No. 2.

3. David M. Raab, Principal, Raab Associates, per quote in *Case in Point,* Acxom Corporation, Fall 1995, p. 2.

4. Harte-Hanks Data Technologies is a leading provider of database marketing software for the financial, automotive, banking, retail, and catalog industries.

5. Ray Jutkins has supervised hundreds of database marketing projects in 41 countries on 6 continents.

6. Scott Hample, "Fear of Commitment," *Marketing Tools,* January/February 1996, p. 8, quoting Doug Porter, Senior Account Director, Leo Burnett.

7. Len Egol, "A Beginner's Guide to Failure," *Direct,* September 1, 1996.

8. Steve Leeds, Ph.D, "The Marketing Investigators (TMI Associates)," *Direct Marketing,* April, 1996, p.52.

9. Michael Schrage, Research Associate MIT Media Lab, "Business alignment: A two-way street," *Computerworld,* September 9, 1996, p. 41.

CHAPTER 27

1. Katherine Lemon, Assistant Professor, Fuqua School of Business, Duke University, focuses her research on customer retention issues—investigating factors that influence a customer's decision to disadopt a product or service and the implications of this customer decision process for marketing managers.

2. Seacord, Stephanie, "Who's Been Sleeping in Our Beds?" *Marketing Tools,* March/April 1996.

3. Katherine Lemon, Assistant Professor, Fuqua School of Business, Duke University, from an MBA course in Marketing Management.

4. Paul Alberta, "NCOA Violates Law, Sez GAO," *DM News,* August 26, 1996, p. 1.

5. Timothy Swigor, co-founder, Database Marketing Resources, "Taking a science to an art form," *Canadian Direct Marketing News,* May 1995, p. 8.

CHAPTER 28

1. Art Hutchinson, Senior Consultant, Northeast Consulting Resources, Boston, *Computerworld Retail Journal,* October 1996, p. R-20, quoted by Jeremy Schlosberg.

CHAPTER 29

1. Larry Jaffee, "Markey's Bill to Extend Online Privacy Protection to Consumers," *DM News,* July 8, 1996, p. 3.

2. Joseph Perkins, "The end of privacy as we know it," *The San Diego Union-Tribune,* September 27, 1996, p. B-7.

3. *The Friday Report,* Hoke Communications, September 6, 1996. p. 3.

4. Brendan B. Read, "Free Opt-In/Out Web Preferance Service Offers Info to Marketers," *DM News,* August 26, 1996, p. 3.

CHAPTER 30

1. Marian Salzman, "Riding with technology to millennium," *Advertising Age,* October 7, 1996, p. 34.

2. "Co-branding," *Advertising Age,* October 14, 1996, p. 20.

3. Bill Dean, "Viking Pillages Office Superstores," *DM News,* February 1996, p. 19.

4. Rebecca A. Fannin, "Neiman Marcus is looking Far East," *Advertising Age,* September 16, 1996, p. 16.

5. Rebecca A. Fannin, "Lands' End extends sales in Far East with local catalogs," *Advertising Age,* September 30, 1996, p. 54.

6. Keith J. Kelly, "'SI' issue to stand alone," *Advertising Age,* September 30, 1996, p. 64.

7. "Strict Requirements for Catalog Display in Japan Post Office," *DM News International,* September 16, 1996, p. 3.

8. "Baier Completes Asian Rim Tour," *Direct Marketing,* September 1996, p. 12.

9. *The Friday Report,* Hoke Communications, September 20, 1996, p. 6.

10. Mathew Rose, "Marriott by Mail: Time to Share in Spain," *DM News International,* August 19, 1996, p. 8.

11. Mathew Rose, "Heinz Targets UK Consumers With 'At Home' Mailings," *DM News,* March 11, 1996, p. 7.

12. "UK Firm Launches Mail Campaign to Attract American Bettors," *DM News International,* September 16, 1996, p. 10.

13. "Coping with list scarcity & other Pacific Rim obstacles," *Direct,* September 15, 1996, p. 27.

14. *DM News International,* January 1996.

15. Cynthia Miyashita. "ICLP To Open In The Gulf In Sept.," *DM News Inernational,* August 19, 1996, p. 17.

16. "Argentine Firm Offers US Mailers 'Hand Cleaned' Lists," *DM News International,* August 19, 1996, p. 15.

17. International Mail Order Direct Marketing Statistics, *Direct Marketing,* August, 1996, p. 57.

18. "UK Direct Mail Volume Increased 123 Percent in Last 10 Years," *The Friday Report,* Hoke Communications, July 26, 1996, p. 1.

19. "Around the World in 80 Channels," *Direct,* October 15, 1996, p. 1.

20. "Dateline Asia," *DM News,* January 22, 1996.

21. Budd Margolis, "Home Order Television Is Germany's Answer to the Home Shopping Trend," *Direct Marketing,* July 1996, p. 55.

22. "Dateline Europe," *DM News International,* October 21, 1996, p. 10.

23. "Direct Response Growing at Healthy Rate in Canada," *DM News International,* January 22, 1996, p. 14.

24. "Software Company: DMers Should Look to The Web For Their Future," *DM News International,* January 1996.

25. *Computerworld,* October 7, 1996.

26. Mathew Rose, "USA Today's Web Site: Ideal For International DMers?" *DM News International,* January 22, 1996, p. 9.

27. *Ibid.*

28. "NBC Goes Online In Europe and Asia," *DM News International,* August 19, 1996, p. 3.

29. Chis Peterson, "Finding Your Orbit," *Direct,* September 15, 1996, p. 31.

30. *Ibid, p. 34.*

CHAPTER 31

1. "The Human Body Is a Valid and Viable Conductor of Electronic Data," *The Friday Report,* Hoke Communications, June 28, 1996, p. 2.

2. Budd Margolis, *Direct Marketing,* January 1996, p. 43.

3. *Advertising Age,* June 17, 1996.

4. "IQ 1996: Fashion at the Net—The Data Game," *Woman's Wear Daily,* March 20, 1966, p. 12.

5. *Ibid.*

6. *Ibid.*

7. *Ibid.*

8. Larry Edwards, "Watching Out for Number One," *Advertising Age,* October 16, 1995, p. S-3.

9. "Analysis," *The San Diego Union Tribune,* October 11, 1996, p. C-3.

10. Editorial, "Having It Both Ways," *DM News,* January 22, 1996, p. 48.

11. *The Friday Report,* Hoke Communications, June 28, 1996, p. 3.

CHAPTER 32

1. Brendan B. Read, "Net Result: Consumers Will Control Electronic Marketing," *DM News,* March 25, 1996, p. 1.

2. Al Reis and Jack Trout, *The 22 Immutable Laws of Marketing* as quoted in *Strategic Direction,* January 1996, p. 4.

3. Ralph Soucie, "Can banks survive the on-line onslaught?," *Computerworld,* September 23, 1996, p. 41.

4. Alan Ehrenhalt, "Main Street Revival: Small towns enjoy new favor in the 90s," *San Diego Union-Tribune,* June 29, 1996, p. A-28.

5. *Yankelovich Monitor®* "Shaking Stress," December 1996, pp. 2,10.

CHAPTER 33

1. Viewpoint, "Forever young," *Advertising Age,* April 8, 1996, p. 16.

2. Horatio Alger Association Poll, reported in *New York Market Radio Update,* September/October, 1996.

3. Chuck Ross, "Children tuning out TV in alarming numbers," *Advertising Age,* October 7, 1996, p. 3.

4. "Viewpoint," *Advertising Age,* October 14, 1996, p. 30.

5. Don Tapscott, "The Rise of the Net-Generation," *Advertising Age,* October 14, 1996, p. 31.

CHAPTER 34

1. Lester Wunderman, *Being Direct: How I Learned to Make Advertising Pay,* Random House, Inc., 1977.

2. Julia King, "Sharing IS secrets," *Computerworld,* September 23, 1996, p. 1.

3. Suzanne E. Gallagher, "Print on-demand could change target marketing," *DM News,* March 25, 1996, p. 4.

4. The Electronic Messaging Association, Arlington, Virginia. *Computerworld,* November 6, 1995.

5. Doug Henschen, "Program personalizes mass e-mailings," *DM News,* September 9, 1996, p. 19.

6. "UPS Announces Partnerships for Electronic Commerce," *The Friday Report,* Hoke Communications, October 18, 1996, p. 3.

CHAPTER 35

1. "Milliken makes money," *Strategic Direction,* MCB Business Strategy Publications, Bradford, England, April 1996, p. 19.

2. "Nonprofit achiever assesses the industry," *DM News,* August 26, 1996, p. 33.

CHAPTER 36

1. Tom Brannan, Chairman,The Chartered Institute of Marketing, "The tower of Babel—communication in the third millennium," *Strategic Direction,* MCB Business Strategy Publications, Bradford, England, January 1996, p. 3.

2. Robert F. Delay, *The Delay Report,* May 1996.

3. "The Insider," *Inter Media,* Wolfe Communications, May 1996, p. 1.

4. Barbara Drimmer, "Aristotle will pay people to read e-mail," *DM News,* September 23, 1996, p. 2.

5. Fred Schneider, Executive Director, SMART STORE, "Hyper Competition in Retailing—Leadership Lessons," at The Center for Retailing Studies Texas A&M, Dallas, Texas, October 18, 1996.

6. Viewpoint, *Computerworld,* October 7, 1996.

7. "Internet Households Are More Valuable Households," *Direct Marketing,* February 1996, p. 2.

8. "Internet Households Are More Valuable Customeres," *Direct Marketing,* September 1996, p. 8.

9. Debra Aho Williamson, *Advertising Age,* September 2, 1996, p. 1.

10. "Where are the marketers?," Viewpoint, *Advertising Age,* September 9, 1996, p. 26.

11. Cathy Asato, "Web ad spending seen exploding by next century," *DM News,* October 21, 1996, p. 21.

12. Beth Negus, *Direct,* September 1, 1996, p. 14.

13. Cathy Asato, "Supplementing the print catalog, Marvel's on-line site does super biz," *DM News,* June 24, 1996, p. 4.

14. Bradley Johnson, "Oh What a Web Site, Toyota," *Advertising Age,* October 16, 1995, p. 22.

15. "Internet, On-line Services Require Businesses to Restructure Sales and Marketing Functions," *The Friday Report,* Hoke Communications, August 30, 1996, p. 1.

16. "Ovitz dream machine and digital newsstands," *Advertising Age,* October 21, 1996, p. 60.

17. *The Friday Report,* Hoke Communications, June 28, 1996, p. 3.

18. Doug Henschen, "Libey sees 'Net nuts," *DM News,* July 22, 1996, p. 42, quoting Donald R. Libey at Direct Media Conference, July 1996.

CHAPTER 37

1. *Direct Marketing,* April 1996.

CHAPTER 38

1. Wendy Lieberman, "Retailing on the Brink . . . How to Survive in the New Millennium," *RAMA Bulletin,* p. 1, published by the Retail Advertising and Marketing Association International.

2. Vernon J. Tirey, "Database Marketing Basics and Best Practices," *DM News,* September 4, 1995, p. 31.

3. Margery Tippen, "Building Customer Loyalty Through Quality Telemarketing," *Direct Marketing,* September, 1996, pp. 14–15.

4. Ernie Connon, "Developing and Retaining Profitable Customer Relationships Through Call Centers," *Direct Marketing,* September 1996, p. 24.

5. "Not change, but revolution," *Strategic Direction,* October 1996, p. 17.

6. Paul Younger, Engineering Manager—Manufacturing Services, Lutron Electronics, "Achieving Mass Customization Through Training and Innovation," at the Mass Customization Conference, Strategic Research Institute, November 18, 1996, Chicago, Illinois.

7. Michael Rollens, "Shopping in the Virtual World," *Arthur Anderson Retail Issues Letter,* copublished by the Center for Retailing Studies Texas A&M University, January,1996, Vol. 8, No. 1, pp. 1, 4.

Index

About the Author

Frederick Newell virtually created the field of database marketing over 25 years ago, and has seen it adopted in one way or another by successful marketers around the globe. Today he is CEO of the international consulting firm Seklemian/Newell, which helps companies of every size develop and implement profitable customer-based marketing programs.

Newell is sought after as a speaker in the U.S., Canada, Mexico, Latin America, and Australia, and serves as columnist, contributing editor, and editorial director for important national and international advertising/marketing trade publications. He was named Advertising Professional of the Year in 1985, and has been elected to the Retail Advertising Hall of Fame. He and his wife live in Coronado, California, where between consulting and writing assignments he disappears on his 50-year-old wooden catboat.